D1786461

ECHOES OF THE GENERAL HOLINESS ASSEMBLY

Chicago
May 3–13, 1901

Edited by S. B. Shaw

Garland Publishing, Inc.
New York & London
1984

BX
7990
.H6
A34
1901

For a complete list of the titles in this series
see the final pages of this volume.

Library of Congress Cataloging in Publication Data

General Holiness Assembly (2nd : 1901 : Chicago, Ill.)
*ECHOES OF THE GENERAL HOLINESS ASSEMBLY,
CHICAGO, MAY 3-13, 1901.*

("The Higher Christian life")
Reprint. Originally published: Chicago, Ill. :
S.B. Shaw.
1. Holiness churches—Congresses. I. Shaw, S. B.
II. Title. III. Series.
BX7990.H6A34 1901   289.9   84-18817
ISBN 0-8240-6442-9 (alk. paper)

The volumes in this series are printed on
acid-free, 250-year-life paper.

Printed in the United States of America

"THE HIGHER CHRISTIAN LIFE"

SOURCES FOR THE STUDY OF THE HOLINESS, PENTECOSTAL, AND KESWICK MOVEMENTS

A forty-eight-volume facsimile series reprinting extremely rare documents for the study of nineteenth-century religious and social history, the rise of feminism, and the history of the Pentecostal and Charismatic movements

Edited by

Donald W. Dayton
Northern Baptist Theological Seminary

Advisory Editors

D. William Faupel, *Asbury Theological Seminary*
Cecil M. Robeck, Jr., *Fuller Theological Seminary*
Gerald T. Sheppard, *Union Theological Seminary*

A GARLAND SERIES

ECHOES

—OF THE—

GENERAL HOLINESS ASSEMBLY

HELD IN CHICAGO,
May 3-13, 1901.

Edited by S. B. SHAW.

"And when the day of Pentecost was fully come, they were all with one accord in one place."—Acts 2:1.

"And the glory which thou gavest me I have given them; that they may be one, even as we are one."—John, 17:22.

CHICAGO, ILL.
S. B. SHAW, PUBLISHER,
275 Madison Street.

Introduction.

The recent General Holiness Assembly was the result of many prayers, and as can be seen by reading the Official Call the chain of providences that led to this great general conference of holiness workers can be traced back to the first General Holiness Assembly held fifteen years ago in Park Ave. M. E. church, Chicago, May 20-26, 1885.

For several years there has been a conviction on the part of many of the leaders of the holiness movement of the great need of deeper union of heart and effort. No one can doubt that thousands upon thousands of souls will praise God to all eternity as a result of what is known as the modern holiness movement; but none can doubt but that much more might have been done and would have been done if the holiness people had at all times been of one mind and of one heart in the work of God and in utter abandonment of self to His will and His glory. Yet, in spite of the teaching that the sanctification of believers will bring about the answer to our Saviour's prayer that His disciples might be one as He and the Father were one, the last few years have witnessed a sad scattering of the holiness people.

Because of this many hearts have been greatly burdened and have been crying to God for union among all of God's children, especially among all those that believe in holiness of heart as possible through faith in the cleansing blood of Christ and by the baptism of the Holy Ghost; yet divisions seemed to increase. The holiness work has been suffering all over the land because of it. Seeing this.

the burden of our heart became an unearthly cry that God would in some way undertake. We felt that something must be done; yet waited for others who were older and more prominent to take the lead.

Reference has already been made to the first General Holiness Assembly of holiness workers held in Chicago in 1885. At that time, as will be seen by reading the Official Call for the recent Assembly, given in another place, a committee was appointed for the calling of another Assembly at such time and place as they might deem necessary; yet the years had slipped away and the prospect of such an Assembly, from the human standpoint, seemed less and less. Our name was the last on the list and we the youngest of the committee, but the time came when we could no longer forbear.

On our way home from evangelistic work in Texas in August, 1900, with our heart full of burning love for our brethren of different movements, and breaking with sorrow over the desolation of Zion, we promised God to wait no longer. On the train we blocked out a Call in harmony with our convictions and soon after reaching home revised it and sent it on to Brother George Hughes, chairman of the committee, urging him to take hold of the matter and see what could be done. His reply was encouraging and immediately both of us began correspondence with other members of the committee and leaders of the holiness work. Some of the answers we received were rather discouraging and showed but little faith, but all acknowledged the great need. Members of the committee and many others readily promised their hearty sympathy and co-operation, and in spite of difficulties that appeared insurmountable, the work went on in answer to prayer. From the first, Brother Hughes took it upon his heart and labored with us constantly and faithfully.

As a result of consultation with Brother Hughes and other members of the committee, some changes were made in the Call and some things added and names agreed upon to fill vacancies in the original committee; and the consent and co-operation of the brothers secured. Thus several months passed before the Call was ready for publication and at times our faith was greatly tested; but from that time preparations went forward rapidly and the work took strong hold upon many hearts and in spite of great opposition on the part of some from whom we expected sympathy, difficulties were overcome, barriers gave way, and interest and sympathy and co-operation increased.

Of our own part in this work, Brother Hughes says in an editorial in the June number of The Guide to Holiness: "Brother Shaw was really the father of this enterprise, and at his earnest solicitation we consented to unite with him in making the preparations. Brother and Sister Shaw worked heroically in the matter, going from church to church, and holdings meetings in the First Church, daily, in the afternoon, for a month, in order to interest pastors and people in the work contemplated by the Assembly."

The Official Call was published in nearly all of the holiness papers of this country and Canada and many of them opened their columns freely for communications regarding the Assembly and published strong editorials in its favor. Several numbers of the "Guide to Holiness" were devoted largely to the interest of the Assembly and large extra editions sent out. Many church papers of different denominations published the Call and encouraged the work. The names of hundreds of leaders representing a score or more of different evangelical denominations were added to the Call, and thousands of God's children took the work to heart and carried it to the throne in earnest and prevailing prayer asking that the Holiness Assembly might result in the greatest revival of perfect love known in the modern holiness movement. Succeeding pages will tell our readers some of the glorious results already seen, but no words can tell and time can not measure all the outcome.

We were authorized by the Assembly to publish its proceedings in book form and an advisory committee was appointed. So far as possible we have consulted not only this committee but others of the leading workers who were present at the Assembly. It has been thought best to condense sermons to eight or ten pages. This has been done by the speakers themselves so that as far as possible the truth brought out might be clearly presented.

Depending upon the work of the stenographer who was to keep an accurate report of all services, we took no notes during the Assembly and when too late found that the reports, given of altar services utterly failed to do them justice. This we greatly regret.

In all this work, God is our witness that we have labored with an eye single to His glory and we earnestly pray that mistakes may be overruled and that our work, by the mercy of God, may be greatly used in the uniting of God's people and the salvation of many souls.

Your brother and servant in Christ Jesus our Lord,
S. B. Shaw.

ECHOES
OF THE
GENERAL HOLINESS ASSEMBLY

The Official Call.

To all the saints and faithful brethren scattered abroad, greeting. "Grace be unto you, and peace from God our Father, and from our Lord Jesus Christ."

Many will remember that in the spring of 1885, there was held in the city of Chicago, a Holiness General Assembly, May 20 - 26.

That assembly represented a score or more of the evangelical denominations; yet regarding holiness doctrine, experience and testimony, it was, practically, a unit. Its sessions (as stated by the committee on deliverances, in the published report) were characterized by Christian fellowship, unity and gracious outpourings of the Holy Spirit; so that at almost every service, persons were converted or sanctified. "At times," as they state, "the Divine communications were overwhelming; the altar and surrounding seats were filled with seekers and the saving work progressed with great power."

So great was the good accomplished, that it was the conviction of those present that some provision should be made to arrange for another similar gathering of the holiness forces, and we, the undersigned, * were appointed members of a general committee of correspondence for

---

*Some vacancies in the original committee have been filled by other names.

the holding of another holiness assembly at such time and place as we deemed expedient. Fifteen years have swept rapidly by since that glorious time and many of those then present with us have gone to join the general assembly of the first born, around the throne in the heavenly city. Great responsibility rests upon us who remain, and upon all who have ever proved that there is power in the blood of Christ to cleanse from all sin, and have ever known in their own hearts the baptism of the Holy Ghost and fire. And while we praise God for the revival and spread of scriptural holiness which has been witnessed in the last few decades, we are firmly convinced that the holiness people (so known) are not measuring up to their glorious opportunity. As a committee, we believe that another general holiness rally, similar in object and methods to the one we have mentioned, will greatly redound to the glory of God in the stirring up and uniting of God's people and in the salvation of a multitude of souls.

Under these convictions the Committee has been led, we trust by the Spirit of God, to arrange for a

GENERAL HOLINESS ASSEMBLY.

to be held in the First Methodist Episcopal Church of Chicago, Ill., of which Rev. J. P. Brushingham, D. D., is pastor, corner of Clark and Washington Streets, May 3 - 13, 1901. To this Assembly we cordially invite members of the Evangelical Church of Christ. And if there be any Christians, who, for any just cause, may be temporarily without a Church home, they will be welcome to meet with us, and the more if we may aid them in selecting a congenial Church home, where the means of grace will contribute to their spiritual life and progress.

In the services of the Assembly, largeness of gospel

liberty will be enjoyed, and there will be abundant opportunities for holy exercise in testifying freely of the great salvation in its varied phases—to lead fellow Christians to the fountain of cleansing, and penitent sinners to the feet of Jesus, that they may know the joy of pardoned sin.

The gates of entrance to the Assembly will be open day and night, to admit the unsaved of all classes, in expectancy that very many will be happily converted and introduced to the fellowship of the saints, during the progress of the services.

The Assembly will be representative in character. Persons will be enrolled as members who bring certificates from some branch of the evangelical Church, or from organizations which maintain a fraternal spirit and attitude toward the Church—such as Holiness Associations, ecclesiastical bodies, Conferences, Camp Meeting Associations, definitely on the line of holiness, Missions and Stated Meetings, and any other organization of like character, said certificates being subject to approval of the Committee on Enrollment or Credentials as the Assembly may appoint. Members will be entitled to participate in the discussions and to vote on questions submitted to the Assembly for its action.

While leaving the Assembly in the main to plan for its own work, we deem it proper to specify the following general objects:

1. Such a Pentecostal waiting upon God in humble, united, prevailing prayer, as will bring about truly Pentecostal results in the outpouring of God's Spirit and the saving of souls.

2. Such prayerful and harmonious consideration of the needs and hindrances of the holiness movement, as shall lead to more hearty co-operation, more thorough

and aggressive work, and more victorious results than in the past.

3. To provide opportunity to again publish to the world, the true mission and object of the holiness movement (rightly recognized as such) and so, as far as possible, remove prejudice that comes from misunderstanding or has resulted from extreme, erroneous and fanatical positions assumed by some so-called holiness workers.

4. It is especially desired that this Assembly shall present a basis for the bringing of the holiness organizations throughout the world, if practicable, into an International Union, so that there shall be an augmented strength, and a mightier advance made upon the kingdom of darkness in the present century, than has yet been known in the history of the modern holiness movement. And in furtherance of this design, all side issues irrelevant to the objects herein specifically stated, will be necessarily excluded from the discussions of the Assembly.

5. Such an Assembly, representing all of the evangelical Churches, will give a blessed opportunity of manifesting to the Church and to the world, the love they have for each other and for the various movements and denominations they represent; thus proving the word of God, "By this shall all men know that ye are my disciples, if ye have love one to another." John 13:35. The most devoted and prominent Christian workers have not been able to see alike in all things, but, by the grace of God, they may be able to feel alike and work in perfect harmony regardless of their many differences.

There is a wide-spread conviction among God's people that we are on the eve of a great revival of Scriptural holiness. Thousands are on their knees every day praying for a deeper type of Christian experience and for more heavenly union among God's people. If the Holy

Ghost is fully honored by all saints in the coming Assembly, we believe it will be greatly used of God in bringing about the greatest revival of holiness witnessed since the days of the apostles; that the fire of God's love will sweep away all barriers that have kept the holiness people apart, and that the saints will be so occupied with God that they will lose sight of human creeds and forms and self importance and whatever else has hindered the outpouring of God's Spirit.

We earnestly recommend the observance of a general fast among the holiness people everywhere. Let special and prevailing prayer be offered for the coming assembly and the cause of holiness. Let prayer be offered daily for God's blessing to rest upon this expected gathering of his people.

We have secured a large church in the heart of the city for the use of the Assembly, and an effort will be made to obtain reduced rates over the railroads.

Through the kindness and co-operation of the holiness people of Chicago, we hope to provide free entertainment for those coming from a distance. Further and more definite information will be published in due time.

Your brethren in the bonds of perfect love,

GEORGE HUGHES,	New York.
W. T. HOGUE,	Illinois.
ISAIAH REID,	Iowa.
JOHN A. WOOD,	California.
A. M. HILLS,	Texas.
J. McD. KERR,	Canada.
CHAS. N. CRITTENTON,	Washington, D. C.
AURA SMITH,	Missouri.
S. B. SHAW,	Illinois.

Donations in aid of the expenses, which will necessarily be large, will be thankfully received. Address, S. B. Shaw, Treasurer, Central Union Block, corner Market and Madison Streets, Chicago, Ill,

The following leading holiness workers gave their names in endorsement of the call:

Rev. Chas. Garnett, Congregationalist, London, England.
Rev. Chas. W. L. Chrisliew, Wesleyan, England.
Rev. I. E. Page, Wesleyan, England.
Rev. E. T. Curnick, D. D., Lyon, Mass.
Rev. A. T. Jennings, Editor Wesleyan Methodist, Syracuse, N. Y.
Rev. A. W. Hall, Publisher Wesleyan Methodist, Syracuse, N. Y.
W. P. Raidabaugh, Manager Friends' Pub. Ass'n., Chicago.
Rev. J. W. Lively, Presiding Elder M. E. Church, Marshall, Texas.
Rev. John G. Fee, President Berea College, Berea, Ky.
Rev. T. C. Reade, D. D., President Taylor University, Upland, Ind.
Bishop N. Castle, of U. B. Church, Elkhart, Indiana.
Rev. B. Carradine, Evangelist, St. Louis, Mo.
J. Walter Malone, Pres. Friends' Bible Training Home, Cleveland, O.
Rev. W. I. Phillips, Gen. Sec. American Christian Association, Chicago.
Rev. Edward F. Walker, Evangelist, Greencastle, Ind.
Rev. C. W. Ruth, Evangelist, Indianapolis, Ind.
Col. F. E. Peck, of Christian Crusaders, Dutton, Mich.
Rev. W. B. Godbey, Evangelist, Perryville, Ky.
Rev. J. L. Glascock, Evangelist, Cincinnati, Ohio.
Rev. Thos. H. Nelson, Leader in Charge of Pentecost Bands, Indianapolis, Ind.
Rev. C. B. Whitaker, P. E. of U. B. Church, Charlotte, Mich.
Rev. John Kirn, P. C., Primitive Holiness Mission, Owosso, Mich.
Rev. Lucius Hawkins, Evangelist, Birmingham, Alabama.
Rev. T. B. Arnold, Publisher, Chicago, Ill.
Rev. F. M. Levy, D. D., Philadelphia, Penn.
Rev. John Parker, Ashbury Park, N. J.
Rev. A. E. Ballard, D. D., President Pitman Grove Camp Meeting Association.
Rev. Bud. Robinson, Evangelist, Greenville, Texas.
Rev. S. Rice, Superintendent Pentecostal Union, Chicago.
Rev. G. A. McLaughlin, Editor Christian Witness, Chicago.
Rev. D. O. Ernsberger, P. E. Raichur, District, South India Conference, M. E. Church.
Brigadier General Fielding, of American Volunteers, Chicago.
J. S. Date, Sec. Des Plaines Camp Meeting Association, Chicago.
Bishop I. W. Joyce of M. E. Church, Minneapolis, Minn.
Rev. L. A. Townsend, Pastor Sedwick St. Cong. Church, Chicago.
Rev. D. F. Brooks, Pastor-Evangelist, Brandon, Vermont.
Mrs. Lizzie R. Smith, Evangelist, Philadelphia, Pa.
Rev. Seneca Howland, Evangelist, New York.
Mrs. Sarah A. Cooke, Evangelist, Chicago.
Deacon Geo. M. Morse, Putnam, Conn.
Rev. A. C. Morehouse, Leader of Tuesday meeting, New York.
Rev. J. B. Foote, Evangelist, Syracuse, New York.
Rev. W. G. Browning, Poughkeepsie, New York.
Rev. J. D. Kelsey, Chicago District Free Methodist Church, Chicago.

W. J. Hadley, Gen'l Supt. Pastoral and Evangelical Department of Iowa Yearly Meeting of Friends' Church.
Rev. Grover C. Clark, P. E. Dixon District Rock River Conference. M. E. Church.
Rev. C. S. Hanley, Pres. World's Faith Missionary Association. Shenandoah, Iowa.
Rev. T. H. Osborn, the "Drummer Evangelist," Union Springs. New York.
Bishop Cyrus D. Foss, of M. E. Church, Philadelphia, Penn.
Bishop Thomas Bowman, of M. E. Church, East Orange, N. J.
Rev. D. A. H. Tuttle, Pastor of M. E. Church, East Orange, N. J.
Rev. Alexander McLean, Treas. National Holiness Association. Brooklyn, N. Y.
Bishop A. Walters, A. M. E. Zion Church, Jersey City, N. J.
Mrs. Julia A. Foote, Evangelist, Jersey City, N. J.
Rev. and Mrs. Jas. Harris, of Methodist Church, Guelph, Canada
Rev. E. E. Reynolds, Secretary of Vermont Holiness Association.
Rev. D. G. F. Oliver, P. E. of M. E. Church, New Philadelphia, Ohio
Bishop D. H. Moore, of M. E. Church, Shanghai, China.
Rev. Dr. A. J. Nast.
Rev. T. C. Ligon, Editor of *Way of Faith*.
Bishop J. M. Walden, of M. E. Church.
Dr. Manley S. Hard, Secretary Church Extension Society of M. E. Church.
Mrs. E. M. Whittemore, Founder of Door of Hope, New York.
Colonel Ray, Missionary to "The Tombs," New York.
Rev. Dr. H. B. Parks, Secretary of Missionary Society of A. M. E. Church.
Mrs. Abbie C. Morrow, Evangelist and Editor of *S. S. Illustrator*, New York.
Bishop B. W. Goodsell, of M. E. Church, Chattanooga, Tenn.
Rev. Egerton R. Young, Indian Missionary, Toronto, Canada.
Mrs. J. F. Willing, W. C. T. U. Training Institute and Settlement, New York.
Mrs. Amanda Smith, Evangelist, North Harvey, Ill.
Mrs. Mary Grant Cramer, Evangelist, East Orange, N. J.
Miss Isabella S. Leonard, Evangelist, Phœnix, Arizona.
Rev. J. P. Brushingham, Pastor First M. E. Church, Chicago.
Mrs. Kate Summer Burr, Editor of *Invalid's Visitor*, Williamson, New York.
Rev. N. Vansant, of Newark Conference Holiness Association, Madison, N. J.
Rev. D. F. Brooks, Pastor and Evangelist, Brandon, Vermont.
Rev. Seneca Hurland, Evangelist, New York.
Rev. H. Grentzenberg, Editor of *German Guide to Holiness*, Cincinnati, Ohio.
Col. and Mrs. Chas. Sowton, Officers in charge of Northwestern Division Salvation Army, Chicago, Ill.
Rev. and Mrs. James Printer, Evangelists, Sarahville, Ohio.
Rev. L. B. Whitcomb, Pastor of F. M. Church, Evanston, Ill.

M. L. Ryan, Editor of *Light,* Salem, Oregon.

Rev. B. F. Roberts, Editor *Earnest Christian,* North Chili, N. Y.

Rev. Geo. W. Ridout, Pres. Fletcher Grove Holiness Camp Meeting Association, Delanco, N. J.

Dr. M. W. Palmer, New York, at whose home the "Tuesday Meeting" is held.

Rev. Dr. C. J. Fowler, Pres. of National Holiness Association, Haverhill, Mass.

Mrs. O. M. Fitzgerald, Newark, N. J., over forty years Leader of Holiness meetings.

Rev. W. B. Osborn, Hackettstown, N. J., Founder of National Holiness Movement, now New Jersey Conference Evangelist.

Mrs. Lucy D. Osborn, Pres. of Missionary Training Institute, Brooklyn, N. Y.

Miss Hester Alway, Vice Principal of Missionary Training Institute, Brooklyn, N. Y.

Bishop W. F. Mallalieu, of the M. E. Church, Auburndale, Mass.

Rev. Dr. A. Carmen, Superintendent of Methodist Church, Canada.

Rev. Dr. John Potts, Secretary of Educational Society of Methodist Church, Canada.

Bishop A. Grant, A. M. E. Church, Indianapolis, Indiana.

Rev. W. N. Ogborn, Chairman, Pitman Grove, N. J.

Rev. J. S. Heisler, Camden, N. J.

Rev. J. B. Westcott, Camden, N. J.

Rev. and Mrs. J. T. Johnson, Evangelists, Perkinsville, Vermont.

Richard Grant, East Orange, N. J.

Mr. and Mrs. Stephen Simonson, Newark, N. J.

Rev. Dr. D. M. Stearns, Editor of *Kingdom Tidings,* Philadelphia, Pa.

A. W. Dennett, Westville, Placer Co., California.

Mother Prindle, late Matron of Florence Crittenton Mission, New York.

Rev. E. D. Whiteside, of Christian and Missionary Alliance, Pittsburg, Pa.

Rev. A. W. Orwig, Evangelist, Cleveland, O.

Jennie Smith, Railroad Evangelist, Washington, D. C.

Mrs. Grace Weiser Davis, Evangelist, Jersey City.

Mrs. R. C. Oliver, Missionary, Columbia, S. C.

Miss Emily E. Oliver, Matron Missionary Training Institute, New York, and Marie J. Smith, Frances Stevens, Minerva L. Guthappel, Maud M. Ralph, Margaret L. Boyer, Florence R. Weiss, Harry Lee, Elizabeth Schwab, Louis M. Daval, Ruth Finch, Louise M. Stead, Henrietta Robins, Althea M. Todd and J. W. Bill, students of the institution, who are in the experience of perfect love.

The Union Revival Services Preparatory to the General Holiness Assembly.

Realizing the great importance of the coming General Holiness Assembly, myself and wife with several others had strong convictions that special meetings should be held in order to prepare the hearts of the people in Chicago for the great work before them. We rented the lecture room of the first M. E. church where meetings were held daily from 2 to 4 P. M., except Sundays, when they were held from 3 to 5 in the audience room. These lasted for one month.

The meetings opened up Friday, April 5th, with an all day meeting. It was a day of great power and there were a number of earnest seekers. The meetings continued from day to day with unabated interest and we do not know of a single service without some seekers. The coming Assembly was kept before the people and the importance of heart union among Christians of all denominations was made prominent in all the meetings. Christian workers representing a dozen or more denominations co-operated in the work. Salvation Army officers and officers of the American Volunteers and all kinds of Methodists, Baptists, Presbyterians, Congregationalists and other denominations assisted. There was a great burden on myself and wife and others to see Christians of different denominations more closely united in heart and in the work of God.

At times the Lord gave us great power in prayer and preaching the word. Many days and nights were spent on our faces weeping and crying to God for the holiness movement and for the General Holiness Assembly. We deeply felt and sought to impress upon others the following truths:

If we expect to return to primitive piety and power, we must come back to primitive consecration and self denial. We must fear God and keep His commandments, for this is the whole duty of man. Not the main duty, as many people think nor the most important duty, but the whole duty. We should cry to God day and night with an unearthly cry for the old time power and glory.

The lack of sympathy and co-operation among the holiness people has been a great hindrance to the holiness movement. So many of the holiness people allow their differences on non-essentials to result in prejudice and lack of Christian charity. We can never hope for union, even among holiness people, by all seeing alike. The most devoted saints, by a careful study of the Scriptures, will come to different conclusions as to the plan of church government, or the mode of baptism, and other church ordinances. The best, and most able writers have not been able to see alike, as to what constitutes worldly amusements, neither can they exactly agree as to what are unscriptural ways of raising money, or what constitutes worldly conformity in dress and living; and so with other things connected with the work of the Lord, and individual practice.

The best people will never see alike on all points; but God's people may be so cleansed from all sin, and so filled with perfect love, that they will think no evil of each other. They may be of one heart and of one mind, touching the vitals of the Christian faith; and whether they think or believe alike or not, they may be able, by the grace of God to feel alike, and work in perfect harmony, regardless of their many differences.

We have labored in holiness conventions, where ten or twelve denominations were represented, and they disagreed on many points, and yet they were perfectly united in love. If we expect others to respect our judgment and convictions of right, we must respect theirs.

If the holiness people would spend as much time praying for each other, as they do in criticising each other, they would soon come together.

Brother Hall from the Moody Institute had a great burden of prayer and was greatly used of God in exhortation and prevailing prayer for the meeting. Brother A. L. Whitcomb of Evanston, preached two powerful sermons that were greatly honored of God. During the meetings we also had an able sermon from G. W. Hanmer of the same place; also from Evangelists John B. Shaw, S. Rice, W. E. Shepard, G. D. Cleworth, Hattie Livingston, Joseph Jamieson. We were also greatly assisted by Rev. G. A. McLaughlin, John Kelsey, Sarah A. Cooke and others. One of the most remarkable conversions during the preliminary meetings was an ex-Catholic monk. After his conversion he told us of the awful tortures that he had endured because he could not conscientiously endorse all the corruption that he witnessed in the various monasteries where he had been for over twenty years. The preliminary meetings resulted in getting the holiness people of Chicago greatly united and interested in the Assembly.

In addition to the meetings held every day from two to four at the First M. E. church, myself and wife held revival services preparatory to the Assembly in Salvation Army and Volunteer halls, Missions and various churches, which meetings were greatly blessed of God and resulted in the salvation of a goodly number of souls.

A Day of Fasting and Prayer for the General Holiness Assembly.

The following notice was widely published and abundant evidence given that the day was very generally observed.

In addition to the request in the Official Call for daily prayer for God's blessing to rest upon the Assembly, we are urged to fix upon a day for the observance of a general fast among Holiness people everywhere, when they shall unite in crying mightily to God for the coming Assembly, to be held in Chicago May 3-13.

We therefore, in the fear of God, set apart Friday April 26, to be thus observed, and request all who will to join in the following petitions:

1—Pray that God in His infinite mercy may grant to all hearts the intercession of the Holy Ghost, that they may prevail with Him in prayer in behalf of the Assembly.

2—Pray that God may open the way for all those whom He would have come to Chicago.

3—Pray that all those that come may come in the fullness of the Spirit, or with hearts hungering after righteousness.

4—Pray that the hearts of the holiness people may be united for the work of God as never before, and that all misunderstandings and all other barriers that have hindered the work may be swept away by the mighty power of God.

5—Pray that the Assembly may be the beginning of the greatest and most thorough revival known to the modern holiness movement.

GEO. HUGHES, Chairman,
S. B. SHAW, Secretary.

First All Day and All Night Meeting.

In harmony with the call for special fasting and prayer we arranged for an all-day service, April 26, to be followed by an all night of prayer. Our report is largely taken from the Christian Witness. This service was in union with the regular Friday all day meeting here in the city under charge of the Pentecostal Union.

The morning service was held in the Wabash Ave. M. E. church, and was led by Bro. S. Rice, Supt. of the Pentecostal Union. The service consisted mainly of prayer and testimony and a good talk by Bro. Hughes, editor of "The Guide to Holiness," who had just arrived to assist in the preliminary meetings of the Assembly. The service was good and the Lord of hosts was in the midst.

The afternoon service was held at the First M. E. church, where the preliminary meetings were held each day. Bro. Hughes was much blessed in speaking to the people. Sister S. B. Shaw read the Scripture lesson. Exhortations, testimonies and a blessed altar service followed. This was a glorious service.

The evening service was at the Wabash Ave. M. E. church again and lasted all night. From 7 till 10 it was in charge of Bro. Rice. Following prayer and testimony, Bro. W. E. Shepard of California preached a very excellent sermon on consecration, which was followed by a blessed altar service with a goodly number of seekers for pardon and holiness, some of whom received the desire of their hearts.

Following this service the Salvation Army came in large force, representing the corps of the city, with a number of the leading officers, and led a very interesting service till about one o'clock, many of them remaining till the close at five o'clock in the morning.

After the time allotted to the Army, Bro. S. B. Shaw took charge of the meeting for the rest of the night. A number of ten minute talks from some evangelists, pastors and Salvation Army officers present, with frequent altar calls for prayer, which were much owned of God, took up a goodly portion of the time.

At about four o'clock in the morning it seemed that the windows of heaven were opened and the glory that shone of old beamed from the faces of the saints, and their testimonies had a heavenly ring.

Among the wonderful uplifts of the night was the sermon of Evangelist Joseph Jamieson. He occupied the last part of the night. As the light of morning began to break in at the windows, the glory of God poured into the saints' hearts.

Sister Lydia E. Brown, evangelist, describes the meetings and sermon as follows:

"The wonderful power of God was felt all night. At times the church seemed to be aglow with divine glory and filled with the presence of the risen Christ. Christians were filled with the Holy Ghost, unsaved souls were brought into the light of sins forgiven, and before morning it seemed as if the time had come for the Second Coming of our Lord and Savior, so manifest was His presence among us. Then came that wonderful closing between the hours of four and five, when God seemed to open the windows of heaven and pour out a blessing which will never be forgotten in this world nor in the world to come. A brother spoke, and as he addressed the audience it seemed to me as if surely the Holy One of Israel was not only in the midst of us but had full control of preacher and people."

During the night a goodly number of souls were entirely sanctified, including six Salvation Army officers, four of whom were captains.

Officers and Committees of the Assembly.

TEMPORARY OFFICERS.
Chairman.
Rev. George Hughes of New York.
Secretary.
Rev. G. A. McLaughlin of Illinois.

PERMANENT OFFICERS.
President.
Rev. C. J. Fowler of Massachusetts.
Vice Presidents.
Rev. E. F. Walker, Ind.
Rev. A. M. Hills, Tex.
Rev. James Harris, Canada.
Rev. M. L. Haney, Ill.
Deacon Geo. M. Morse, Conn.
Secretary.
Rev. A. L. Whitcomb, Ill.
Assistant Secretary.
Rev. W. E. Shepard, Cal.
Treasurer.
Rev. G. A. McLaughlin, Ill.
Railroad Secretary.
Rev. T. B. Arnold, Ill.
Assembly Reporter.
Rev. Isaiah Reid, Iowa.

COMMITTEES.
Committee on Permanent Methods.
Rev. Alexander McLean, Chairman, Brooklyn, N. Y.
Rev. T. K. Doty, Cleveland, Ohio.
Rev. Aura Smith, Seymour, Ind.
Rev. T. H. Agnew, Virginia, Ill.
Rev. G. A. McLaughlin, Evanston, Ill.
Rev. J. R. Allen, Waterloo, Iowa.
Rev. J. B. Foote, Syracuse, N. Y.

Committee on Deliverances.
Rev. W. T. Hogue, Chairman, Chicago, Ill.
Rev. L. B. Kent, Jacksonville, Ill.
Rev. E. F. Walker, Greencastle, Ind.
Rev. Hiram Ackers, Big Prairie, Ohio.
Rev. A. M. Hills, Greenville, Texas.
Rev. M. L. Haney, Normal, Ill.
Rev. W. E. Shepard, Los Angeles, Cal.

Committee on Music.

Rev. G. A. McLaughlin.
Rev. J. M. and M. J. Harris.
Rev. J. B. Shaw.
Rev. C. B. Jernigan.

Committee on Mail.

Mrs. Hattie Livingston.

Committee on Books.

Rev. S. B. Shaw, Chairman.
Rev. J. P. Brushingham.
Rev. S. Rice.

Committee on Pulpit Supply.

Rev. A. D. Traveller.
Rev. S. Rice.
Rev. H. Hunt.
Rev. S. B. Shaw.

Committee on Credentials.

Rev. J. B. Foote.
Rev. James Harris.
Rev. A. C. Morehouse.
Rev. A. M. Hills.
Rev. G. M. Morse.

Committee on Press.

Rev. A. M. Hills.
Rev. W. T. Hogue.
Rev. C. J. Fowler.

Committee to Report Nominations.

Rev. E. F. Walker.
Rev. L. B. Kent.
Rev. James Harris.
Rev. J. B. Foote.
Rev. Wm. G. Hanmer.

Committee on Street Meetings.

Sarah A. Cooke.
Beatrice Beaseley.

Committee on Finance.

Rev. S. B. Shaw.
Rev. John Kelsey.
Rev. E. C. De Jernett.

Committee on Entertainment.

Rev. Herbert Hunt.
Mrs. Etta E. Shaw.
Rev. F. C. Hall.
Mrs. C. W. Brown.

Committee on Preparation.

Rev. C. J. Fowler, Mass.
Rev. A. M. Hills, Tex.
Rev. H. C. Morrison, Ky.

Rev. A. L. Whitcomb, Ill.
Rev. M. L. Haney, Ill.
Rev. J. M. Pike, Ga.
Rev. John McD. Kerr, Canada.
Rev. P. F. Bresee, Cal.
Deacon Geo. M. Morse, Conn.
Rev. Isaiah Reid, Iowa.
Rev. E. F. Walker, Ind.
  Committee to Draft Constitution for Holiness Bands and Associations.
Rev. Alexander McLean, New York.
Rev. L. B. Kent, Illinois.
Rev. C. W. Ruth, Indiana.

Assembly Roll.

Ackers, Rev. Hiram, Big Prairie, Ohio.
Agnew, Rev. T. H., Virginia, Ill.
Allen, Rev. Jacob R., Waterloo, Iowa.
Alling, Rev. J. H., Evanston, Ill.
Anderson, Erick, Nordness, Iowa.
Anderson, Rev. Alfred, 1345 Noble Ave., Chicago, Ill.
Applegate, Mrs. J. F., 406 W. Illinois St., Indianapolis, Ind.
Arnold, Rev. T. B., 104 Franklin St., Chicago, Ill.
Atkinson, Mrs. J. F. —— Dearborn St., Chicago, Ill.
Armstrong, Rev. J. B., Norwood, Ga.
Baker, Rev. L. H., Delaware, Ohio.
Barnes, Wilson, 173 Park Ave., Chicago, Ill.
Barrett, C. L., Indianapolis, Ind.
Beaseley, Mrs. Beatrice, Chicago, Ill.
Beebe, J. W., 811 University Place, Evanston, Ill.
Behner, Rev. Geo., St. Charles, Ill.
Benkert, Rev. Wm., 1912 Main St., Davenport, Iowa.
Birdsall, Miss Fannie, Indianapolis, Ind.
Boyce, Mrs. C. B., Office of Christian Witness, Chicago, Ill.
Boyer, Rev. J. W., Coloma, Mich.
Bradley, Rev. C. L., Cohoctah, Mich.
Brengle, Brigadier S. L., New York City.
Brookmiller, Rev. F. H., Red Oak, Iowa.
Brooks, Jonas, Des Moines, Iowa.
Brooks, Rev. John P., Fort Scott, Kansas.
Brown, Rev. B. J., 3343 State St., Chicago, Ill.
Brown, Della, 523 Lord St., Indianapolis, Ind.
Brushingham, Rev. J. P., 108 Washington St. Chicago, Ill.
Bryant, Mrs. Geo., Riverdale, Mich.
Buck, Rev. Geo. R., Bloomington, Ill.
Buck, Mrs. R. C., Bloomington, Ill.
Buck, Miss Mary L., Bloomington, Ill.
Burleson, A. E., 526 —— 66 Place, Chicago, Ill.
Blanchard, Henry C., Boscobel, Wis.
Burpee, Laura, Woodstock, N. B.

Cadwell, Rev. J. R., 1093 West Grace St., Chicago, Ill.
Cain, C. N., Cerrogordo, Ill.
Casper, Rev. C. C., Salem, Wis.
Clark, Mrs. M. B., Sioux City, Iowa.
Cleworth, Rev. C. D., Wabash Ave. and 14th St., Chicago, Ill.
Cook, Rev. D. W., Lebanon, S. Dakota.
Cook, Mrs. Sarah A., 22 Aberdeen St., Chicago, Ill.
Crabbs, Mrs. V. E. Shenandoah, Iowa.
Collinge, Rev. J. A., East Troy, N. Y.
Crampton, Mrs. Mary, Evanston, Ill.
Coleman, Rev. J. J., Bryant, Ind.
Colby, Mrs. J. S., Storey, Wis.
Day, Mrs. M. E., 1232 W. Addison St., Chicago, Ill.
De Foe, Rev. M., Hartford, Mich.
De Foe, Mrs. M., Hartford, Mich.
De Jernett, Rev. E. C., Greenville, Texas.
Dempster, Rev. Joseph, Washington, D. C.
Donovan, J. L., Chicago, Ill.
Doty, Rev. T. K., 36 Lowell St., Cleveland, Ohio.
Dudman, Mrs. Charlotte, 1475 W. Congress St., Chicago, Ill.
Duryea, Rev. C. M., 355 Harrison St., Holland, Mich.
Dustman, Rev. J. M., Urbana, Ind.
Eclenger, Mary E., Demotte, Ind.
Edwards, Rev. Wm., Paxton, Ill.
Entorf, Rev. S. T., Naperville, Ill.
Evans, Rev. W. T., Concord, Ill.
Felmlee, Mrs. C. L., 265 Park Ave., Chicago, Ill.
Ferris, A. L., Paxton, Ill.
Flower, Rev. J. H., Greenville, Ill.
Floyd, H. R., Saugatuck, Mich.
Foote, Rev. J. B., Syracuse, N. Y.
Fowler, Rev. C. J., Haverhill, Mass.
Funk, Rev. H. W., Danville, Ill.
Gilbert, Mrs. A. T., Chicago, Ill.
Goff, W. Roy, Evanston, Ill.
Goodman, E., 276 E. North Ave., Chicago, Ill.
Grentzenberg, Rev. H., Kinsey Place, Cincinnati, O.
Hall, Rev. F. C., Fryburg, Maine.
Haney, Rev. M. L., Normal, Ill.
Hanmer, Rev. W. G., 2010 Darrow St., Evanston, Ill.
Harris, Rev. J. M., Evanston, Ill.
Harris, Mrs. M. J., Evanston, Ill.
Harris, James, Guelph, Ontario.
Hayes, Rev. D. A., Evanston, Ill.
Hewitt, Rev. S. M., Tallula, Ill.
Hewitt, Mrs. S. M., Tallula, Ill.
Hills, Rev. A. M., Greenville, Texas.
Hogue, Rev. W. T., 14 N. May St., Chicago, Ill.
Hughes, Rev. George, Orange, N. Y.
Hunt, Rev. Herbert, 1678 Flournoy St., Chicago, Ill.
Hurlock, Mrs. A. J. Cleburne, Texas,

Hodgkins, Mrs. A. J.
Jacobs, A., 5817 Emerald Ave., Chicago, Ill.
Jacobs, Mrs. F. A., 5817 Emerald Ave., Chicago, Ill.
Jernigan, Rev. C. B., Greenville, Texas.
Jones, Rev. H. L., Wild Cherry, Ark.
Kean, Mrs. S. A., 1815 Chicago Ave., Evanston, Ill.
Keithly, Mrs. F. M., 4618 St. Louis St., St. Louis, Mo.
Kelsey, Rev. J. D., 14 Nebraska Ave., Chicago, Ill.
Kelsey, Rev. W. M., Evanston, Ill.
Kelsey, Mrs. W. M., Evanston, Ill.
Kent, Rev. L. B., Jacksonville, Ill.
Kerr, Rev. J. McD., Toronto, Ontario.
Kirn, Rev. John, Owosso, Mich.
Kirn, Mrs. Etta, Owosso, Mich.
Klaus, John W., Earlville, Iowa.
Kletzing, Rev. H. F., Naperville, Ill.
Lamb, H. C., Dennison, Iowa.
Lafgren, Rev. A. J., 151 Oak St., Chicago, Ill.
Laird, Samuel, Mt. Vernon, Ill.
Lafontaine, Rev. C. V., Ada St., Chicago, Ill.
Landon, C. K., 972 Adams St., Chicago, Ill.
Lee, John Wesley, Plymouth, Ind.
Leek, Rev. J. D., Englewood, Chicago, Ill.
Livingston, Mrs. Hattie, 500 Chestnut St., Des Moines, Ia.
Loring, Rev. W. T., Knox, Ind.
Love, Mrs. Belle, 152 S. Wood St., Chicago, Ill.
Lyman, Rev. C. W., 435 Carroll Ave., Chicago, Ill.
Lyman, Mrs. C. W., 435 Carroll Ave., Chicago, Ill.
Lyon, Daniel D., Woodbine, Iowa.
Marsh, Rev. J. D., 981 N. California Ave., Chicago, Ill.
Matlack, Rev. J. A., 68 De Kalb St., Chicago, Ill.
Mayhew E., Talona, Ill.
McClung, Rev. T. M., Spring Green, Wis.
McBride, Rev. H. C., 150 Fifth Ave., New York City.
McCoy, J. F., Danville, Ill.
McFarland, Rev. Wm., Maples Mill, Ill.
McGeary, Rev. J. S., Greenville, Ill.
McKinnon, Mrs. M. J., Dallas, Texas.
McLaughlin, Rev. Geo. A., 1109 Ayers Ct., Evanston, Ill.
McLaughlin, Mrs. Geo. A., 1109 Ayers Ct., Evanston, Ill.
McLean, Rev. Alexander, 5 Seeley St., Brooklyn, N. Y.
Mitchell, Mrs. S. J., 2322 N. 43d Ave., Chicago, Ill.
Millican, Rev. Wm., Ross, Washington.
Morse, Deacon Geo. M., Putnam, Conn.
Moorehouse, Rev. A. C., 150 Fifth Ave., New York City.
Morris, B. S., Derby, Iowa.
Morris, Mrs. B. S., Derby, Iowa.
Murdick, Rev. P. H., Clinton, Mass.
Musselman, M. H. J., Wheeler, Ill.
Nelson, Rev. J. O., 214 N. May St., Chicago, Ill.
Nelson Rev. Thomas H., Indianapolis, Ind.

Nelson, Mrs. Flora B., Indianapolis, Ind.
Nickel, Rev. F., 7930 Chauncey Ave., Chicago, Ill.
Nickel, Mrs. F., 7930 Chauncey Ave., Chicago, Ill.
Olmstead, Rev. W. B., 14 N. May St., Chicago, Ill.
Palmer, Mrs. M. E., Lincoln, Neb.
Parry, Rev. A. W., St. Charles, Ill.
Parker, F. J., Blue Island, Ill.
Peck, Col. F. E., Dutton, Mich.
Peck, Mrs. Agnes, Dutton, Mich.
Peck, Mrs. Kate, Dutton, Mich.
Pledger, Rev. C. P., Des Plaines, Ill.
Reid, Rev. Isaiah, Des Moines, Iowa.
Rice, Rev. S., 6323 Ellis Ave., Chicago, Ill.
Ridout, Rev. G. W., Manahawkin, N. J.
Roberts, Rev. E. J., Milwaukee, Wis.
Roberts, Rev. B. H., North Chili, New York.
Rothermel, M. F., Adaline, Ill.
Rose, Rev. W. B., 932 N. Kedzie Ave., Chicago, Ill.
Rose, Mrs. W. B., 932 N. Kedzie Ave, Chicago, Ill.
Roeder, Rev M., Moberly, Mo.
Ross, Mrs. Fannie, Lincoln, Neb.
Ruth, Rev. C. W., 33 Hamilton Ave., Indianapolis, Ind.
Ruth, Mrs. C. W., 33 Hamilton Ave., Indianapolis, Ind.
Schirmer, Wm., Brooklyn, N. Y.
Schuetz, Rev. H., Springfield, Ill.
Schuh, Rev. C. G., 157 Fremont St., Chicago, Ill.
Schuh, Mrs. C. G., 157 Fremont St., Chicago, Ill.
Scott, Rev. C. J., Nappanee, Ind.
Sergeant, Rev. A., Wilmington, Del.
Shaw, Rev. S. B., 1306 W. Montrose Ave., Chicago, Ill.
Shaw, Mrs. S. B., 1306 W. Montrose Ave., Chicago, Ill.
Shaw, Rev J. B., 116 Seeley Ave., Chicago, Ill.
Shearer, C. B., Blue Island, Ill.
Shearer, Mrs. C. B., Blue Island, Ill.
Shepard, Rev. W. E., Los Angeles, Cal.
Shepard, Mrs. W. E., Los Angeles, Cal.
Showerman, Capt. R. E., Tolona, Ill.
Showerman, Mrs. Capt., Tolona, Ill.
Smead, Nina L., 3438 Wabash Ave., Chicago, Ill.
Smith, Mrs. Amanda, Harvey, Ill.
Smith, Mrs. Lizzie, Woodstock, N. B.
Smith, Rev. Aura, Seymour, Ind.
Smith, Mrs. Aura, Seymour, Ind.
Smith, Jennie, Washington, D. C.
Sniff, A. B., Derby, O.
Snow, Rev. O. L., Peiro, Iowa.
Speicher, D. L., Urbana, Ill.
Spruill, Rev. W. F., Evansville, Ind.
Stambaugh, Mrs. Emma, Colchester, Ill.
Stevenson, W. F., Lovington, Ill.
Swahlen, S. J., Evansville, Ind.

Talbot, Thomas B., Louisville, Ky.
Taylor, Rev. B. S., Stuart, Iowa.
Terrell, Loranat., Albia, Iowa.
Traveller, Rev. A. D., 57 Washington St. Chicago, Ill.
Vasey, F. T., Menominee, Wis.
Vetchistain, Mary, 72 74th St., Pittsburg, Pa.
Vincent, Rev. B. J., Knox, Ind.
Vischer, Irving V., Cohon, N. Y.
Walker, Rev. E. F., Greencastle, Ind.
Warren, T. F., Eola (Du Page Co.), Ill.
Watson, Mrs. M. R., 1208 Lexington Ave., Chicago, Ill.
Wendel, Rev. O., Peiro, Iowa.
West, Mrs. C. A., 11 Seeley Ave., Chicago, Ill.
Wheaton, Mrs. E. R., Tabor, Iowa.
Whitcomb, Rev. A. L., 1814 Ridge Ave., Evanston, Ill.
Whitcomb, Mrs. A. L., 1814 Ridge Ave., Evanston, Ill.
White Mrs. Kent, 2348 Champa St., Denver, Colo.
White, Rev. Levi, 1111 Lexington Ave., Indianapolis, Ind.
Whitaker, Rev. C. B., Charlotte, Mich.
Whitaker, Mrs. C. B., Charlotte, Mich.
Wilson, Rev. Isaiah, Constantine, Mich.
Wilson, Rev. John, Stormburg, Iowa.
Willing, Rev. H. S., Indianapolis, Ind.
Willing, Mrs. H. S., Indianapolis, Ind.
Wisler, R. L., New Carlisle, Ind.
Winget, Rev. B., 14 N. May St., Chicago, Ill.
Winget, Mrs. B., 14 N. May St., Chicago, Ill.
Woertendyke, Rev. J. H., Freeport, Ill.
Wortheim, Mrs. R. L., Denver, Colorado.
Young, Geo. W., Epworth, Ia.
Young, Mrs. F. R., Epworth, Iowa.
(Total 229.)

Holiness Assembly General Address.

1. SALUTATION.

This address was unanimously adopted by the Assembly.

The members of the Holiness General Assembly in session in Chicago, Ill., May 3-13, 1901, unto all in every place who "have obtained like precious faith with us through the righteousness of God and our Savior Jesus Christ. Grace and peace be multiplied unto you through the knowledge of God and of Jesus our Lord."

Beloved, we who, in the providence of God are convened in the second general or international assembly ever held in this country in the interest of promoting the spread of experimental holiness have neither forgotten nor failed in our devotions and deliberations to bear in mind and carry upon our hearts the large and varied constituency of holy men and women scattered throughout the land unable to be with us, and whom we have the honor to represent. On behalf of all such "we bow our knees unto the Father of our Lord Jesus Christ, of whom the whole family in heaven and earth is named, that he would grant them, according to the riches of his glory, to be strengthened with might by his Spirit in the inner man; that Christ may dwell in their hearts by faith; that they, being rooted and grounded in love, may be able with all saints to comprehend what is the breadth and length and depth and height, and to know the love of Christ, which passeth knowledge, that they may be filled with all the fulness of God. Now unto him that is able to do exceeding abundantly above all we ask or think, according to the power that now worketh in us, unto him be glory in the church, by Christ Jesus, throughout all ages. Amen."

2. DOCTRINAL STATEMENT

It is fitting that we should, in our assembled capacity, not only send greetings to the saints who are scattered abroad, but present in a simple form a statement of those doctrines of divine grace particularly related to the experience and life of holiness on which we are agreed.

Concerning what are commonly regarded as the fundamental doctrines of revealed religion, we wish to declare ourselves in full and hearty accord with the views which are held in common by all evangelical churches. Touching those doctrines which we consider more immediately and vitally related to experimental and practical holiness, the following is a brief summary of what we regard as scriptural and essential:

1. Repentance, which is the sinner's first step toward God, consists in such a sorrow for sin, arising from a divinely wrought conviction of its exceeding sinfulness, as leads to its hearty confession, entire abandonment, and a turning to God with purpose of heart, through Jesus Christ, for salvation; all of which will ever be manifested in bringing forth fruits meet for repentant state, particularly in the direction of restitution and reparation for wrong done to one's fellow men, wherever practicable.

2. Conversion, in its comprehensive scriptural sense, includes (a) justification, which is that relation of acceptance before God into which the repentant sinner, on the sole condition of faith in Jesus Christ, is introduced by the Holy Spirit, including the pardon of sin—a remission so full and free that all past transgressions are, by this act of divine mercy, blotted out, and the individual, notwithstanding all his former sinfulness and guilt, is accounted as righteous before God. (b) That regenerating work of the Holy Spirit upon the heart of the believer whereby he is morally and spiritually so quickened and renewed in the spirit of his mind that he is said in Scripture language to have "passed out of death into life," to have been "born again," "born of the Spirit," "born from above." (c) Adoption into the family of God, and consequent joint heirship with Jesus Christ; the fact of pardon and adoption being witnessed directly to his consciousness by "the Spirit of adoption whereby we cry, Abba, Father."

3. Entire Sanctification, more commonly designated as "sanctification," "holiness," "Christian perfection," or "perfect love," represents that second definite stage in Christian experience wherein, by the baptism with the Holy Spirit, administered by Jesus Christ, and received instanta-

eously by faith, the justified believer is delivered from inbred sin, and consequently is saved from all unholy tempers, cleansed from all moral defilement, made perfect in love and introduced into full and abiding fellowship with God. The sole condition of its attainment is that of appropriating faith in the blood of Jesus Christ as efficacious for present, complete and abiding purification from sin; but this faith is preceded by a special, definite, comprehensive and detailed dedication of the individual to God in all the added light accompanying his conviction for the advanced and deeper work of grace.

In our apprehension and reception of them, regeneration and sanctification are DISTINCT, though related, works of grace. Both are included in the one covenant of grace into which God has mercifully been pleased to enter with all his children. They are so closely related, as stages in the working out of our personal salvation, that it should never be considered necessary for any particular length of time to elapse between the two experiences. On the contrary, young converts should be encouraged at once to seek the sanctifying baptism of the Spirit as the blood-bought heritage of all believers. To reaffirm the utterances of the Holiness Assembly of 1886 on this point, "We record it as our conviction, that only those who are walking in the clear light of justification are prepared to seek entire sanctification. If, through unfaithfulness, any have lost the witness of their personal acceptance with God, their first work is to seek the restoration of their forfeited inheritance; and when this is regained they may intelligently and successfully advance to the second stage."

4. We deem it fitting that we should declare our unqualified and hearty belief in the personal return of the Lord Jesus Christ for the final redemption of his

saints as one of the strongest Scriptural incentives to holy living and to zealous and aggressive evangelism, and also as the very "pole-star of hope" to the church of God in all ages.

5. We wish to declare it as our belief that the sick may be healed through the prayer of faith, and that if God's people generally would measure up to the New Testament requirement in the matter of holy living, including particularly the matter of consecrating their bodies to the Lord, marvelous instances of divine healing would be far more numerous than they now are, God would be better glorified and the general testimony of the church would be much more effective upon the outside world.

6. While devoutly believing in sanctification as set forth in the foregoing statement, and that its obtainment and realization are essential to fulness of Christian character and life, we rejoice that great interest is being awakened in recent inquiries and movements contemplating the deepening and spiritualization of Christian life and experience among God's people by the fuller recognition and reception of the Holy Spirit; though we greatly regret the failure on the part of many to discover that, only as we become sanctified by the Holy Spirit, can he make us spiritual and practically holy; as also the disposition on the part of some earnest and worthy teachers, in connection with these movements, to discredit the doctrine and deny the fact of present deliverance from sin through faith in Christ our Sanctifying Savior. We also deem it important to say that much that is set before us, especially in the Epistles, as for us in Christ Jesus, and to be given us through the personal ministry of the Holy Spirit, will be unknown in experience so long as we fail of being saved from sin, or sanctified; while all of the highest and best things

of spiritual experience may be realized by those who are fully saved.

3. WITNESSING.

"Ye are my witnesses, saith the Lord." It is the bounden duty of all who are made partakers of the saving grace of God in any degree to witness modestly and unassumingly to the same. The testimony of the church is second only, if second at all, to the preaching of the word, as a means of promoting the work of God. Testimony to entire sanctification should be clear, and definite, but never boastful or irreverent. It is important that we keep to the use of scriptural terms in such witnessing as much as possible. Our testimony should always exalt Christ and abase self; and, though courageously borne, should be borne in such a spirit of humility, reverence, and tender charity for others as to carry to all who hear, the conviction that we magnify not self but Christ, and that our spirit accords with our utterances. Withholding testimony to sanctifying grace, when once that experience has been wrought in the soul, is almost sure to be followed by spiritual darkness and relapse.

4. HOLY LIVING.

True holiness is eminently practical. Wherever experienced it will hallow every action and relation of the life. "As he who hath called you is holy, so be ye also yourself holy in all manner of living." If we are truly holy, it will be manifest by separation from the world; by heeding the injunction which says, "be not conformed to this world;" by abstaining from all appearance of evil; by a life of daily self-denial and cross-bearing in the name of the Lord Jesus; by keeping aloof from all worldly alliances, and particularly in abstaining from connection with oath-bound secret orders; by eschewing all unseemly and injurious habits, such as the use of intoxicants, tobacco and opium;

by modesty and simplicity in dress, conforming to the apostolic injunction, twice repeated in the New Testament, which prohibits the adornment of the body with "gold and pearls and costly array;" and, finally, by heeding the scripture injunction, "Whether therefore ye eat or drink, or whatsoever ye do, do all to the glory of God."

The lives of all who profess to have been sanctified wholly should be especially modeled after the Sermon on the Mount, the twelfth chapter of Romans and the thirteenth chapter of First Corinthians. Moreover, every wholly sanctified life should constantly eminently manifest "the fruit of the Spirit," which is "love, joy, peace, longsuffering, gentleness, goodness, faith, meekness, temperance, against which there is no law." Above everything else sanctified men and women should "put on love, which is the bond of perfectness."

5. CHURCH FELLOWSHIP.

In respect to the matter of church fellowship we observe that the church is the institution of Christ, having many members in one body, himself being the living Head. He has redeemed it with his blood, and engraven it upon the palms of his hands. Membership therein is a precious privilege, and always to be highly esteemed. Wherever practical, every saved man and woman should be connected with some church. Holiness is not a disintegrating, but a conserving force; it is not intended to tear down, but to build up. Hence, professors of holiness are not excusable in voluntarily surrendering their church privileges for trivial causes. But, if oppressive hands be laid upon them in any case by church authority, solely for professing holiness, or for being identified with the work of holiness, depriving them of the privileges of Christian communion or public testimony and service, they should then, in whatever way seems best, so adjust themselves to cirin the service of Christ. Should humble fidelity to the cause of holiness make them the objects of persecution on the part of church authorities and cause their expulsion from church fellowship, or, should conditions in the church become such as to necessitate voluntary severance of the relation in order to the maintenance of a good conscience, they should be regarded with charity, treated with tenderness and consideration, and not disfellowshiped by the holiness brethren or branded with epithets of an unpleasant and reproachful character. Our advice to such would be in all cases to seek affiliation as early as possible with some organized body of Christian people who believe in and are committed to the holiness work. We declare it to be our purpose in the future, as in the past, to maintain the "unity of the Spirit in the bond of peace," hoping through this wide-spread revival of Bible holiness ultimately to lay a molding hand upon the great body of Christian people and bring the church at large to the realization of the New Testament ideal of "a glorious church, not having spot, or wrinkle, or any such thing, but that it should be holy and without blemish."

6. CO-OPERATION.

Inasmuch as holiness or Christian perfection is a uniting and cementing principle, designed to bring all believers into the unity of the faith, holiness people the world over should be one in faith and heart, and also in endeavoring to spread scriptural holiness over the land. Of all people in the world they, more than any others, should study the things that make for peace, and things whereby they may be mutually edified and made strong and fruitful for the Master's service. Though their work may be within the various churches, associations and organizations, yet neither ecclesiastical nor geographical limits should ever cumstances as to secure for themselves the continued enjoyment of the ordinances of our holy religion and freedom be barriers in the way of their hearty and constant co-operation in the work of God.

While there are subordinate points of doctrine and particular forms and usages in respect to which holiness people, as the representatives of different churches, associations and organizations, may differ, we would earnestly counsel that these should in no instance be allowed to become matters of contention, or barriers to fellowship and co-operative efforts to promote the holiness work. In matters of lesser importance about which we may differ, and particularly in matters on which the churches of Christ in general have declared no dogma and equally good men hold divergent views, let us not contend with each other, but agree to think and let think, to "love as brethren," and to concentrate all our forces in one united, grand and unceasing endeavor to storm and overthrow the strongholds of sin, and the devil, and to promulgate the gospel of free and full salvation rapidly through all the earth for a testimony, that so the way may be prepared for the actual and full realization of the end we pray for in the petition, "Thy kingdom come; thy will be done, in earth as it is in heaven."

7. QUESTIONABLE EXPEDIENTS.

We sincerely deprecate the modern questionable expedients extensively resorted to in the churches of to-day for the purpose of raising money, and as entertainments with which to draw and hold the masses, particularly the young. We regard the holding of fairs, festivals, dramatic and other worldly entertainments for either of the foregoing purposes as inexcusable profanations of God's cause and a reproach to our holy Christianity. Holy people should not only refrain from connection with all such questionable expedients for carrying on the work of God, but should unitedly and strongly bear their testimony against the same. While taking this stand, however, consistency would require that of all men those professing holiness and enlisted in the work of its promotion should be illustrious examples of New Testament consecration and liberality in respect to supporting the work of God, and particularly in contributing to the work of definitely promoting the experience and practice of Bible holiness. While abounding in faith, in love, in zeal, and in patience, let us diligently see to it that we "abound in this grace also."

There are necessary pecuniary expenses connected with the work of spreading holiness, and this matter we recommend to the earnest and prayerful consideration of the holiness people, praying that God may put it into their hearts to devise liberal things.

With regard to the support of the ministry, the scriptures declare that the "workman is worthy of his hire;" and, while we would deprecate in the evangelist, as in the pastor and layman, a spirit of covetousness as utterly inconsistent with true holiness, we earnestly recommend that God's people provide for those who serve them in the gospel that financial support which their needs may demand.

8. HOLINESS LITERATURE.

Concerning the subject of holiness literature, we can do no better than to reaffirm substantially the utterances of the holiness assembly of fifteen years ago, as follows: "The times imperatively demand a wide circulation of holiness literature in the form of books, tracts and periodicals; but our periodicals should not be imprudently multiplied. Friends of holiness having their Lord's money in their keeping should contribute liberally for the circulation of books and periodicals, so that none of these interests shall languish. And to this end, those who are now conducting the periodicals should adhere closely to the thirteenth chapter of First Corinthians, excluding uncharitable controversy and unbrotherly personal references; seeking to build up their readers in the knowledge of the truth as it is in Jesus. And we further advise the exclusion of all advertisements which do not accord with holiness."

9. COMMITTTEE OF CORRESPONDENCE.

In our judgment it is desirable that a committee of nine be appointed, to be composed of representatives of the holiness work in various sections of the United States and Canada, which shall be known as the General Committee of Correspondence, to confer with reference to the holding of another Holiness General Assembly, and to call and arrange for such a gathering in the year 1902, at such place as they shall deem expedient.

WILSON T. HOGUE,
A. M. HILLS,
E. F. WALKER,
HIRAM ACKERS,
M. L. HANEY,
L. B. KENT,
W. E. SHEPARD.

Report of Committee on Permanent Methods.

Whereas, we have a great number of holiness people scattered throughout this and various holiness organizations, and, knowing that in unity there is strength, your committee deem it would please God to have one general association for the promotion of holiness, embracing all our people and organizations for more aggressive work and better conserving the work already accomplished; therefore,

Resolved, First: That, since the divine approval

has so manifestly rested on this Assembly, we recommend its continuance with its present officers, and that we look forward to another Assembly in the year 1902, at which a permanent General Association for the promotion of holiness may be perfected, which may include this Assembly and all holiness organizations.

Resolved, Second: That this Assembly now create a committee of seven members, one of which shall be the President of this Assembly, to be called The Committee on Preparation, which shall confer with other organizations for the promotion of holiness, in the interest of the above general affiliations, and which shall make the necessary preparations for the meeting of the Assembly in 1902.

Resolved, Third: That all holiness people and all holiness bodies be invited and urged to attend individually, or by delegation, the Assembly provided for in the above resolution.

A. McLean, Chairman.
T. H. Agnew, Secretary.

The committee provided for in the above report was afterward enlarged and the following brethren elected as the Committee on Preparation to arrange for the next Assembly.

Rev. C. J. Fowler, Mass.
Rev. A. M. Hills, Texas.
Rev. H. C. Morrison, Ky.
Rev. A. L. Whitcomb, Ill.
Rev. M. L. Haney, Ill.
Rev. J. M. Pike, Ga.
Rev. John McD. Kerr, Can.
Rev. P. F. Bresee, Cal.
Deacon Geo. M. Morse, Conn.
Rev. Isaiah Reid, Iowa.
Rev. E. F. Walker, Ind.

DAILY PROCEEDINGS

Friday, May 3.

MORNING SESSION.

This was devoted largely to an informal service. The time was occupied in prayer, testimony and song. Bro. Geo. Hughes presided. A goodly number of delegates were already present, and the number rapidly increased.

AFTERNOON SESSION.

Bro. Geo. Hughes, chairman of the committee who issued the Official Call, called the meeting to order. After devotional exercises, Bro. Hughes was chosen Temporary Chairman, and Bro. G. A. McLaughlin, Secretary Pro Tem.

Bro. Hughes: I think it would be in order to hear a word from some of our brethren. Let us hear from our Texas brother—Bro. Hills.

Bro. Hills: "I feel greatly honored. I love to tell my experience. I was born in Michigan of parents that were Christians. Was converted at eleven years of age and went to leading meetings at sixteen. I became a student of Oberlin College at nineteen and graduated at twenty-three. I felt conviction for holiness, and sought Bro. Finney that I might be enabled to teach it, but this dear man seemed unfortunately unable to impart this peculiar knowledge to others. He would pray with me, but it didn't seem to help me. After Oberlin, I attended Yale Theological Seminary, and, although somewhat shaken, I never lost the great impulse I had to be a soul winner. God gave me revival after revival until I had led twenty-five hundred souls to Jesus Christ. My heart was hungering for something else that I wanted, and didn't know how to get. I thought it was something to grow into. By and by, after two pastorates, lasting sixteen years, God gave me the blessed experience but, because I preached it, I was driven out of the charge. I was crushed and heart-broken. God shook me out of the pastorate. A Doctor of Divinity said: 'You have had two short pastorates. God wants you in the evangelistic work.' I said: 'If God can keep my family from starvation in these panicky days of '93, I will try it.' Right where the blessed Finney preached, and where I had sung in the choir, I had two hundred conversions. The most blessed thing about it was the fact that I was trying to preach holiness, and a little, despised, holiness man came and prayed for me. I was preaching fifteen times a week, meanwhile reading everything in the way of holiness literature, for sixteen long months. I began to see how people got it, and I said if God ever gave me that blessing I would write a book and make it plain. That was the inspiration of my book, 'Holiness and Power,' which a good Methodist Bishop was kind enough to recommend to his conference in Texas. I thought it was a very gracious thing for a Methodist to do with a Congregational book. God has permitted me to write four books, given me four thousand souls, helped me to teach three years in a theological seminary, and in another college one year."

Bro. Hughes: "Let us hear from the East, where the sun rises,—from Deacon Morse of New York."

Bro. Geo. M. Morse: "Praise the Lord! I am glad to be here. I want to say the blood cleanses me from all sin. I have come out from everything the devil has of every character. I am clean along those lines. I started in a Baptist Church, forty-two years ago. I am at peace with all men. I have nothing against anybody. I don't have to go across the street to get away from my enemies. I want to say that I have to keep trusting in the name of

GEORGE QUINAN,
Redlands, Calif.

J. O. NELSON,
Chicago, Ill.

F. E. MOREHOUSE,
Napoleon, Mich.

T. M. McCLUNG,
Spring Green, Wis.

W. C. PALMER,
(Deceased).

WM. McDONALD,
(Deceased).

B. WINGET,
Chicago, Ill.

MRS. B. WINGET,
Chicago, Ill.

Jesus. I ought to have done better in view of what Jesus has done for me. He that is least shall be the greatest, and it yet remains to be seen what God will do in Chicago and New York with the people. It may be that the devil will tempt some of you big preachers to put yourselves on exhibition. Let us keep low at the feet of Jesus, and keep full of the Holy Ghost. I am here to spend and be spent. I expect to see souls saved in Chicago. This morning, when I arose I had to begin preaching Christ to the waiters and bell boys."

Bro. Hughes: We will now hear from the North, from Bro. Harris of Canada, one of the old time workers.

Bro. James Harris: "For 50 years I have been a standard-bearer for Christ. Looking through Leslie's biography, I see that he was baptized by Wesley. Leslie took me in his arms and baptized me, and I have always been a disciple of the Wesleyan kind of holiness. There I stand to-day by the blessing of God, and I am ready to do anything to further the cause of God."

Bro. J. B. Foote of Syracuse, N. Y.: "I think we ought to constitute ourselves a committee of the whole to go into the homes, the shops and offices, or wherever we go, and do something for the furtherance of God's work. The beginning of one of the greatest national camp meetings was at the dinner table. It has been said in the past and is being said yet that holiness people don't care for sinners. We want to convince them that we do care for sinners. A man was asked if he was saved. He said 'no.' That was the first convert for the National Camp Meeting. One spoke to another, and from that time the work went on until five hundred were converted."

Committees were then appointed on Music, Mail, Books, Pulpit Supply, Credentials, Press, Organization, and Street Meetings.

On motion, the committee on organization was requested to be prepared to report at 10:30 Saturday morning.

On motion the Assembly adjourned to meet in business session at 10 A. M., Saturday, May 4; it being understood that this motion had no bearing on the evening devotional session at 7:30 P. M.

EVENING SESSION.

Rev. George Hughes presided.—He announced the arrival of Bro. P. H. Murdick of Drew Theological Seminary, who had come as a representative of a little holiness band of students in that institution.

Bro. Hughes: I have been fully persuaded, from the time of the initiation of this movement, that, if we were to have victory, it would be along the prayer line. That is my solemn conviction; hence, we have men and women of God interested in prayer, all over this country, for this Assembly. Thank God! We have succeeded in this matter of enlisting prayer, far beyond our expectations. The members of the committee have been praying, every day at noon, for each other. It occurred to me that I would ask fifty of the men and women that I knew were people who would pray up into heaven, to join with the committee at noon, so there has been an outside committee surrounding the committee. I think these prayers have been heard.

Then it came to us to put forth a request in the April Number of the Guide to Holiness, asking for the names of one thousand who would pray for this Assembly, and asking all who would to send their replies to my residence in New Jersey, stating that they would join in the prayer service. From the time that was put out, the mail began to bring answers to the request. Several times a day the postman came with the letters. I have them in a box in my trunk. Someone said: "Why don't you ask for 10,000?" I thought my faith ought to have gone so high. The letters keep coming and I am receiving them at my lodging place.

Then we have asked for requests for prayer to come up before this Assembly for unsaved friends, or any object for which the writer desires prayer. That box is a great deal fuller.

Now, we have been looking around to find somebody to take these requests for prayer and put them on an International Prayer Roll, to be added to day by day, as the prayer requests come in, and we expect them in still greater numbers.

It was Inskip who taught me to use the prayer roll many years ago, and I am making good use of it. I have 1,500 prayer requests, that came in on other occasions, that I wouldn't part with for anything. I want you people to join in this thing. Those that hear me to-night, if you have an unsaved friend that you want saved, write the name on a slip of paper and hand it in. We will hold these requests up before the Lord, as we used to do in National Camp meetings. I will ask you all to stand up and offer silent prayer that God will bless everyone mentioned in those boxes.

(The congregation arose and engaged in a brief silent prayer.)

Bro. Alexander McLean: "I am deeply impressed with the occasion which has brought us together, and I trust the Holy Spirit will so come upon us that we will be led of God, if possible, more than we ever were before. ("Amen") This is an extraordinary moment for us and the people of God, generally. I cannot help but go back in my recollection, as I am here now for the first service of this convention to the time a few years ago, when I attended the early sessions of a Methodist Conference in the room across the hall. If I speak of the Methodist denomination, it is not because I am not in sympathy with others. God bless you all! ("Amen!") One of the bishops cried frequently, 'We have them, those who weep.' Bishop Janes was always present at that 8:00 o'clock meeting. I remember how he used to urge the brethren to come into the prayer meeting in the morning. The thing that we need here most is prayer. Bishop Clarke was there. One morning I saw him as he was lifting up his heart in prayer. His eyes were wet with tears. I said: 'Bless God! There is a bishop who can weep as he prays.' · A few years ago, I was in London, and I couldn't refrain when standing by the grave of John Wesley, from uncovering my head, under the solemn blue skies and taking a solemn vow to labor to the end that we may have a race of holy people, and, God being my helper, I will be true to that trust. In beautiful Greenwood Cemetery, between the graves of John Inskip and his wife, I renewed this solemn vow, before coming here, to be true to holiness, and I would be glad to renew it to-night. ("Amen!") The occasion is solemn and impressive. It is a momentous hour for all of us, and for men and women of God all over the land,—a very momentous hour. And, for one, I feel like getting down on my face before Almighty God and asking divine help."

Brother Hughes: "Let us go down on our knees before God. Let us dismiss all formality that might otherwise come into the services and usurp the place of the blessed Holy Ghost. Is it not the blessed Holy Spirit urging you to come and get down before God? Let us have a melting time. Beloved, God does not want you left out. Let us have a moment of silent prayer."

Silent Prayer was followed by prayer led by Bro. A. McLean: "O, Lord, Thy Spirit is here. Thou art in our hearts. Thou art leading us. We will put aside all possible formality. Help us to get down in the dust before Thee. O, Lord, look upon us, we pray Thee, and if there be any disposition to prefer one to another, or to have our own way, help us infinitely to prefer Thy blessed way. O, God, search my heart. Come in infinite mercy into our midst. We want to be knit together in love—united with bonds of holy love. We want, blessed Spirit to ask God to take this matter in hand and lead on and out for His glory and for His honor. Lord, help us to have the spirit of John the Baptist, when he said, 'I must decrease but He must increase.' O, that we may have the grace to go down, down, out of sight of self and have Jesus exalted. Our hearts cry out 'All hail the power of Jesus' name. Lord, we are in the dust; we desire to get very low,—clear out of sight, but we must have Thee present. We must have Thy guidance; we must have a baptism of real, genuine Holy Ghost fire and power. O, Lord, banish everything contrary to Thy will. Whatever there be that hinders, help us to get rid of it in this place made memorable in years gone by. We are here before Thee in the depths of our humility and meekness of spirit, and we know that Thou dost answer prayer. Now Lord, let a re-anointing of Thy Spirit come upon us. Lord, if we did nothing but praise Thee, it is counted a very excellent thing. But we would have a growing tide of spirit life and power to date from this very service. Thou art hearing us and answering us, but answer in thine own way, we beseech Thee, and we will give Thee the praise and glory forever."

Bro. Hughes: "Now, friends, I am going to turn this meeting over entirely to Deacon Morse. I told him to tell his experience,—what the Lord has done for him; to take whatever course he sees fit, only that he should lead us into a battle for souls. The cry of my heart is for souls. We hope a good many people will be sanctified tonight."

EXPOSITION AND EXHORTATION BY DEACON GEORGE M. MORSE.

I thank my dear brother Hughes for the honor he has given me. It's a wonder he shouldn't have selected some sermonizer or preacher. The time we have left this evening is limited.

Are we ready for the battle? Are we where God wants us? Are we full of love and fire? Are we in it, heart and soul? I am certain that holiness people can backslide, and get in a state of lethargy, waiting for Sunday to come, as though all the work was to be done on Sunday. We have, thank God, men and women in the cause with tears running down their cheeks. O God, give us a burning love for souls. O, Lord help us, for Jesus' sake to get on ground where we will say it shall be done. I tell you a great deal depends upon our keeping low before God, and preaching Jesus beside all waters. ("Lord help us.") I don't mean that we shall fire too many random shots The Lord is with those that fear Him. We must keep our eyes single to God's glory, and see to it that there is no stumbling in us. We should be up and at it, subject at all times to His beck and bid, and something will happen. Press on for souls and somebody will get converted to God, or believers led into entire sanctification.

We are living in a marvelous age. Oh, what a great work for God, to my observation and reading, has been done up and down this continent and in England in the last twenty-five years. Now, if we all look to God and keep in the spirit of prayer, we shall see results in this meeting.

I will read, and perhaps make a few comments on the

prayer of Jesus, as found in the 17th Chapter of St. John's Gospel.

I want to call special attention to the 17th verse: "Sanctify them through Thy truth: Thy word is truth," and the 19th verse: "And for their sakes I sanctify myself, that they also might be sanctified through the truth."

This prayer as breathed by our dear Savior and given us in this chapter, is in harmony with the Apostle Paul's prayer—(1 Thess. v: 23), "And the very God of peace sanctify you wholly: and I pray God your whole spirit, soul and body be preserved blameless unto the coming of our Lord Jesus Christ." It is also in harmony with John xv: 2, "Every branch that beareth fruit, he purgeth (which means sanctifieth) it, that it may bring forth more fruit." I met a gentleman (who may be within the hearing of my voice now,) on the sidewalk last evening who said he received all that anybody ever receives, at conversion. I didn't argue with him. I don't believe in too much argument. But I didn't happen to get sanctification in that way. I was three days and three nights—seventy-two hours under the power of Holy Ghost conviction, and God converted me through and through. I had no living sacrifice to offer to God. I was dead in trespasses and sin, and no good thing was in me, and I cried to God for mercy. I could neither eat nor sleep. I was driven to the wall. I cried unto God to have mercy upon me a poor sinner. God heard my cry and regenerated me with the power of the Holy Ghost, and made me alive from the dead. I then ran about everywhere, so to speak, thirty, forty or sixty miles from home, telling everybody what a dear Savior I had found. I never came to the point of offering a living sacrifice to God for thirteen years. Phoebe Palmer and the Guide to Holiness had a great deal to do with my sanctification. Somehow a copy of this magazine came into my hands, and it gave me instruction in the way of Holiness. Then I heard Sister Phoebe Palmer deliver a prayer at a camp meeting at Martha's Vineyard away back in '59 or '60, and I never got rid of the impression that prayer made until God sanctified me wholly. I was brought up, strange to say, under this character of instruction: that we were sanctified at death, and that we were sanctified by reading the Bible through and through, are sanctified by the truth. Another teaching was, that we were sanctified at conversion and regeneration. The above was the character of teaching I sat under for thirteen years in my own denomination, and to a great extent the above teaching is very prevalent to-day among us as a denomination.

I saw a notice of a three days' convention for the promotion of Holiness, at New Bedford, Mass., Nov. 14, 15, and 16, 1870. I attended the meetings. They were under the leadership of W. T. Harlow, a godly Methodist minister. Under his clear teaching of the way of faith in offering a living sacrifice, holy and acceptable to God, I saw my privilege, made the offering, believed, and entered in, and God sanctified the offering and illuminated my entire being, filled me with the Holy Ghost and love, and gave me a revelation of the plan of Salvation such as I never had before, and from Love's constraining power I have been a worker for Jesus in this line ever since. All glory and praise to His holy name. We are living witnesses to the fact that God did, subsequent to our conversion, sanctify us wholly to Himself. These witnesses raised their hands and asserted this fact to-night. "I am sanctified now—wholly sanctified" means the extracting of all carnal appetites from the soul. After the Lord came into my soul, I had no want or appetite for the things that were a hindrance to my Christian experience. He lives in us, instead of we trying to live—we have God's life come into us. Jesus lives in me to-night as I stand on this platform, and, wherever I may be, I don't want anything the devil has. God makes me a free man. I have Him with me everywhere. I never complain when it rains or blows! This blessed salvation brings us into harmony with God in everything. Our time and talents are the Lord's, loaned us for a season, and we should dispose of them according to His plan. No good thing does He withhold from a man that walks uprightly and stands by the truth, honoring God everywhere. Hallelujah, blessed be His name! I wouldn't exchange my hold on Christ and Christ's hold on me with any man, nor for a whole planet like this.

We have had a good time to-day, and Jesus has sent His angels to minister to my spiritual necessities, and he gives me the approving consciousness of His Love.

You say: "I don't believe in sanctification, or holiness?" Then you don't believe in the power of God. We have read: "All power is given unto me (Christ) in heaven and earth," and, "Where sin abounded, grace did much more abound." Cannot He that made the skies and all there is in them take sin out of our hearts and purge us from moral depravity? I am here to declare that He can do it (Amen), and I know of my own personal experience that He does it.

Does holiness go with business? ("It does"). I have had God in my business for years. I do not deal in any stocks or stuff that I can't ask God's blessing on.

Sometimes the bright light gets dim from the fact that we do not wait on God or because of the trial of our faith. At all times we have got to take up our cross and confess Christ. They were saved "by the blood of the Lamb, and by the word of their testimony."—

I presume I have obeyed God and let $150,000 go in one direction and another for His glory, and the advancement of His kingdom. It is more blessed to give than to receive. It is a delight to give of one's possessions toward the advancement of the kingdom of heaven.

O, Jesus, help us to get the people under conviction for entire sanctification. Help the people to read their Bibles. ("Amen.")

Glorious victory crowned the altar service which followed. It was a time of deep humility and of weeping and crying to God for the guidance and blessing of the Holy Spirit and the salvation of souls.

Saturday, May 4.

MORNING SESSION.

9:00 A. M. Prayer and Testimony service led by Bro. E. F. Walker.

10:00 A. M. Bro. George Hughes presiding.

Singing by the congregation, "Blest be the Tie that Binds."

Scripture Lesson, read by Bro. M. L. Haney, 1 Cor. xiii.

Prayer, led by Bro. H. C. McBride: "Blessed be the God and Father of our Lord Jesus Christ, which according to His abundant mercy hath begotten us again unto a lively hope by the resurrection of Jesus Christ from the dead, to an inheritance incorruptible and undefiled, and that fadeth not away, reserved in heaven for us, who are kept by the power of God through faith unto salvation, ready to be revealed in the last time; wherein we greatly rejoice, though now for a season, if need be, we are in heaviness through manifold temptations; that the trial of our faith being much more precious than of gold that perisheth, though it be tried with fire, might be found unto praise and honor and glory at the appearing of Jesus Christ;

whom, having not seen, we love; in Whom, though now we see Him not, yet believing, we rejoice with joy unspeakable and full of glory; receiving the end of our faith, even the salvation of our souls. Glory! Glory! Glory! O Lord! Make our hearts bigger this morning; enlarge our capacity. We have so much for which to be thankful. We hardly know where to begin, so we say with David: Bless the Lord, O our souls, and all that is within us, bless His holy name. Bless the Lord, O our souls, and forget not all His benefits: Who forgiveth all our iniquities; Who healeth all our diseases; Who redeemeth our lives from destruction; Who crowneth us with loving kindness and tender mercies; Who satisfieth our mouths with good things, so that our youth is renewed like the eagle's. Thou preparest a table before us in the presence of our enemies, even in these days of higher criticism, skepticism, worldliness, formality, and forgetfulness of God. Thou anointest our heads with oil; our cup runneth over. Glory to God! We know, O God, that there is no room for the devil when our cup runneth over. There is therefore now no condemnation to them which are in Christ Jesus, who walk not after the flesh but after the Spirit. For the law of the Spirit of life in Christ Jesus hath made us free from the law of sin and death; for what the law could not do in that it was weak through the flesh, God sending His own Son in the likeness of sinful flesh, and for sin condemned sin in the flesh, that the righteousness of the law might be fulfilled in us, who walk not after the flesh but after the Spirit. To be carnally minded is death, but to be spiritually minded is life and peace. For as many as are led by the Spirit of God, they are the sons of God. Hallelujah! Glory be to the Father and glory be to the Son and glory be to the Holy Ghost. As it was in the beginning, is now, and shall be for all eternity. Glory be to God most high.

"We thank Thee for this convention; we thank Thee for the communion of the saints, and if our fellowship below in Jesus is so sweet, what heights of rapture shall we know when around Thy throne we meet.

"Bless those who have come here seeking Thy perfect love; bless those who have come expecting to reach more liberty in Thee; bless those of us who have come expecting to be led out into the light. Make this the greatest occasion that this wicked city has ever seen. Give us the victory, O God. Let somebody step out into the light even during the opening of our preliminary service. Bless our dear Brother Hughes. We thank Thee that Thou hast preserved him so long, and that he has been the instrument of blessing to so many. We pray not only for him, but that Thou wilt bless all who gather here, that they may go home as flaming fire-brands, setting fire to everything they come in contact with. Lord help us! We are going to pass by this way but once. Help us until we have preached our last sermon, sung our last song or given expression to our last sigh, and to Thee we will ascribe the honor and praise forever. Amen."

Singing, by Sisters Flora B. Nelson and Fannie Birdsall, "Some Blessed Day."

OPENING REMARKS, BY BRO. GEORGE HUGHES.

"I think, if you will indulge me, I will spend a brief time in making a statement in regard to the origin and purposes of this Holiness General Assembly. It is fitting for me to do so at this time, so that it may be as clearly as possible understood what we aim to do in this unregenerate city."

Fifteen years ago, we had a Holiness General Assembly at Park Avenue M. E. Church, of which church the Rev. Davies was pastor,—one of the noblest men of God, who has since passed to his reward. He went on his way rejoicing to the eternal throne of God. We had a blessed time at that meeting. The work of the Lord went on gloriously. Believers were sanctified and sinners were converted. It was a very gracious and powerful time, but it was a much smaller gathering than we have together at this time. At the close of that Assembly a committee of nine was chosen to prepare for another such gathering when, in their judgment and the indications of providence the time had come for another Assembly. We had no idea that fifteen years would roll away before another Holiness General Assembly would come, but such has been the fact. The Lord put it on the hearts of this committee that the time had come for another gathering of His people.

Our minds go back to those exciting times when our country was in a very critical state. I do not know how others regard it, but it seems to me that now we are passing under a very serious state of things, amidst these epidemics for the past two years striking our cities, towns and villages, and I have been amazed that so little has been said about it, even in our religious papers, as well as the secular press. It seems to me, that during the past winter, God has been thundering upon our country and upon the heads of the people, and yet they have gone on making money, not caring, and these things have made no impression on the popular mind, and not even upon the church as I expected to see. Then again, since the opening of the new century, there has sprung up in every denomination, a great cry for the giving of hearts and souls to the Lord Jesus Christ, and a deep interest in the coming of His kingdom. The cry has come up from these hearts: "Lord revive thy work!" It has been clearly seen by those of discerning mind that we must have a revival of pentecostal power, and with all our churches baptized with the Holy Ghost, we ought to take the world for Christ. That is the Pentecostal order. In reading the Acts of the Apostles we learn that they were not permitted to move until they were filled with the Holy Ghost, and, when the day of Pentecost came they were all filled with the Holy Ghost, and the artillery of Mount Sinai was opened upon the multitude. Kings witnessed it too. And I do not believe the day of Pentecost has ever passed. I think it is continuing to this day. If we are assembled along Pentecostal lines, we have a right to expect a revelation of the Holy Ghost, a fit opening of the 20th Century,—a world-rocking revival of religion. We should have such a revival that it will shake the very foundations of earth; an awakening that will lead this whole country and the world to understand that the God of Glory has risen up out of His holy habitation.

At the time the call was issued for this Assembly, an invitation was issued to Christian people of all denominations to come together and wait upon God. We need to do a great deal of waiting upon God. We need to get down before Him as we did yesterday afternoon, in the depths of our souls,—deeper, deeper, deeper yet! I tell you, if we can get this whole Assembly down on their knees and cry out for the manifestation of the Spirit, it will surely come, and the glory of the Lord will be revealed among us. ("Amen").

Henry Belden, one of the noblest men along holiness lines once said, That when the woman of Samaria asked Jesus for a drink of living water, He not only gave it her but He let her take the well with her. We ought to have that well within us distributing water all over the land. (Amen). For my part, I am disposed to go down just as far as the Holy Ghost will lead me. I want the Holy Ghost to lead me, and give me understanding. I believe it is possible, brethren, to have the very windows of Heaven opened, and that there may come down on this company of Christian people a marvelous enduement of the Holy Ghost, making everyone a charged battery,—a mighty agency of God to the pulling down of the stronghold of the devil. Do you say "Amen" to that? (Cries of "Amen," and "Hallelujah," from all over the house.) We have the first installment here already, but it will be better as we go along, and the coming days of this Assembly will be marvelous days that will pass into Christian history.

I believe it is possible for these holiness forces here to be brought nearer together, knit with love and Christlike bonds, and riveted by the Holy Ghost so that we may go out in unity to do His work. We want the evil forces in this world to be afraid of us. We want this Assembly to give notice to the legions of the devil that we are going forth under the banner of Emmanuel, from the north and the south, from the east and the west to do battle for God. (Amen.)

We need so to be filled with the spirit of love that we will neither think evil nor speak evil; that we will be ready to endure all things for Christ and to suffer whatever comes upon us in the name of the Lord Jesus Christ. Let the test of our fellowship one with another be not whether we are Baptists, Presbyterians, Congregationalists, or members of some other denomination, but rather, Have we the love of Christ in our hearts? and to all such I want to give my hand and bid you God-speed. I want every heart and soul in this Assembly to have the 13th Chapter of 1 Corinthians burned into them, that you may be so filled with love that it will go leaping out to the humblest man, woman and child of Chicago. ("Amen"). O, my God, by the power of the Holy Ghost, put in the heart of George Hughes and everyone of us love, with humility alongside of it.

Another thing is meekness. O, may there no harsh words come out of our mouths. Fill us with gentleness, meekness, long-suffering, brotherly kindness and love toward all. ("Amen").

I tell you, it is high time that the people of God got the shaking power, just as in the day of Pentecost. They prayed and the place was shaken. Let this be a great company of heart-to-heart Christian people, knowing no denomination, no sect, no theology and no creed but Jesus Christ, that we may march in solid columns and take the world for Him. (Amen! Hallelujah!) Look at this big prayer roll stretched from gallery to gallery. This whole country is praying for this Assembly, and requests for prayer are coming in every mail, saying, "Put me down for prayer," and asking for prayer for a mother, father, sister or brother.

On the way over here, not far from Chicago, we stopped at a place, and I asked the conductor what was going on there. He said, "We are going to put on a larger engine." I said, "That means more force and greater speed." Now the time has come for the people of God to put on a larger engine. Now, brethren, we have come this morning to the most solemn and important duty. We appointed a committee yesterday to report upon credentials and other things, and I say to you, Don't let us get in a hurry. We want to approach this work in solemn prayer to God that he will direct us and lead us, enabling us to do business as if in the immediate presence of God, that we may be led in the light of the truth. Will Bro. Haney lead us in prayer?

Prayer, by Bro. M. L. Haney.

On motion, Committee on Credentials were given an extension of time in which to report.

The Committee on Permanent Organization made the following nominations: For President, C. J. Fowler of

S. A. KEAN,
Evanston, Ill.

MRS. S. A. KEAN,
Evanston, Ill.

H. GRENTZENBURG,
Cincinnati, Ohio

G. W. RIDOUT,
Manahawkin, N. J.

S. B. SHAW,
Chicago, Ill.

MRS. S. B. SHAW,
Chicago, Ill.

E. C. DE JERNETT,
Greenville, Texas.

J. B. FOOTE,
Syracuse, N. Y.

Mass. For Vice-Presidents, E. F. Walker, Ind., A. M. Hills, Tex., James Harris, Ontario, M. L. Haney, Ill., and Geo. M. Morse, Conn. For Secretary, J. D. Marsh, Ill., Assistant Secretary, W. E. Shepard, Cal. For Treasurer, G. A. McLaughlin, Ill. For Railroad Secretary, T. B. Arnold, Ill. For Assembly Reporter, Isaiah Reid, Iowa.

The report of the committee was accepted and all officers nominated by the committee were elected.

Upon taking the chair, Brother Fowler spoke as follows: "I want to say that I very greatly appreciate two things: First, the privilege of being here. I signed the call originally, because I thought it was a consistent thing to do, although at the time I signed the call I did not expect to be here. However, the circumstances changed, so, by the good will of God, I am permitted to be with you. I greatly appreciate that, and I greatly appreciate your full and standing vote to make me president of this body.

"There are several things I would like to say. I want to say that I am blessed already. ("Amen"). When I first struck the atmosphere this morning I scented something that was not of this world. I was fully alive to the sense that God was here. I expect to have my thought quickened and be better informed for being here. I expect to have my heart more and more refreshed.

"Now I hesitated in taking this position. The hesitation is with me still, and yet that hesitation is consistent with victory. My soul claims the victory. My faith is exceedingly optimistic, and it takes hold on victory in all the phases of this assembly. I have some hesitation because I am not an expert parliamentarian. I recognize that the position is at times a delicate and difficult one, but I can get along with these people. Then I have a genuine hesitation because of the responsibility attached, and again my faith comes to my rescue.

"This gathering is two-fold in its bearing. It is evangelistic. It ought to be that; it must be that. May God give us the power to do something that will be felt forever. But it is more than evangelistic in the ordinary acceptance of the term. It is deliberative. I do not think any of us begin to properly appreciate the weighty responsibilities that will crowd into these days. There will be things said and done here that will tend either to wreck or help the holiness movement in this country.

"Not a little is expected of this Assembly, and there must be a formulating and framing of matters here that will put things where they ought to be. Let us be much in prayer. Let us hand something down to future generations that will be worthy an occasion like this. As Bro. Hughes says, If you like that, say 'amen.'" (Cries of ("Amen.")

On motion, the regular services of the Assembly were arranged as follows: 8:00 A. M., People's Meeting (or prayer service); 9:30 A. M., opening of Assembly, proper; 2:00 P. M. and 7:30 P. M., of each week day, it being understood that the Committee on Program had the power to settle the time and character of public services.

AFTERNOON SESSION.

Call to order by Chairman, C. J. Fowler.

Singing by congregation: "There is Power in the Blood," and "Make Me a Blessing Today."

Prayer by Bro. John Norberry of Conn.:

"We read in Thy Word, blessed Lord, that if our heart condemn us not, then have we confidence toward Thee, and whatsoever we ask we receive of Thee, because we keep Thy commandments and do those things which are pleasing in Thy sight. O, Lord! We read that this is the confidence we have in Thee, that, if we ask anything according to Thy will, Thou hearest us, and, if we know that Thou hearest us, whatsoever we ask, we know we have the petitions that we desire of Thee.

Lord! as one man, we pray. We look to Thee, at this afternoon service, and pray that God will have His way in this convention. We pray Thee, that Thou wilt be in this meeting. May the power of the Holy Ghost be in Thy servant, who shall deliver the message this afternoon. May the Holy Ghost, the real, genuine Holy Ghost conviction come upon the people, and many here come up for pardon and purity this afternoon. May we have a great victory, and to Thee we will give all the glory. We ask it all in Jesus' name. Amen.

Song by Bro. and Sister Harris: "Let Him Have His Way with Thee."

Brother M. L. Haney preached a very excellent sermon, the report of which was sent him for correction but he was unable to do this at the time and requested, us to omit it. We still hoped to receive it in time for publication but have not and are obliged to omit it.

EVENING SESSION.

By some strange oversight we have no report of this service except of Bro. Hogue's sermon which we give.

SERMON BY REV. W. T. HOGUE.

After trying to get the mind of the Lord as to what He would have me say tonight, I am led to invite your attention to words recorded in Acts, second chapter, and the first four verses.

"And when the day of Pentecost was fully come, they were all with one accord in one place.

"And suddenly there came a sound from heaven, as of a rushing mighty wind, and it filled all the house where they were sitting.

"And there appeared unto them cloven tongues, like as of fire, and it sat upon each of them.

"And they were all filled with the Holy Ghost, and began to speak with other tongues, as the Spirit gave them utterance."

That was the birth-day of the Christian church. It was the birth-day of Christianity itself. The Christian church, Christianity itself, I may say, was born of the Holy Spirit. Just as the individual to be a Christian must be born of the Spirit, so must any Assembly to constitute it any part of the church of Jesus Christ be born of the Spirit. It takes the Holy Spirit to constitute it a living organism in the beginning—to preserve it as a living organism to the end. Nothing short of such a baptism and empowerment as came to the one hundred and twenty disciples at Pentecost can put and keep that church in a normal condition, and make it the proper representative of Jesus Christ and constitute it the body of Christ in the spiritual sense.

It becomes very important therefore to know something about the Holy Spirit and His operations; to know something about the dispensation of the Spirit and what it represents. The Spirit of God is the very soul of the church, as it is of every individual spiritual life. I am sorry the church of this period has found it necessary to look back to the primitive Pentecost as though the like were never to be expected again on earth. As I understand it, that was but an instance or illustration of what ought to prevail with God's people always and everywhere. I do not know of any place in the New Testament where God has expressed Himself as satisfied with the Christian church, only as that body has been filled with the Holy Ghost; and I have given considerable attention to the studying of God's measures of grace as set forth in the New Testament. Whether it be the Holy Spirit, divine love, the knowledge of His will, or the fruits of righteousness, God's measure is a full measure.

I am glad to be assured that what the disciples got in the upper room, the wonderful manifestation and fulness of divine light, love, grace, power and victory that came to them on that memorable day—is for God's people through all time. It is not because God is straitened or limited that some fail to get it now. It is because they fail to meet the conditions. If we measure up fully to the conditions, we may have Pentecost repeated. I care not for the visible signs, nor for the sound as of a rushing mighty wind, nor that the Holy Spirit shall come down on us like a tornado; though you might suppose I would, being a Free Methodist! (Laughter.) I am here to respond to the blessed Holy Spirit in all His movements, whatsoever those movements shall be.

The important thing on that occasion was not the sound from heaven, not the fiery manifestations, but the thing spoken of in the last verse of my text—"They were all filled with the Holy Ghost." That is what we ought all to recognize; and the moral and spiritual results ordained by God will invariably follow if we get and retain this blessed fulness provided for us in Christ.

I want to call your attention to several things connected with the Pentecostal baptism with the Holy Ghost.

I remark in the first place that the original Pentecostal baptism with the Spirit was a second work of grace. I mean by this that the disciples who received it had already experienced the preliminary operations of the Spirit in regeneration; that they were already men of God. Some tell us that the hundred and twenty disciples did not receive their conversion until the baptism with the Holy Spirit on that day. Let me call your attention to what Jesus said about them long before the day of Pentecost.

Turn to John, fifteenth chapter. Here I read (verse nineteen) "If ye were of the world, the world would love his own; but because ye are not of the world, but I have chosen you out of the world, therefore the world hateth you." I cannot conceive of Jesus Christ talking that way to unconverted men. They were so distinct from the world, that the world hated them. That is the testimony Jesus Christ bore concerning these disciples long before the day of Pentecost. Speaking to them again in the same connection, He said: "Ye have not chosen me, but I have chosen you, and ordained you, that ye should go and bring forth fruit, and that your fruit should remain." He had called, chosen and ordained them, that they should go forth and preach the Gospel and bring forth fruit, and their fruit should remain. Have you any such idea as that He chose unregenerate men to preach His gospel? It cannot be.

You will also remember that as Jesus met Peter and the other apostles in the coasts of Caesarea Philippi, He said: "Whom do men say that I, the Son of man, am? Peter answered: Thou art the Christ, the Son of the living God. And Jesus answered and said unto him, Blessed art thou, Simon Barjona; for flesh and blood hath not revealed it unto thee, but my Father which is in heaven." There had been a revelation of Christ to one of these disciples, at least, just such as constitutes a real and radical conversion. St. Paul tells us, that "No man can say that Jesus Christ is Lord but by the Holy Ghost." No man can say it in a true and spiritual and experimental sense, unless it has been divinely revealed unto him in his own salvation.

Some tell us this baptism was simply a gift of miracle-working power. I would have you notice that these disciples had the power of miracle-working before the day of Pentecost. In sending out His apostles on their mission to the lost sheep of the house of Israel He said: "As ye go preach, saying, The Kingdom of heaven is at hand. Heal the sick, cleanse the lepers, raise the dead, cast out devils: freely ye have received, freely give." Thus they were empowered to heal the sick, cast out devils and perform various miracles in His name before the day of Pentecost. The seventy also received a like commission to work miracles when they were sent out upon their ministry of preaching and teaching. They exercised that power, wrought a few miracles, and, overjoyed with their success, they came back like little children exulting over a new-found toy, and said: "Lord, even the devils are subject to us through thy name." And Jesus said to them, "I beheld Satan as lightning fall from heaven, Behold I give unto you power to tread on serpents and scorpions, and over all the power of the enemy: and nothing shall by any means hurt you. Notwithstanding, in this rejoice not, that the spirits are subject unto you, but rather rejoice because your names are written in heaven."

Note again that before He left them, our Lord told those followers of His, who had been in His own school, under His own instruction for three years or more, and who had walked in personal fellowship with Him, to tarry in Jerusalem for something further. As the time of His ascension drew near, "They asked of Him saying, Lord, wilt thou at this time restore again the Kingdom to Israel? And He said unto them, It is not for you to know the times or the seasons, which the Father hath put in His own power; but ye shall receive power after that the Holy Ghost is come upon you: and ye shall be witnesses unto me both in Jerusalem, and in all Judea, and in Samaria, and unto the uttermost parts of the earth." He told them to wait for it, and they did. The text tells us the result: "And when the day of Pentecost was fully come, they were all with one accord in one place. And suddenly there came a sound from heaven, as of a rushing mighty wind, and it filled all the house where they were sitting. And there appeared unto them cloven tongues like as of fire, and it sat upon each of them." These were the outward phenomena; but better than the sound from heaven and the fiery manifestations, "they were all filled with the Holy Ghost."

There is a second installment of the Holy Spirit for all believers. His preliminary office work is accomplished in our conversion and justification. In the Pentecostal baptism, He comes in abiding fulness to dwell in us as our abiding Comforter, Illuminator, Sanctifier, Guide, and Stand-by. The original word translated "Comforter" means a "Stand-by." Blessed be God! You can stand anything if you have that "Stand-by" enthroned within you always. ("Amen!")

I call you to notice in the second place, that this Pentecostal baptism was the fulfillment of a supreme promise. What do I mean by that? I mean to say, that of all the glorious promises of former dispensations, that which referred to the bestowment and dispensation of the Holy Spirit was of supreme excellence—the climax and glory of the whole. It is called emphatically "The promise of the Father" just as though it were the only promise He had given. This is because it contains the sum of all the rest.

Go back to the prophetic age and see this verified. The prophets sang in wondrous raptures concerning the coming of Christ to redeem this world, and with the deepest pathos they described His humiliation and sufferings. But in more enrapturing and inspiring strains they sang of the future outpouring of the Holy Spirit. Of the Spirit filled messengers of the New Dispensation, Isaiah sang: "The wilderness and the solitary place shall be glad for them; and the desert shall rejoice, and blossom as the rose. It shall blossom abundantly, and rejoice even with joy and singing: the glory of Lebanon shall be given unto it, the excellency of Carmel and Sharon; they shall see the glory of the Lord, and the excellency of our God." Isaiah further speaks of it as floods poured out on the dry ground, and rivers upon the thirsty land—not as a single river but rivers of water upon dry ground. The Psalmist tells us that when God's people "go through dry places they shall make it a well, and the rain also shall fill the pools." Ezekiel, in his vision, foresaw the glorious dispensation of the Holy Spirit. He likened it to a river beginning with the issuing of waters out from under the sanctuary. Mere droppings which flowed together, and, without any visible tributary from without, increased in depth and volume until it became a mighty and impassable river. He says the angel led him forth to measure the river, and when he had measured a thousand cubits the waters were to the ankles: another thousand cubits and the waters were to the knees; another thousand and they were to the loins; and still another thousand and it was a river that they could not pass over; "for the waters were risen, waters to swim in, a river that could not be passed over." It was also said that everything should live whithersoever this river should come, and by it even the waters of the Dead Sea were healed.

Now, note this peculiarity about that river. It was

characterized by a perpetually accumulating flow. In this it symbolized the law of the bestowment of the Spirit. Instead of looking backward to Pentecost for the greatest manifestation of the Holy Spirit we ought to be ashamed to be obliged to take a backward look of that kind. We ought to have Pentecost repeated and augmented to-day. "But," you say, "we don't hear any sound from heaven. We haven't felt the place shaken. We don't have the visible manifestations 'like as of fire.'" Very well. But these were not essential. They were mere accompaniments. That fire was only a symbol of the divine fire, the Shekinah flame, the divine light and power of the Holy Ghost enthroned within, and spiritually enabling us, wherever we come in contact with the dead to bring them to life. ("Amen!") This gift of the abiding Comforter, not the accompanying phenomena was the thing promised in the Old Testament in connection with the Gospel Pentecost.

The supreme promise in the ministry of John the Baptist related to the gift of the Holy Ghost. He preached the two-fold work of grace. First, he preached Christ as the Atoner of sin, by Whom we come to God. He cried "Behold the Lamb of God, which taketh away the sin of the world." Having acquainted them with Him as the atoning Lamb, He began to tell them about "a mightier than I, whose shoes I am not worthy to bear," and added. "He shall baptize you with the Holy Ghost and with fire." His supreme mission was to point to Jesus Christ as the Baptizer with the Holy Spirit. To preach Christ fully we must present Him in both of these offices—as the great Atoner for the sins of the world and the Baptizer of believers with the Holy Spirit. To preach Him as the Atoner only is to preach but half the Gospel.

Coming now to the ministry of Jesus, we find that He also preached the two-fold work of grace. First, He taught His disciples as they were able to bear it concerning the mystery of the death He was to accomplish on the cross. He said to them, "Except ye eat my flesh and drink my blood, ye have no life in you." Later, however, He proclaimed to them the gospel and mission of the Comforter which is the Holy Ghost. Speaking to them of His departure as recorded in John 16, He said:—"Because I have said these things unto you, sorrow hath filled your heart. Nevertheless, I tell you the truth: it is expedient for you that I go away; for if I go not away the Comforter will not come unto you; but if I depart, I will send Him unto you." That was the promise of something better than to be favored with His visible presence and to listen to the gracious words that proceeded from His lips. It is better to have an indwelling, though invisible Comforter than to have with us the visible Jesus. He must depart, but He was to send another Comforter, Advocate, Intercessor, which meant the gift of the Spirit in a general sense to all believers for all time and not to a few only. The culminating and supreme thing in the ministry of Jesus Christ was to be this bestowment of the Comforter. The one thing He strove above everything else to impress upon His followers was that this was their heritage, to the end that all might receive the baptism of the Holy Ghost and fire. ("Amen!")

I call your attention next to the fact that the baptism of the Holy Ghost was received in answer to prayer.

In Acts 1: 9 we read, "And when He had spoken these things, while they beheld, He was taken up; and a cloud received Him out of sight." They stood and gazed until two men in white apparel appeared and said:

"Why stand ye gazing up into heaven? This same Jesus, which is taken from you into heaven, shall so come in like manner as ye have seen Him go into heaven." Then they went back to the upper room, where "all continued with one accord in prayer and supplication, with the women and Mary the mother of Jesus, and with His brethren." They prayed. They all prayed. They all continued to pray. Ten days were spent chiefly in this exercise. "And when the day of Pentecost was fully come they were all with one accord in one place" and suddenly came the sound from heaven, and the fiery emanations, "and they were all filled with the Holy Ghost." This wonderful baptism and enduement with power came upon the infant church in answer to prayer.

And yet there are many people who go up and down the land assuming to be so wise, and who say it is an insult to God Himself to pray for a baptism with the Spirit. They tell us that when the Holy Spirit came at Pentecost He came to stay, hence, we err in praying for His coming again. That may be true as to His coming to the church at large but not as to personal experience. Jesus taught that we should ask the Father for the gift of the Holy Spirit. He it was Who told His followers the Father was more willing to give the Holy Spirit to them that ask Him than earthly parents are to give good gifts unto their children.

I have read about Hicks, the village blacksmith, who went into a Quaker meeting. After a prolonged period of stillness which was very painful to Sammy, he got up to testify. A Quaker brother said, "Sammy, sit thee down until the Spirit moves thee." The silence began again to be oppressive to Sammy, and he arose once more only to be told to wait until the Spirit moved him. Sammy waited a few minutes longer, and, rising, said:

"Friends, the Spirit doesn't move, let us pray for the Spirit." That is a sensible way to get the Spirit.

We must cry unto God for the fulness of the Spirit. David cried unto the Lord for heart cleansing and the Lord gave it to him. He said: "Create in me a clean heart, O God, and renew a right spirit within me." God heard his cry. A great many who are trying to seek the Holy Ghost might as well get a Chinese praying machine and set it in motion. They are not sufficiently in earnest. They do not cry to God for Him. We need to seek Him earnestly, as on the day of Pentecost, where they were all in one place with one accord, most earnestly praying to God, and not praying at each other. They prayed "with one accord." The instrument was in perfect tune. There was no jar, no discord, no disturbing vibrations, but all was in perfect harmony. That is what we need here. It is good and blessed for brethren to dwell together in unity. I never knew a marked degree of the Holy Ghost to come down where there was discord manifested among the brethren. I knew a place once where the members of a small church took particular pains to come in at separate doors, and seat themselves as remotely from each other as possible. I had occasion to preach to them, but I didn't preach to the empty seats. I preached first to those on one side of the house, and then to those on the other. I said: "You all profess holiness, but when you get it you will love one another enough to come in at the same door, sit together in the same sanctuary and worship God in brotherly love. You will shake hands together, and, once in awhile you will call at one another's homes. Then people will say, "See how these brethren love one another." In that prayer meeting of the early church, they all prayed, and they all got the blessing. The women prayed and the men prayed;

the preachers and the lay members. They were all after the blessing and when the Spirit came He came upon them all. ("Amen!" "Glory!")

I remember in 1861 when God sanctified my mother and converted me on the Alleghany camp ground in Western New York. During those days very few professed it unless they got it, it cost so much. I remember how they prayed too. Bless you! They would pray all night. They prayed through and the Pentecostal power and fire came. Just so there is no better way to seek the Pentecostal baptism now than that of earnestly and persistently crying unto God for it.

Again, I remark that the primitive baptism with the Spirit was given at a peculiarly appropriate season—"when the day of Pentecost was fully come." Why was it given at that particular time? We may not know all the reasons. This we know however; Pentecost was the anniversary of the giving of that law which originally was written in tables of stone by the finger of God. The law under the Old Testament was outward and objective—a set of rigorous, external exactions. The distinguishing characteristic of the New Covenant is the promise that under its provisions the law is to be written on the mind and heart. It is the work of the Holy Spirit to do this. Baptism with the Holy Spirit baptizes the very essence of the law into the mind and heart. It is not the abolition of the law, but a new promulgation of it. It does not release from obligation to keep the law, but makes us all the more sensible of that obligation. At the same time it puts within us the constant disposition and ability to keep the divine requirements. Blessed be God!

There is a sense in which a sanctified believer is not under the law. He doesn't obey through fear any longer in a servile spirit or from feeling "I must." Of course he has to recognize the law. The law is not taken away. The law is put in the heart however, and so becomes his thought, desire, will and activity. It is this that makes it a kind of second nature, for to do the things required by the law, and so to delight in it as to say, "O, how love I Thy law! It is my meditation all the day." Some people seem to be fond of living in the seventh chapter of Romans, where they are ever in a vain struggle to keep the law. Paul, in this chapter says: "O, wretched man that I am! Who shall deliver me from the body of this death!" I don't see how any one can want to live where there is nothing but wretchedness, where they have always to say, "The good that I would, I do not: but the evil which I would not, that I do." This "when I would do good, evil is present with me" is too often excuse for living in some known sin. Thank God there is a more excellent way. Paul, in the eighth chapter of Romans, tells of another law which counterworks this law in the members which enslaves us. He says: "There is therefore now no condemnation to them which are in Christ Jesus; who walk not after the flesh, but after the Spirit."

Holding this book in my hand, I let it go. According to the the law of gravity, it goes down. But I have the ability to bring in the operation of another law and thereby to overcome the operation of that downward law and send the book heavenward. If my ability were infinite, I could send it upward forever. God is able by His Spirit to reverse the downward law of our depraved natures as to bring our wills, affections and affinities to perfect harmony with Himself, and to keep them there forever. Moreover He will do this, when we meet the conditions. This is what is meant by putting the law in the heart. "Ye shall therefore be perfect, even as your Father which is in heaven is perfect." Then the law of God in all its requirements will become very sweet. You will not get offended if the minister preaches ever so closely, if what he preaches is from the Word of God. You can take the strongest things in this Book and say of them, "How sweet also are Thy words unto my taste! Yea, sweeter than honey and the honey comb." Thus, by the sanctifying baptism of the Spirit the law is written on fleshly tablets of the heart, not by pen and ink, but by the Spirit of the living God. As the New Testament Pentecost signifies this new writing and promulgation of the law how fitting that its inauguration took place at Pentecost, the anniversary of the original publication of the law.

I call you to notice further that the outpouring of the Spirit was attended by peculiar and significant phenomena—a voice like a rushing mighty wind and cloven tongues like as of fire. These phenomena were symbols of the Holy Spirit's operations. As the divine breath swept down upon that upper room assembly there was a sound as of a rushing mighty wind. Wind is a symbol of the Spirit. It is independent in its operations, "Thou canst not tell whence it cometh or whither it goeth, so is every one that is born of the Spirit." You must let Him come in His own way. He will submit to no dictation, to no formula of yours or mine.

An Ogden pastor prayed "O Lord we beseech Thee to send us the Holy Spirit, send Him upon us very graciously. Send Him upon us very quietly, send Him upon us very beautifully." Do you suppose He came? By no means. He was insulted to His face. I like the old Methodist way of putting it better, as when we sing "Come as Thou wilt, but Holy Spirit come." ("Amen.")

Wind is also a reviving, inspiring and purifying agent, and in all these respects is a symbol of the Holy

F. H. BROOKMILLER,
Red Oak, Iowa.

BRIG. S. L. BRENGAL,
New York, N. Y.

H. S. WILLING,
Indianapolis, Ind.

MRS. H. S. WILLING,
Indianapolis, Ind.

S. RICE,
Chicago, Ill.

W. M. KELSEY,
Evanston, Ill.

J. H. MARSH,
Chicago, Ill.

JOHN KIRN,
Owosso, Mich.

Spirit. Then came the fiery manifestaticn. Fire has ever been the symbol of divine presence. It is a symbol of ardor. It is illuminating, inspiring, refining, purifying and penetrating. Dr. Parker says, that what is received by each is to be communicated to the whole world. It is always for utility that the Holy Spirit is given.

If God gives the Spirit to you it is that you may be His agent to convey it to others.

I call you to observe finally that this Pentecostal baptism with the Spirit was a universal bestowment. "They were all filled with the Holy Spirit." How glorious it must have been! I have often thought I would like to live to see one church of whose membership it could be truly said, "They were all filled with the Spirit." Brethren this sanctifying baptism is for us all, ministers, laymen, old and young, learned and unlearned, rich and poor. It is for all. Moreover all ought to have it. Have you ever been to a church where every member was filled with the Holy Spirit? Some would be afraid of such a people. Most people are afraid to get where there is much spiritual light and life and power. It is the carnal in them that thus shrinks at the phesence of the Holy Spirit. We need whole churches that are sanctified and spirit-filled to overcome the opposition of the world.

What marvelous results follow when God's people are filled with the Holy Spirit! What a change it effects in their own hearts and lives! How much God wrought through those who were filled with the Spirit at Pentecost! Spectators mocking said, "These men are full of new wine!" but Peter said, "These are not drunken as ye suppose, seeing it is but the third hour of the day." Then he began telling, in a simple way, their experience: how God had raised Jesus from the dead who had shed forth upon them the Holy Spirit as foretold by the prophet Joel. He charged upon them the murder of Christ and fervently exhorted them to repentance toward God, and faith in our Lord Jesus Christ. Three thousand were cut to the heart, and cried "Men and brethren what shall we do?" Peter exhorted them to repent and be baptized in the name of Jesus. They did so, and there were added to the disciples that day about three thousand souls. Following this there ca   ermnent revival and the Lord added to the church daily such as should be saved.

My friends, if you are without this baptism, seek it now. You can afford to forego eating and sleeping to obtain this blessing, and give yourself in prayer until God baptizes you with the Holy Spirit. To seek it successfully, however, you will need have to hunger and thirst after righteousness. You will have to be in accord with spiritual people and love your neighbors. If you are indulging any hard feelings against anyone, you cannot get the Holy Ghost. "He cannot endorse any thing of that kind. Don't say, "My neighbor is to blame." If you would be right with God, get right with your brother; meet the conditions, and see how God will baptize you. Pray for the blessing. Pray until the heavens part and distil their blessings upon your head. There is such a thing as praying through and touching the arm that moves the world. God grant us to see Pentecost repeated at this Holiness Assembly. Amen!

Bro. B. S. Taylor followed with an earnest exhortation of about twenty minutes, after which a large altar service was held, a number seeking a deeper, larger experience.

Sunday, May 5.
MORNING SESSION.
LOVE FEAST IN CHARGE OF BRO. J. B. FOOTE.

Bro. Foote: I wish to read and pass a few comments upon the Scripture as found in 1 John 1. (Reading chapter entire).

" 'That ye also may have fellowship with us.' What a blessed experience, to have fellowship with God. ("Amen!") What is heaven? A great German student collates all the verses of the Bible, where the word "heaven" is used in a religious sense, and brings out this definition: "Fellowship with God, unobstructed by sin." When I got that, I said a big "Amen." ("Glory!") It went all through me like lightning. I came to know this heaven on earth. Perfect union,—fellowship with God, God in me.

" 'And these things we write unto you that your joy may be full.' Our joy cannot be hindered, if we have this fellowship with Him. I have the 23rd Psalm in my experience. The Lord is my shepherd, and I lack nothing. This psalm is present tense until the last verse, and that is glorious. I am restored; I am in the banquet house in the presence of mine enemies. I have victory. Twenty-three years ago, I was converted and sanctified in a holiness meeting,—converted at 9:00 o'clock and sanctified next day at 3:00 o'clock. Twenty years ago, I read Bro. Doty's "Lessons in Holiness," whch meant a great deal to me, but it meant a great deal more to be taught by experience. I believe there are a great many things that go along with holiness, but holiness is first. I am here to learn the best methods for getting sinners converted and believers sanctified."

Bro. G. W. Chapman: "This experience brings a thrill and a halo of glory on my soul that no tongue can tell. I believe in a holiness that gives a man a clean heart. I was a great sinner, but God took all jealousy and bitterness out of my heart. Many are praying, 'Lord, give us more power.' When I got free, I got the power. God always fills a place that is clean. ("Amen!") It is a great thing to be clean from the top of the head to the soles of the feet. You don't have to keep priming your old pump. You have the power. All the powers of evil in hell and on earth cannot keep the power of God out of your soul, if you are clean." ("Amen!")

Sister Kent White: "My well of living water is still flowing. ("Amen!") The Lord sanctified my soul after three days of fasting and prayer. The Lord didn't let me rest until I got it. ("Amen!") The Rocky Mountain preachers are all on fire since they got the baptism of the Holy Ghost. I want to preach it out. I realize that holiness is power. Some folks get down and cry for power. After they get purity, they get power. ("Amen!") When I got a clean heart, it came in streams. It was a deluge. I am free in any place. Glory to God! I don't know why I am here. I got my ticket, and my folks sent me. I have sanctification and the Holy Ghost in my heart. Bless God!" ("Amen!")

A delegate: "The blood cleanses me. Jesus accomplished this work in my soul to make me His temple. I have learned the secret of abiding. He is waiting anxiously to find an abiding place in our souls."

A Sister from Denver, Colo.: "For twenty years, I was in a blackslidden state. I cried: 'God save me, or I perish,' and I handed up the key of my heart to Jesus, and He came in. ("Amen!") When I thought of coming to this meeting, I said, 'O, God, if you want me to go out there 1500 miles, take me,' and I am here. I came here to pray, and I believe that we have to pray without ceasing. My faith takes hold for never-dying souls.

A Brother: "I don't want to take any time from any child of God. I do know something about the Holy Ghost, and something about the Holy Ghost giving a man patience and help. If we have the love of God in our hearts, the people with whom we come in contact will know it, and it will have its influence to lead them to Him."

A Delegate: "Pardoned, sanctified, and kept by trusting in the Saviour."

Deacon Morse: " 'In Him we live, and move, and have our being.' If any heart will clean the temple, He will move in. He will make us His temple, and live in us, giving us rivers of living water in our souls." ("Amen!")

A Brother: "I found when I got the baubles of this world out of my heart. I got the blessing. If we want full salvation, we must get pure. We must get rid of all thought of worldliness."

Sister Jacobs: "I thank God, when I was ready to receive Him, He came into my heart. I tell you He did something for me. If you say you are justified or sanctified, and there has been no change in you, you haven't got it. ("Amen!") I gave the Lord everything else He wanted, and finally I said: 'Lord take me.' I tell you, friends, if you don't know what the second blessing is, get it today." ("Amen.")

A Chicago Brother: "I said I wanted the pure cream and essence of salvation. I had been taught, that if I had a little of this world's goods, I could go through purgatory. I thank God that I was able to break the shackles and chains that held me to popery. I had to be crucified with my Lord. I praise God, 'There is none other name under heaven, given among men whereby we must be saved,' except through the Lord Jesus Christ. ("Amen!") 'If the Son, therefore shall make you free, ye shall be free indeed.'"

A Texas Brother: "There used to be a drawing back in my heart. I praise God that this perfect love will cast that out, and make us love the colored man as well as the white man. ("Amen!") My father used to be a slave-holder, and I knew what it was to be associated with the slaves. After I got this experience, I used to hold meetings and get these colored folks to come, and many of them were sanctified. Bless His name forever!"

Bro. John Kirn: "I am saved of God. When I got converted, I want to say that I was a new creature in Christ Jesus. I swung out into a new realm. Some time after my conversion, I sought for cleansing of heart—for this purity the Bible speaks about. When the blessing came, I knew it. I was naturally timid, but God took the timidity all out and I long to face the world and tell what Christ will do for sinners. It was the 14th day of January, about 15 years ago, that I got this blessing, and, by the help of God, I will press on, through thick and thin to the end." ("Amen!")

A Brother: "I have much to be sorry for that I didn't start sooner. I have a lot to be thankful for that I did start at all. I put it off until I was forty-seven years old. The devil used to be in—looking out, but now I have him out—looking in. ("Amen!") I am on a through train that doesn't get side-tracked; the frogs are all pointing the right way. I am on a train that is moving rapidly, and I am praying that the bridges may be burned behind me. ("Amen!") I am serving God with all my heart."

Bro. F. H. Brookmiller of Iowa: "I praise God for victory in my soul. At the age of nineteen, while walking in the clear light of a justified experience, I first learned of holiness, and I said, 'Lord, I want it.' I was a happy boy, but I wanted to get closer to God. Every night, I knew I was nearer it. One day, in the town of Jefferson, the experience came upon me quicker than I can tell. What occurred, I can never tell. I felt it go through me like a shock from head to foot. All I know is, that God sanctified me then and there; and I bless Him for the faith through which I have claimed the victory in His name. I want all that He has for me. I have never had any wish to be great or wise, in any but my Savior's eyes." ("Amen!")

Bro. A. M. Hills: "I am glad to be here. The Lord saved me when I was eleven years of age. I went through the schools, colleges and seminaries, and didn't know that it was my privilege to be sanctified. When I first went into the ministry, I was without this blessing, and I couldn't get anybody any further in experience than I was myself. The providence of God took me out of the ministry into evangelistic work, and I found myself back at the college where I had graduated twenty years before. There I met a humble farmer, who had stood for twenty-five years with the finger of scorn pointed at him. Sentiment had been against him, his name derided and ugly things said about him, all those years; but he stood for God and holiness. He loaned me some books, and those books brought me into the experience. I am in the experience today. Bless His holy name!" ("Amen!")

Brother A. C. Morehouse: "Sixty-four years ago, this month, I was converted. Fifteen years after I was converted, God sanctified me. I found I was where the Israelites were, and that I would perish unless I got into my Promised Land. God so filled me with His blessed, perfect love that I could hardly eat or work for months, and He has been leading me all the way."

Bro. T. K. Doty of Cleveland, O.: "I was converted about forty-five years ago. I became a business man in Cleveland, Ohio. It was there I was introduced to a Mrs. Farmer, who said to me: 'Do you enjoy the blessed experience of holiness?' She added looking me straight in the eye, 'You may have as beautiful an experience as St. Paul.' I began to think about it. For about three weeks I was praying and under deep conviction, when I heard a brother get up and testify. I saw it was for everybody; that it was the Father's will that we should be sanctified. I gave up everything. I died out to self. I didn't have any great emotion, but I knew I had the experience. I went to a camp meeting, and found that they had the same thing. I didn't know but what they had something better! God cleansed my heart, and I felt so clean. I have been testifying to it for twenty-four years. Let us pray mightily that God may make this Assembly a great blessing, and that He may put His seal on this meeting."

Bro. T. H. Nelson of Indianapolis, Ind.: "I want to thank God that He saved me. I want to thank God for a religion that cost everything. For years, I worshiped God with a string of beads in my pocket. Sixteen years ago, I took these out of my pocket, to find peace in Jesus. After that though I was not up and down in my experience, and was constantly victorious, I found an involuntary shrinking, an involuntary rebellion, until I became sanctified. I think we ought to be more definite. There are some who think they are sanctified, but are only justified. There is that involuntary rebellion still there. When God sanctified me, He took out that disposition to walk limpingly. Thank God it had to go, and now I have deliverance through the blood of Jesus." ("Amen!")

SERVICE AT 10:45 A. M.

Singing by congregation, "Come Thou Almighty King."

Prayer, by Bro. A. M. Hills: "O, Lord, our blessed God, Author of our being, we come into Thy presence this morning with loving and grateful hearts, to bow before Thee in thine holy temple. O, Lord, let all the earth keep silence before Thee, and worship Thee in the beauty of holiness and in the fear of the Lord. We bless Thy name for the privilege of Thy sanctuary. We thank Thee for this pleasant Sabbath morning and, as the sun rose so beautifully over the earth this morning, so may the Son of Righteousness arise in every heart. We thank Thee for a living God. We thank Thee for the assembly of the First Born. We thank Thee for the privilege of worshiping Thee. We pray Thee Father, to take out of our hearts everything that offends Thee. As we come and bow before Thee, this morning, and offer up our supplications and songs of gratitude and praise before the Lord, we call upon our souls and all that is within us to bless Thy holy name and forget not all Thy benefits. We praise Thee for Thy Gift of gifts— the blessed Son of God, who died for us. We praise Thee for that other Gift to be our Guide, our Leader, Comforter and Sanctifier,—the indwelling Holy Ghost. O Triune God, we call upon our souls this morning not to be unmindful of Thy benefits and blessings innumerable. The Lord God Omnipotent reigneth! O, come into our souls and reign this morning, God Supreme, and sway Thy sceptre over every faculty of our being. O, Lord, set our heart's affection on Thee, that we may love Thee with all our heart and soul and mind and strength, and that we may love those for whom Thou didst die, as ourselves. Sway Thy sceptre over all our being, that our will may ever more be submissive to Thy will. Rule over our natures, that every desire and appetite shall be in sweet conformity to the perfect will of God.

"We pray Thee to remember the pastor of this church. Rejoice his soul, and water it with the dews of heaven, and may he have all that God wants to give him, and all that was purchased for him with the precious blood of Jesus. We pray Thee for a blessing upon his family and upon his church. Bless all who are accustomed to worship here from Sabbath to Sabbath. O, Jesus! Every congregation represents so much of weakness and longing unsatisfied, hope deferred, and heart sickness. Thou knowest how to minister to these people. Remember, O Lord, all sin-sickness; this sickness that Thou didst come to save the world from. Minister to these sin-sick hearts that may be here this morning. Point them to Thyself and the five wounds that bought their salvation.

"O God, hear us for this prayer roll, stretched across this church. It represents so much of agony, heart-ache and longing. O, Jesus, come in mercy and bless all these souls. Some of them are poor wives, who have wrestled long, and their hearts have grown sick with waiting for the salvation of their husbands. Fathers and mothers want their children brought to Thee. O Christ, Thou knowest the feelings of the parental heart, for Thou didst make it. Thou knowest what it is for fathers and mothers to wait and weep before Thee in supplication for their dear ones. Have mercy upon them. Then there are the brothers and sisters praying for loved ones. Even children, doing the unnatural thing, are praying for parents, when their parents ought to be praying for them.

We beseech Thee to hear these prayers that are now being lifted up for these precious ones all over the land.

"Thousands are praying for us. O God, come down on this convention. We want the holiness forces united. We want them melted down, melted together and fused until every heart beats in sympathy and unison, laboring together for the cause of holiness. Jesus, Thou Almighty God, we pray Thee to give us a Pentecostal blessing in this Assembly. Let not a week pass, until God comes in mighty power, and multitudes are saved and sanctified. Almighty God, come down and help us and this great city. Let Thy kingdom come. Let Thy will be done in our hearts. Sanctify all of our hearts until this world shall be redeemed to our Lord and His Christ, and He shall reign forever, and Thou shalt have the glory, world without end. Amen."

Scripture Lesson, Isaiah 55, read by Bro. A. M. Hills.

SERMON BY BRO. J. P. BRUSHINGHAM.

Text: "Sir, we would see Jesus." John xii:21. "Tarry ye in the City of Jerusalem." Luke xxiv:49.

Some of the Greeks that were proselytes, came up to Jerusalem to the Feast of the Passover. And they came with the exclamation on their lips: "Sir, we would see Jesus!"

After Philip and the others had been converted, Jesus the Divine Master, who conversed with him on this occasion said: "This is not all there is for you. 'Tarry ye in the City of Jerusalem, until ye be endued with power from on high.'"

There is no word appropriate to express the present climacteric state of things. We are not here simply for dress parade.

Christ's Personal Power.—I call your attention to the power and influence of a personal Christ on our salvation. I want to say to you in the first place that Jesus and His personal power on the lives of men can never die out. It is impossible. Pharaoh tried to put Moses to death, but failed. Herod tried to put him (who came from that obscure village of the Roman Empire) to death when a babe, but could not do it.

If there is anything in your voice or heart of testimony to the consistency of holy living, the world wants it. "And I, if I be lifted up," said Jesus, "will draw all men unto me." We need no argument; we need no demonstration; we need no proof in a logical formal way —all we need to do is to hold Him up faithfully, both by word of mouth and exemplary life, presenting Him to the world, and He will win His own way.

Enthroning Christ.—If I understand the meaning of this assembly, it is to enthrone the living Christ in the hearts of the people. You cannot have a photograph of Christ. It doesn't appear that photography had reached its present stage in that day. Nor have we a phonograph of Mr. Edison's to reproduce His precious words as they fell from His lips. But you and I may reproduce His Spirit and present Him to the world as a Saviour and Redeemer. We are here waiting for a baptism of His Holy Spirit.

Holiness the Climax of Christianity.—What is the climax of all Christianity? Holiness and Sanctification. That includes the Holy One. That includes the Sanctifier. Of course there is no preaching greater than the preacher. There is no doctrine greater than the teacher. There is no salvation greater than the Saviour. I believe in the possibility of full salvation. I know something of it by experience. I believe in the Saviour. I believe in a Holy God, because I believe a Holy God will not have unholy people as His chosen ones. We want nothing less than an indwelling Christ and a baptism of the Spirit resting upon us.

To see Jesus.—In what sense would men want to see Jesus,—from what view-point? He is interesting from many points of view. I have no patience with the modern sneer at theology. Jesus Christ is God manifest in the flesh, and any phase of the science of God is interesting and profitable.

It is profitable for us to come and see Jesus historically. We see Jesus blessing little children; feeding the multitude; standing by the pool restoring the impotent man, when there was nobody to help him; hearing the cry of blind Bartimaeus; turning to the poor invalid of 12 years, who touched the tassel of his robe, and saying: "Be of good cheer. Thy faith hath made thee whole;" healing the sick and raising the dead. What a field for the study of an historic Christ! Strauss and Renan planted their guns of attack along the lines of an historic Christ. You might as well expect to see the sun and stars fall from heaven, as to see Christ taken out of history.

People might come to see Christ from various aspects and points of view, but let me hasten to say that the view point which is most precious is that of experience—that of a personal, present Saviour, cleansing us from all sin. Some would like to see Jesus on the throne of Judgment, judicially, when great and small, high and low shall ascend with a shout and at the voice of the trumpet all shall be raised from the dead. Others would prefer to see Jesus in glory. What we want to see, is Jesus as a present, personal Saviour from all sin, and then:

"We'll have heaven below,
Our Redeemer to know."

Brother John McNeill was in Chicago preaching on the transfiguration of Jesus. I remember his saying "I am glad, brethren, that I am not preaching on the Atlantic coast. 'And when they lifted up their eyes, they saw no man save Jesus only.' If I were on the Atlantic coast and lifted up my eyes, I would want to go home and see mother." We can all stay a little longer in sin-cursed Chicago, or New York, or Boston in the service of the Master.

Personality of the Saviour.—Why do we come together? Why do we come to church? You say: "I can read my Bible at home." You say: "I want time to read the Sunday morning paper." God pity that kind of diet! It is the personality back of the words of the preacher, that causes us to prefer the spoken word. God pity the preacher that doesn't put anything back of the printed page of his sermon! When Dr. Storrs was preaching a memorial sermon in honor of the great Brooklyn divine he said: "Read Beecher's sermons? You might as well go back to the 4th of July with its exploded sky-rockets and broken wheels, after it was all over." He said you would miss the life and power and spirit. I am thankful that God sent His Son, that we might know a personal Saviour. Frank Bristol, when passing through Chicago, said that his church in Washington was always full on account of the people coming to see the president. He said you might think it foolish, but you would be surprised at the number who come up and say: "I wish you would take me up. I want to sit in President McKinley's pew." They want to have the honor of saying that they have sat in his seat. W. T. Stead of London was writing a letter, and started to say "Be a Christian." He got to the last word, and had gotten down "Be a Christ——" when he was called away. When he came back and found what he had written, he said "I'll not finish that. I'll let that stand." There is a sense in which we are to be a Christ and represent Him.

Christ cannot fall.—The religion that is centered around Jesus Christ cannot fall any more than the sun can fall from heaven. We are not to come with small questions, but in all seriousness, asking "What must I do to be saved,"—to be fully saved? We are not to come sarcastically or ironically asking, for those who do, do not want an answer. And we must not come like the rich man, who went away sorry because the Master said to him: "One thing thou lackest: go thy way, sell whatsoever thou hast, and give it to the poor." We must come prepared to give away everything,—to lay everything upon the altar, in honest and whole-souled sacrifice.

Death then Life.—"Sir, we would see Jesus." So Philip took them to Jesus. Jesus told them: "Except a corn of wheat fall into the ground and die, it abideth alone: but if it die, it bringeth forth much fruit." He said, if you have come to have a good time and simply to see me on my throne of glory, you are mistaken. We put a kernel of corn into the earth, out of sight, covered all over, in contact with the lowly earth. They run wagons over it, the children play above it. It begins to decay,—to die. Presently there is a little opening in it the size of a pin point. Somebody raps at the door and says: "Let me in and I will help you." And the grain of corn says: "O, I am of no account. I am dead. I am of no use." "Just let me in," and Mother Nature goes in and begins her work. The kernel of corn sends its little roots down into the soil and shoots a tiny blade up. "First the blade, then the ear, after that the full corn in the ear." So Christ knocks at the door of your heart that he may enter in and do a work which you cannot possibly do for yourself. First dead to self, alive to God and eternal glory! ("Amen.") A man can afford to be trampled on and covered up out of sight, if the mighty Christ comes in and becomes his "Mother Nature." Christ wants us to be faithful even unto death. Col. Turner said when he went out to battle he told a drummer boy he must go out, saying to him, "Boy, you will take care of my pocket-book and watch and those boots. I think a great deal of those boots." When he came back he saw that a stray shot had left a dent in the boy's head and he was dying. He looked up and said, "Colonel, I have kept the boots." God wants us to keep our trust even unto death. There are worse things than dying. It is a thousand times worse to live to sin than to die to self. ("Amen.")

To Be Like Him.—Paul said: "Let this mind be in you which was also in Christ Jesus, who, being in the form of God, thought it not robbery to be equal with God, but made Himself of no reputation." He emptied Himself of Himself and humbled Himself. Reputation is what we seem to be. Character is what we are. Reputation is what men think of us. Character is what God and the angels know of us. Reputation is the frescoed adornment. Don't worry about your reputation if your character stands unimpeached. "Wherefore God also hath highly exalted him, and given him a name which is above every name; that at the name of Jesus every knee should bow, and that every tongue should confess that Jesus is Lord, to the glory of God the Father." We are to be like Him in humility. "Let this mind be in you which was also in Christ Jesus." That is a very simple statement: Just to be like Jesus. Yes, it is, but it is the profoundest thing in the world to be like Jesus. ("Amen.") You say "I am only human. I cannot aspire to anything like that." But he was human. Take the words of Pilate

JOSEPH H. SMITH,
Redlands, Calif.

B. CARRADINE,
St. Louis, Mo.

ISAIAH REID,
Des Moines, Iowa.

WILSON T. HOGUE,
Chicago, Ill.

S. A. KEEN.
(Deceased)

M. D. COLLINS.
Rapid City, S. D.

MRS. J. M. SHERBURNE,
Chicago, Ill.

MRS. LYDIA E. BROWN,
Chicago, Ill.

"I find no fault in this man." There is hope for us if "our life is hid with Christ in God." ("Amen.") O, the glorious opportunity of sinless manhood and sinless womanhood through the power of Jesus Christ! Let Jesus Christ, the mighty healer come in and cleanse, and, after He has emptied you of all sin, let Him fill the vacuum. Jesus Christ didn't always stay at Jerusalem. Jesus Christ ascended and left this world. But, before He ascended there came two historic scenes of His life. First, He died and was buried. Second, He arose again from the dead. First, let us be dead to self, and rise again unto life in God. ("Amen.")

Spiritual Dynamics.—We are living in an electric age. The age of triumph and progress in the material world. When F. B. Meyer was here, he told how somebody asked a famous electrician if there wasn't more electricity in the world than ever before. He said: "No. We simply know how to utilize the electricity now." Mr. Edison proposes to build an equipment to send dispatches without the intervention of wires through from dynamo to dynamo. Give us a Christian dynamo charged with the full power of the Holy Ghost! Jesus Christ can do more for us in the spiritual world than all the skill and science for the material world. "But ye shall receive power after that the Holy Ghost is come upon you." Christian Dynamics does not mean Christian apologetics! ("Amen!") We have no answer to make to our enemies but Jesus Christ and the Holy Ghost which He promised to give us.

A Critical Time.—It is said this is a critical time for the Holiness movement. If it is, it is a critical time for Christianity, too. We have seen three great temples erected in this city, within a very short space of time, dedicated to the most absurd and erratical doctrines. It is a critical time, but thank God, we are not discouraged. (Cries of "No.").

We catch the glorius optimism of our Lord, when He said to His disciples after He was risen: "All power is given unto me in heaven and in earth. Go ye therefore and teach all nations, baptizing in the name of the Father and the Son and the Holy Ghost; teaching them to observe whatsoever I have commanded you, and lo, I am with you alway, even unto the end of the world."

Back to Christ.—What we want in religion is to go back to Spurgeon, back to Wesley. Back! Back! Back to Jesus Christ! ("Amen!" "Glory!"). There was a wavering in the army. They were falling back before the enemy. Gen. McPherson had fallen dead in battle. Who would take his place? There was a wavering and falling back under the terrific fire of the enemy. It was a critical hour for the "Boys in Blue." They didn't know what to do, but the "Black Eagle of Illinois," Logan, stepped forward, caught up the starry flag, unfurled it above his head and cried: "Rally! Rally! Rally! to the colors." As the men in blue rallied around the flag they were saved from dismay and led to victory. Is there a wavering in the ranks of the Holy Ghost hosts anywhere? Is there a falling back in the face of the enemy? In the name of this great assembly we unfurl this morning the Banner of Jesus, blood red, the flag of the redeemed, and we cry from the depths of our hearts, Rally! Rally! Rally! to the cause of Jesus Christ. "More love to Thee O Christ! More love to Thee." Will you join me in that song as if you meant it?

Singing.—(Congregation joining heartily.)

> "More love to Thee, O Christ,
> More love to Thee,
> Hear Thou the prayer I make,
> On bended knee.
> This is my earnest plea,
> More love, O Christ, to Thee,
> More love to Thee.

"Once earthly joy I craved,
 Sought peace and rest;
Now Thee alone I seek,
 Give what is best:
This all my prayer shall be
More love, O Christ, to Thee,
 More love to Thee.

"Then shall my latest breath
 Whisper Thy praise;
This be the parting cry
 My heart shall raise.
This still its prayer shall be,
More love, O Christ, to Thee,
 More love to Thee."

AFTERNOON SESSION.

Singing by congregation: "The Half has Never yet Been Told," "Sunlight," and "There is Joy in My Soul."

Prayer, by Rev. G. W. Ridout of New Jersey: "We praise Thee Lord, for this Sabbath day in Chicago. We praise Thee for the privilege of being associated with this assembly on this blessed Sabbath day. We praise Thee for the Holy Bible and the doctrine of holiness. We praise Thee for those who preach this precious Gospel of salvation. We praise Thee that this doctrine has not died out, but that it is alive and shall live.

"We pray Thee that this Assembly may be blessed from heaven; that it may be instrumental in unifying and harmonizing the holiness people; that greater impetus may be given to the holiness movement everywhere. We praise Thee that this is not a matter of creed, nor of doctrine, nor of dogma, but a matter of experience. We bless Thee for salvation, justification and sanctifiction; for a real, cleancut conversion, and a conviction for holiness and inward purity, and that Thou hast delivered so many from inbred sin. We bless Thee that so many can sing to-day that they are over in Beulah Land.

"We pray for Thy blessing on this afternoon service.

We want this service to be blessed of God. We want, this afternoon, that such a baptism of celestial fire may fall in our midst that all present may get an enduement of Thine holy unction. Assembled here, we trust with one accord, we calmly wait before Thee. Come, Holy Ghost, and fill this place, and Thou shalt have the praise and the glory, now and forever more. Amen."

Song by Bro. and Sister Harris: "The Old Fountain."

SERMON BY BRO. C. J. FOWLER.

Text: 1 Cor. iii. I hope that we will remember that the objective end of this afternoon service is not the sermon, but that it is soul salvation that is all-important. The sermon I expect will be related to that, but your prayers and attention will be very essential.

The passage I have selected as a text is Paul's first letter to the Corinthians, Third Chapter. (Reading of Chapter.)

Christian experience is life—soul life. "And you hath He quickened, who were dead in trespasses and sins." And this life is spiritual,—effected, sealed and controlled by the Holy Spirit of God; born of the Spirit. "As many as are led by the Spirit of God, they are the sons of God."

This spirituality, this life, is fruitful. "The fruit of the Spirit is love, joy, peace, long-suffering, gentleness, goodness, faith, meekness, temperance." Our initial experience then is divine, and, for a time is profoundly satisfactory, but only for a time. This leads me to say that, usually, Christian experience is contradictory. One is not only conscious of the presence of the fruits of the Spirit, love, joy, peace, etc., but he becomes conscious of the presence of the opposite of these in his heart. While he knows love is there, he is conscious of the presence of envy; while he knows joy is there, yet there is a tormenting fear; while peace is there, there is an inner conflict; while there is long-suffering, yet there is impatience; while there is gentleness, there is something of self-will; while there is goodness, there is a mixture of pride; while there is meakness, there is anger; while there is faith, there is a condition of unbelief; and while there is temperance there is something of inordinate desire. While the fruits of the Spirit are there, there is something of the opposites. I have said that, usually, Christian experience is contradictory. I do not mean to say that there is any exception. John Wesley said that often in conversion the "old man" got such a blow between the eyes that he didn't rally for awhile, but it is only a question of time and a very limited time before the regenerated heart will awaken to the consciousness of these untoward things. This is so real as to suggest doubt that he ever came into the light. So real is this as to suggest inquiry on his part as to the why of it and the how of it. He says: "Why, if I am converted, do I feel this thing? Why do I have these untoward things in me?" Right here is laid the foundation that may wreck that soul; or here is laid the foundation of truth on which that soul can build a structure that will stand forever. Let that soul go to a religious teacher and raise this question: "Is a man that feels pride, unbelief, self-will and anger unconverted? Or does it mean the absence of spiritual life?" The answer may effect the condition of that soul forever. To say to that person "You are not converted. Converted people never feel anger, pride, unbelief or self-will." To tell him that, is liable to discourage him forever. But say to that person: Yes, you may have been converted. The presence of those things is not evidence that you have not been. You want to thank God for the things He has done for you. You must remember that this is not a normal condition. God has something better yet for you. He not only can convert you He proposes to cleanse this away.

I have just read that which has to do with this contradiction of experience. These people addressed by the apostle are "brethren,"—evidently not unconverted sinners, but brethren in Christ. You will note he calls them "babes in Christ." It is true they were babes in Christ. The babe is in the human family, coming through the door-way of natural birth, just as much as the mother that holds it. These babes were in Christ, and were brethren in Christ. They are spoken of as God's husbandry. They are God's tilled land; God's productive soil. And they were God's building. Building carries the idea of ownership and occupancy. "Know ye not that ye are the temple of God, and that the Spirit of God dwelleth in you." And He says they are holy. Every Christian is holy. Not that every Christian is unmixedly holy. Before you and I were converted, we were unholy. The power of unholiness possessed and guided us. When we were born again, the principle of holiness was put in us and guided us. In that sense, every Christian is holy. I say, to be a Christian at all is to have a principle of genuine divine holiness within you. "Therefore if any man be in Christ, he is a new creature: old things are passed away; behold, all things are become new." Now the will of God is enthroned in that soul, and that soul says "yes" to the divine will; but when we are first converted, we don't always say "yes," without a protest.

The apostle in the text is giving a large place to conversion, regeneration or justification. He says: "Brethren," "Babes in Christ;" God's productive land, holy and belonging to Christ, showing clearly a condition as being children of God, and yet he said he could not speak unto them as spiritual, but as carnal. And that distinguished minister and reformer of New York has scriptural basis for his phrasing when he says "Carnal Christians." When one says there is no such thing as a carnal Christian, he breaks with Paul. Paul says they are "Babes in Christ," but are carnal.

I want to ask your attention to the popular and usual method of dealing with carnality. There are two great systems of theology, with which we are pretty familiar. I refer to Calvinism on the one hand and Arminianism on the other. Both of these great systems teach that which I am trying to emphasize. I would like to read you something that may interest you from the Calvinistic Catechism:

"Question. From whom does God defend his people?

"Answer: From all their enemies.

"Question: Who are their enemies?

"Answer: Sin, Satan, the world and death; the worst of which is indwelling sin.

"Question: How does Christ defend believers from sin?

"Answer: By keeping alive the spark of grace in an ocean of corruption.

"Question: What is meant by dying to sin?

"Answer: Ceasing more and more from the love and practice of it.

"Question: "Do not the remains of sin in our old man oppose this death?

"Answer: Yes. Most vigorously.

"Question: How do they oppose it?

"Answer: By secret lusting and violent fighting against grace in our hearts.

"Question: Does indwelling sin ever prevail against grace?

"Answer: Yes. Very often * * *."

There is a clear statement, strong enough to show that what I am undertaking to convey is scriptural from the standpoint of Calvinistic doctrine.

I next quote you from the Arminian doctrine:

"Original sin is the corruption of the nature of every man, whereby man is, in his own nature inclined to evil and that continually. And this infection of nature does remain in them that are regenerate, and, although there is no condemnation to them that believe, yet this lust has, in itself, the nature of sin."

The position taken in these statements is not peculiar to the Methodist, Baptist or any other denominational credal statement.

Now, when you come to the Arminian statement and ask when sanctification is to be complete, the answer is: It may be before death. How? There ought to be uniformity of answers here. All who claim to be adherents to Arminian theories ought to agree, but they do not. You know there is a double answer. Some say you get deliverance by growth in grace,—a long drawn out process. (Cries of "No.") Others say you get it by faith, a sudden and instantaneous process. Let me give you a statement that is clear and interesting. A writer, very prominent in Methodist circles is writing concerning what Methodists believe. He says:

"Some believe and even assert that it is a matter of personal experience, that following regeneration by a special and separate act of the Holy Ghost in answer to prayer and faith that claims it, the soul may immediately and consciously be raised to a state in which all evil tendencies will be eradicated. Others believe that, by continuous growth it may ultimately come into this state while yet in the body."

For a few moments I want to consider this last thought; growth in grace as a method of getting sanctification,—as a process of eliminating this old man, carnality, and becoming every whit whole. Some say, "but you do not believe in growth in grace." We do believe in it, and we think as nobody else believes in it. Why we allow, brethren, that a baby that has pronounced consumptive tendencies will grow, but a baby that has no unhealthy tendencies at all will grow much better. We believe an apple with a worm hole in it can grow, but an apple without the worm hole will grow better. We are not denying growth in grace, but we are insisting on it and insisting upon the right conditions unto growth in grace. What do people mean by growth in grace as a way of getting rid of the old man? May I put it in this way: What is the philosophy of it? There is a philosophy of salvation. The Bible is full of the philosophy of salvation.

I confess that I do not know what this "grow in grace" means. I have no way of knowing. Nobody has ever told me. I have never read it in any book, or heard it in any sermon or testimony. I do not know what these dear men and women mean by growth in grace as a method of getting sanctified and getting rid of the old man. I can only imagine. If I accepted this idea, I would have a theory. I am not an advocate, or believer in it. I want to suggest that growth in grace as a means of getting rid of the old man and being sanctified wholly is unreasonable for me to believe and inequitable for God to require. Here is a man converted when twenty years of age. He dies when he is eighty. Sixty years to grow out carnality. Another is converted at twenty and dies at forty years of age, and the distance is twenty years. Another is converted at the age of twenty and dies at the age of twenty-one, and the distance is twelve months. Still another is converted at twenty years of age and dies within a week. His opportunity to get sanctified by growth or any other method is limited to one week. To tell me that God would allow it, to say nothing of requiring one man to wait twenty years for what another gets in a week is unreasonable. Things are exactly equal here. For God to allow one man to struggle up across the years with this thing, to the end, and let another man get it in six days or one day would be unequal. It is also a misnomer. People who say we get sanctified by growth in grace do not mean what they say. Here is a man present this afternoon, eighty years of age,—an old man, tottering and feeble it may be. One of you holiness workers has talked with him. That dear man says he was converted away back sixty years ago. He says: "I don't understand what you are saying about getting sanctified. I had not been a Christian long before I noticed them, these wrong things in my heart and I am just as conscious of the presence of them in my heart now." Now it is four o'clock, I will say, when you have this conversation with that venerable Christian brother. In going down yonder steps he slips and falls and breaks his neck. Five minutes after you were talking to him he was in eternity. His opportunity to get rid of those things which existed in his heart was just five minutes. His opportunity to outgrow that condition was five minutes. The sixty years absolutely counted for nothing in getting rid of the old man. We do not say that he does not get rid of his carnal nature in the five minutes, but we do insist that he does not get rid of it by growth in grace. ("Amen.") Every state of grace is clearly experimental. Every phase of spirituality has two sides, which for the sake of trying to make it plain, I shall designate as positive and negative. I can remember when I was awakened. I was not an infidel, nor an agnostic. I could have preached not a little truth before I was converted. There was a day when God spoke to me in my inner consciousness. It was the testimony of the Holy Ghost to my soul that I was a sinner and doomed to hell. There was the negative side and there was the positive. There was the consciousness of being a sinner and the divine testimony to my soul that I was a sinner.

If we get sanctified we know it. I am not saying now whether we get it by growth, or death, by purgatory, or how! I just as naturally found myself in with the world as does water run down hill, but the moment God spoke peace to my heart, God's people were my people. ("Amen.") When I was sanctified, I just as naturally took to the holiness people.

You never heard of a case in your life where a man got the divine attestation of this thing we are speaking of, who said "I got it by growth." Here is a man that rises and says he was converted 20 years ago, out back of his good old father's barn, about 4 o'clock in the afternoon. He hadn't been converted a great while before he found in his heart something that led him to do things he knew he ought not to do. He went to his class-leader and minister, and they told him that was the way we all felt, and that he mustn't conclude that he was not converted. They said to him: "You must read your Bible, be careful to attend Sunday School, and enjoy all the means of grace." He says: "I did. I read my Bible; I attended all the means of grace the best I could, and I found I was growing in grace, but these things that so distressed me were still there. I still kept on. I was very active in church and Sunday School. I was instrumental in doing much good, and by and by it all became clear and I was sanctified wholly, all through the growth of grace." You never heard that kind of testimony in your life. ("Never.") If this idea of growth in grace is correct, you ought to hear it every day.

Here is a man that gets up and says: "I was converted 20 years ago, back of my good old father's red barn, about 4 o'clock in the afternoon. I had not been converted a great while before I ound these things in my soul. I went to people about it and they said 'we are glad you came. We have watched you with interest. We thought you were converted. We are glad you came to us with this. We want to tell you there is another work just as definite as this.' ('That begins to sound natural!') If you will go and ask God to sanctify you wholly, He will do it." I didn't know any better. I went right at it and said: "Come now and do this work in me, and God did it, just as definitely as I was converted out back of the barn, and I have had it all these years. Halleluljah!" You have heard that experience everywhere. ("Yes "Amen!") The next time somebody says the way to get it is through growth in grace, very courteously ask him if he got it in that way.

I want to bring two witnesses; two men, not from the common walks of life. I want to bring one of the greatest men Methodism has ever had, Wilbur Fisk. This man of God was twice elected bishop, once in the United States and once in Canada, but he declined the office, feeling, as he said, that he could do more good devoting himself to the education of the young. This marvelous man went down to Cape Cod in August, 1819, to attend a small tent camp meeting, among a few poke-bonnet old women; got down in the straw and asked God to sanctify him. He said he was instantaneously delivered from inbred sin and all doubts, and in after life he bore witness to what he got in the straw in that old Plymouth Camp Meeting on the shores of Cape Cod.

Take the next witness, Stephen Olin, whom the historian says stands forth with commanding prominence in the annals of the Methodist Church. That man, with broken health, went across the seas and visited the coast of Africa in the hopes of improving his condition. While standing one afternoon in the white sands by the Nile, looking up in the skies, with nobody about but the donkey boys and a few Arabs to look on, he received the witness and broke forth in shouts over the marvelous and magnificent life he got in the fullness of the gospel of Christ.

I was brought out from darkness into light as clear as day. I can say that I was never tempted from that minute to this to doubt that I was converted, that night in the old Methodist Church in the White Hills of New England. I got conversion in that little old church. I need not tell you; I could not tell you those heavenly sensations that accompanied it, and God has used me as an instrument to bring thousands of precious souls to Christ. On the occasion of my sanctification, I went into a service and they were praying for somebody. I didn't know who. I knew it fitted me. I was pastor of a large church at the time. I went forward and Deacon Morse came and knelt by my side and began to pray. He said: "O, God, we are unworthy to pray for this preacher. He has been a successful preacher." I hate to say this, but this is what he said: "He has been a successful preacher a useful preacher. He is pastor of a commanding church. We are unworthy, etc." I knew that man wasn't working along God's line. That prayer enhanced my suffering. He seemed to be conscious of this. He stopped to take a breath and said: "God take the devil out of this fellow." Here I was, pastor of a large church, and here I was down on the floor, but I said: "If the devil is in me, I want that prayer answered; if he is not he must not come in now," and I stuck to it and God brought me in and I am in now.

My soul is on the stretch for victory here. Give us such a victory as shall be felt all over the world, that the angels in heaven may rejoice, and you and I have cause to shout hallelujahs for thousands of years without taking breath! O, that somebody might get deliverance!

When the invitation was given, about twenty-five seekers came forward and half the congregation crowded around the altar.

EVENING SESSION.

At the opening of this session, report came from the street meeting in charge of Sister Cooke, that, with ten requests for prayer and five seekers kneeling on the pavements, the meeting had been broken up by a saloon-keeper, who had turned in a call for the police patrol.

Singing by congregation: "There's Power in the Blood."

Bro. Fowler:. "God has put my soul on top for something. I have been praying and fasting for 24 hours, and He has told me that He was going to bring great things to pass. God is going to answer our prayers. It would be in order, I think, at this time, to listen to a few testimonies."

Sister S. B. Shaw:—"I am first on my feet, because I haven't yet testified in this Assembly. I do know in my inmost soul that the blood of Jesus does cleanse from all sin, and that the blessed Spirit takes possession and does come into a poor human heart. ("Amen!") God does at times give promises of victory to His own. I, too, am confident that God is going to work mightily among us."

A Sister:—"I praise the Lord that He took the man-fearing feeling out of my soul. I found a sister, to-day, who was longing for this second blessing. I brought her down here, and, bless the Lord, she got it this afternoon." ("Amen! Glory!")

A Delegate:—"While we were singing 'There's Power in the Blood,' it seemed to me that I was in heaven's border land. This is heaven's border land to me. There's victory here."

Bro. Fowler:—"Get your cup right side up!" ("Amen!")

A Sister:—"I do praise God, because He is such a wonderful God, and Jesus Christ such a wonderful Savior. I praise Him to-night for salvation. I praise His name that He can cleanse me from all sin. I am wholly His, and He is wholly mine."

Bro. J. B. Shaw:—"You may think it strange when I tell you that I have been looking for this meeting for two years. The moment I read the announcement for this Assembly, I said: 'That is it.' I have been trying to preach salvation for many years. I preach it because I enjoy the experience in my soul. When I can't preach that way, I will quit." ("Amen!")

A Brother:—"I got a wonderful victory down on the street. I can say that I am justified, and sanctified. I am glad that Jesus is able to satisfy. I am satisfied with the quality, but I want more of it." ("Amen!")

Prayer by Bro. J. R. Allen of Waterloo, Iowa.

Song by Brother and Sister Harris: "The Riches of Love."

SERMON BY BRO. J. S. DEMPSTER.

Subject: The Two Baptisms.

Text: "I indeed baptize you with water unto repentance, but He that cometh after me is mightier than I, whose shoes I am not worthy to bear, He shall baptize you with the Holy Ghost and with fire." Matt. 3:11.

The anointed eye can see at a moment's glance that there are two baptisms spoken of in my text. The first is the baptism of John, which is the baptism with water unto repentance; the second is the baptism of Jesus, which is the baptism with the Holy Ghost and with fire. You can also discern that the baptism of John, which is the baptism with water unto repentance, is received before the baptism of Jesus, which is the baptism with the Holy Ghost and with fire; or in other words, the baptism of Jesus is not received at the same time that we receive the baptism of John, but is received subsequent to the first baptism. Here we can see that the baptism of John represents "the first blessing" and that the baptism of Jesus is "the second blessing;" so that Mr. Wesley was correct when he said that we are justified before we are sanctified.

We notice in the first place, that in order to receive the first baptism, it is necessary to comply with the Scriptural conditions of repentance, which may be summed up in Holy Ghost conviction, godly sorrow, which implies an utter detestation of all willful transgressions against a known law, complete, open-hearted confession to God, reparation to Him and to our fellow man as far as lieth in our power; an utter abandonment of all occasions to sin as far as our vocation in life will permit, and faith in the Lord Jesus as our personal, present Savior.

You will also notice in the word of God several symbols or types of The Holy Spirit, such as water, oil, wind and fire. This is why we baptize with water; because it is

R. L. SELLE,
Denton, Texas.

J. McD. KERR,
Toronto, Ont.

T. K. DOTY,
Cleveland, Ohio.

G. D. CLEWORTH,
Chicago, Ill.

THOS. H. NELSON,
Indianapolis, Ind.

MRS. T. H. NELSON,
Indianapolis, Ind.

E. GOODMAN,
Chicago, Ill.

H. ACKERS,
Big Prairie, Ohio.

the outward symbol of the inward work of regeneration, in the moral nature of those who have received John's baptism. Water of itself makes no change in the moral nature of any individual; whether we are sprinkled, poured upon or immersed. I am at a loss to know why so many lay such stress on water baptism, who utterly ignore the work of the Holy Spirit in the repentance and regeneration of the soul. It seems strange to any spiritually anointed teacher, why some should lay such stress on water, as if oxygen and hydrogen could work any change upon the spiritual nature of man. What we need to preach to sinners is not that they "come and join our church and be baptized," but come down in the sackcloth of humiliation to the cross of Jesus, and with contrite and broken hearts, cry out to God in the language of the publican's prayer, "God be merciful to me a sinner," and on their faces before God, with hearts lifted unto Him, the friend of sinners, pray until the voice of heaven would speak into their hearts, "son, daughter, thy sins are forgiven thee; arise and go in peace;" until they would be able to say, down in the depths of their very hearts "being justified by faith, we have peace with God through our Lord Jesus Christ." Rom. 5: 1. And know that He the blessed Spirit, has given them the witness that they are His children, His adopted sons and daughters. "For as many as received Him, to them gave He power to become the sons of God."

Secondly, you will notice that oil is also a symbol or type of the Holy Spirit; for the psalmist speaks of the oil of the joy of gladness, and we notice that kings and priests in the Old Testament dispensation were anointed with oil on entering into their offices.

Thirdly, that wind is another type of the Holy Spirit;

for in the upper room we read, in the second chapter of Acts, that when the day of Pentecost was fully come they were altogether in one place, and that suddenly; mind you not by development or culture or growth or gradual process, but suddenly, "there came from heaven a sound;" (I like those sounds from heaven, there is something sublime, heavenly, divine about them,) "as of the rushing of a mighty wind and it filled all the house where they were sitting." There was a heavenly cyclone there. O Lord send some such-like mighty cyclones through all the churches.

Fourthly. Fire is a symbol of the Holy Spirit. It were a foolish thing to say that the Holy Ghost is fire or wind or oil or water. These are but the symbols or types of the Holy Spirit. It would be a foolish thing to say that the baptism of repentance was one blessing, and that the baptism of water was the second blessing; for every careful Bible student knows that the baptism of water is but the outward symbol of the inward baptism of repentance. So we see that it is a foolish thing for some to teach that the baptism of the Holy Ghost in the sanctification of the soul is a second blessing, and that the baptism of fire is a third blessing. It would be just as sensible to teach that when we receive the baptism of water, that we receive the subsequent blessing to repentance.

How foolish it would be to say, "I baptize you in the name of the Father and of the Son and of water" or to dismiss a congregation by saying, "may the blessing of God the Father and of God the Son, and of fire, remain with you"!

The Holy Ghost is a divine person. He is not merely an attribute or an operation or influence. He is very God. Certainly the attributes of God are ascribed to Him, as eternity, Heb. 9: 14, omnipresence, Psalm 139: 7, omniscience, 1 Cor. 2: 10, 11, power, Rom. 15: 13-19; The Holy Spirit is God. I say it reverently, if He is not God, the church is deceived; the Bible deceives us, and if the Holy Spirit is not God, we have no way to be undeceived. But blessed be God! He is truly God, while yet the third and distinct person in the Godhead. It is His office work to witness to the forgiveness of the pardoned sinner; and He is the executive agent in the sanctification of every believer who has abandoned all to God, purging, purifying, filling, setting him on fire with His own blessed presence, revealing unto us Jesus in a fuller and grander and deeper sense in the sanctification of our souls.

So that we see in our text not three baptisms, but two; not three blessings, but two blessings; the baptism of John, which is the baptism of water unto repentance, and the baptism of Jesus, which is the baptism with the Holy Ghost and fire.

Some may ask me, "Is it right to be immersed?" to which I answer that after close and critical study upon the subject, I fail to find any command within the lids of the Bible as regards the mode of baptism; and the Methodist Church has very wisely given free liberty to all her children to be baptized in whatever mode they so desire.

As it is necessary to comply with the scriptural conditions in order to receive the first baptism, so also is it necessary to comply with the scriptural conditions in order to receive the second baptism. As the willfully impenitent can never know Jesus as their personal Savior, so also the believer unabandoned to God as a living sacrifice, can never know Jesus as their sanctifier or baptizer with the Holy Ghost.

You will notice the word He in the text; not it but

He, a personal pronoun. He is the baptizer. He is the One that will baptize you with the Holy Ghost and with fire, if you will "yield yourselves unto God as those that are alive from the dead." Rom. 6: 13. If you will present your body a living sacrifice, (mind you, not a dead sacrifice,) but present your body as a living sacrifice, holy acceptable unto God, which is your reasonable service." Mind you, it is not unreasonable, but your reasonable service. And be not conformed to this world so that ye may be transformed by the renewing of your mind, that you may prove for yourself what is that good and acceptable and perfect will of God concerning you.

Many fail to receive Christ as their baptizer with the Holy Ghost, and with fire because they will not make this complete and unreserved abandonment to the will of their heavenly Father. But if ever you do receive it, it will be only on the conditions which are laid down by the Apostle Paul in the 12th chapter of Romans, 1st and 2nd verses. All conformity to this world must be abandoned. You must get to the end of your entire consecration, and in earnest, believing prayer beseech Him, the mighty impowering baptizer, to sanctify your heart, to fill you with His personal presence, and to make you a living flame of fire.

I have said before that the Holy Ghost is not a mere attribute, influence or operation; but that He is a distinct person; that He is a divine personality; that He is not water or oil or wind or fire; but as Malachi 3: 2 states, "He is like a refiner's fire." And this is what He seems like unto to every believing child of God who has entered into the gracious experience of the second baptism: first, He comes in, taking away the stony heart, and giving you a heart of flesh. You find your heart all breaking up before God in great tenderness, and as the gold in the refiner's crucible is melted up by the fiery baptism it receives in the furnace, so also you find your heart all melted up in the fiery baptism which He the baptizer baptizes you with. Glory to God! But He not only comes in to melt you all up, but He comes in to purify your heart and to bring your moral nature into perfect harmony with His own blessed self; destroying all the ifs and buts and maybes and guess-sos and hope-sos and think-sos, giving you the divine assurance in these words "for by one offering He hath perfected forever them that are sanctified, whereof the Holy Ghost also is a witness." Heb. 10: 14, 15.

But He not only comes in to purify you; for having sold out all, so that in the language of the Apostle Paul you can say "I am crucified with Christ, never-the-less I live, yet not I but Christ liveth in me, and the life which I now live in the flesh I live by the faith of the Son of God who loved me and gave himself for me;" He comes in to make you valuable. As the fire purifies the gold and makes it precious, so you become one of the precious valuable ones in the sight of God, who cannot be bought, who will not compromise with evil in any shape or form, but in the spirit of your loving Lord will become a living witness or martyr both by life and testimony to declare boldly what He the mighty Baptizer has done for you.

Fourthly. He comes in as the mighty attractor of human souls; not to attract people merely to you, but to himself. Here is a lesson.

Some think that learning, culture, sentimental affectation, put-on-smiles, so-called politeness, oratorical eloquence, large organized choirs, a great display of ecclesiastical pomp, the writing up of elaborate reports in worldly newspapers, the uniting of a lot of ecclesiastical force, the systematic arrangement of plans, expensive advertising, the great show of five or six hundred people signing cards as make-believe conversions will attract souls to Jesus; but alas! alas! What a fruitless failure this has all been! O precious ministers of God! Workers in the Lord's vineyard! O that we would learn the lesson that He, and He only, is the mighty attraction! If all these things would attract, then we would have the glory; but He is a jealous God, and whatever we do must be done only to glorify Him. He puts an attraction, a shine upon us such as Stephen had, who in the face of death out of love for the Lord Jesus wins the most hardened to Calvary's Christ. But then He not only melts and purifies, makes valuable and attracts, but He puts a move in us (somehow I like the name, the holiness movement) like a mighty host of heaven's artillery, we are moving on on our white horses of swiftness and with our message of purity declaring to the whole world, or at least to that part committed to our care, that Jesus died, not only to save the sinner from hell, but to sanctify His believing children; not only to give them a birthright of victory over the world, the flesh and the devil, but to make them more than conquerors through Him who has loved us and washed us from our sins in His own blood; who has made us kings and priests unto God, and His Father, to Him be glory and dominion forever and ever. Amen.

Monday, May 6.
MORNING SESSION.

Devotional exercises commenced at 8 a. m., conducted by Bro. G. R. Buck.

The Assembly convened in business session at 9:30 a. m., Bro. C. J. Fowler, presiding.

Bro. Geo. Hughes reported that he was in receipt of a letter addressed to the Assembly from the Oxford Club of Drew Theological Seminary, at Madison, N. J., and that Bro. P. H. Murdick, of that institution, was present to represent said Oxford Club at this Assembly. On motion, the Secretary was ordered to read the letter to the Assembly, and Bros. Geo. Hughes and A. McLean, were made a committee to respond to same. By consent of the Assembly, Bro. Murdick was introduced, and he addressed the Assembly, to which the President, C. J. Fowler, briefly responded.

On motion, it was decided to appoint two committees of seven members each,—one to be a Committee on Deliverances, to formulate an expression of the sense of this Body on questions of Doctrine; the other, to be a Committee on Permanent Methods, to prepare a report on the best methods for advancing the kingdom of God, and, especially that part which relates to the spread of Scriptural Holiness over these lands.

Bro. T. K. Doty moved, and the motion prevailed, that a committee of five be appointed by the chair to nominate the members of the Committees on Methods and Deliverances.

On motion the business session adjourned.

Song by Sisters Nelson and Birdsall: "Christ Loved Me."

Prayer by Bro. C. J. Fowler: "Our Heavenly Father, may Thy servant have the anointing of the Spirit as he presents the message this morning, and may all of us who hear the Word of God have the anointing we need for the great responsibility of hearing Thy truth. Have we not read: 'Take heed therefore how ye hear'? Bless, we pray Thee, him who shall speak and all who hear. Bless all that is done here in the days to come, and may this Assembly, in all things, redound to Thy glory. We ask it in the name of Jesus. Amen."

SERMON BY PRES. A. M. HILLS.

Text: "Like as He which hath called you is holy, so be ye holy in all manner of conversation; Because it is written, Be ye holy; for I am holy." 1 Peter 1:15-16.

We have been distracted, somewhat, by our business session, and the Lord has seen fit not to let me use any text, or any sermon that I have ever preached in my life, and I bring you the message from God as He shall give it to me. I want you to help me, during the few moments you shall listen to me, by your sympathies and prayers.

The first word of the text is suggestive: "Like." God has made us imitative beings for a divine purpose. The little boy not two years old will imitate papa's voice and papa's gestures. The pupil in school will imitate his chosen professor, and will seem to do it unconsciously. The preacher will grow into imitating his ideal preacher. They tell us the woods of the South are full of "would-be Sam Jones." God never made but one, but people will imitate him. The officer will imitate the superior officer that he admires. And God appeals to this divinely planned impulse, and holds up as our ideal "Like as He which hath called you is holy, so be ye holy." All men are moved by ideals. The student of warm heart and generous impulses in college, through literature, gets an ideal which transforms and shapes his whole life and holds him steady to a line of activity. The artist has an ideal and that ideal makes him a painter and brings out the best that is in him. The sculptor has an ideal; and that somehow gets into every stroke of the mallet and every touch of the chisel and shapes the future statue. God is holding before His imitative child the ideal of excellence, and that ideal is lifted up in the infinities of the very heavens, and is none other than the infinite God Himself.

My text leads me first to describe this holiness which God holds up to us; second, to show why we should have it; third, how to get it.

I. You will pardon me if I say something under this first head, that many of you have heard so often that it has become stale to you. In every assembly there are some new souls that have not heard of some of these things. Although I was a graduate of two of the most famous universities, I didn't know the A, B, C's of holiness. After I had preached twenty-one years, I was still ignorant of it. It may be there is some one here that does not know more about it than I did six years ago. If so, let me tell what this means and what we are talking about. We have to state negatively and positively.

1. People are all the time going about and saying we teach that we get above temptation. Bless your souls! Adam was tempted in Paradise in the Garden of Eden. The angels no doubt were tempted in heaven. Jesus Christ was tempted, and God said we were to count it all joy when we fell into diverse temptations. There is not a spot this side of Glory where there are no temptations.

2. Again people say we teach that we get where we cannot sin. No intelligent holiness teacher has ever said such a thing. I have read eighty or ninety holiness books. I have read everything I could get my eyes on. I agree with Bro. Reid, when he says "We may sin but we do not have to sin." I do not suppose there is a brother present in this body who will not say that.

3. Sanctification does not give us Adamic perfection. Dr. Fowler may be as holy this morning as Adam was be-

fore he fell; but Adam had a body so perfect as it came from God that even after he had fallen it would live a thousand years. Our beloved moderator may not have as sound judgment, or as retentive a memory as Adam had; but he may have as clean a heart. How we have been slandered! But we bear it the best we can.

4. I want to say in the interest of God's blessed truth that we do not teach that we get so holy that we do not depend on the atoning work of Christ. I have never met any Christians so consciously and constantly dependent on the atoning work of Jesus as these holiness people. Glory to God! If they will tolerate me, I will them. Frances Ridley Havergal said: "Every moment, Lord, I need the merit of thy blood."

But positively, what is this blessing? Well, to cut the matter short, I will say that it brings deliverance from inbred sin. In regeneration, you had something put into you that you never had before, a trend of the will towards God and righteousness; but there was something left in you that you had always had, and that was the old carnal mind, the law of sin and death, the old man,—just like the old fellow himself, and you ought to know what it means. I was up in Michigan doing revival work, stopping in a minister's family. He seemed to be a very godly man and his wife a Christian woman, and yet there was their boy—the little fellow had some big sores and lumps on his head. I asked her about it, and she said, "O, he has a temper, and gets mad and bunts the door-knob with his head." That is inbred sin. That is the stuff that re generation does not take out. I have known a bald-headed doctor of divinity and theological professor with world-wide fame as a scholar and author lose his temper in the class room. Didn' a Chicago doctor of divinity of national reputation a few years ago go before a national body and make an exhibition, giving himself away, causing his brethren to grow heartily ashamed of his display of temper? Regeneration didn't take it out of them. It has got to go out before we get to heaven. ("Sure.") It is that which puts the "peacock" strut in men, and makes women proud of their apparel and proud of their beauty. It is that which makes the heart flash with temper, bringing the flush to the cheek, and causes us to spit out words as sharp as a dagger. That is what it is; that old man that crops up in the heart; and if we will let Him, God will look down in love and cause that to be taken out of us. ("Amen.")

A few years ago we had a war with Spain, and when one of our gunboats was on the way to the scene of action a Catholic Spaniard, who had been for years working on one of the gunboats, was seen in a place where he had no business to be, in a coal bunk. And that man was putting a stick of dynamite in the coal to blow up that vessel. That is the old man in the ship of your soul. Get him out if you don't want him to put a stick of dynamite in your soul, ready to go off at any moment. Beloved! Sanctification will take the Spaniard out of the Lord's ship and put him over in the ranks of the enemy. We will have foes to fight, but they will be on the outside. The citadel and all within will be loyal to God. That is what all Christians want. God wants that traitor in the ship taken out forever. That is done by sanctification through the power of the Holy Ghost. ("Amen.") Then we will not be obliged to sing:

"Prone to wander, Lord I feel it,
Prone to leave the God I love;
Here's my heart, O take and seal it;
Seal it for thy courts above."

May the day come when God's children shall be free from proneness to wander, or to turn their back on the blessed Lord!

II. Let us now consider some manifest reasons why we ought to be holy, and why God wishes us to be holy.

1. God is holy. Our sun shines with unutterable brilliancy in the sky, so brilliant we cannot look at it except with prepared glasses; but as glorious as our sun is, there are great spots on it many thousand miles across. But our holy God is an undimmed sun, shining in the sky of the universe, and there never has yet been and never will be, one spot on His ineffable holiness. He is a holy God and the angels and cherubim and seraphim look up in His face crying "Holy! Holy! Holy! Lord God of Hosts." That is the admiration of heaven. That is our God and Father. He wants His children to be like Him. You never saw a father or mother in your life that wasn't pleased to have their little child show the benevolent traits of its parents. If father is active or energetic, he likes to see that trait in his little son. If mother is sweet and affectionate, she likes to be told that little Mary has mamma's sweetness. Mamma is pleased to have little Susan show mamma's musical gift. If father is a literary man or an orator, he likes to see indications of these cropping out in his child. Our Father is holy, and He wants His child to be like Him. There are just two great families in this moral universe of ours, and they both have the great unfailing family resemblance. One is the family of sin; and they have all got it stamped on their being. The other is the family of holiness, and they have the image of God stamped on their being. God is holy. "Be ye holy."

2. God commands us to be holy. O, how men that are trained to obey commands will execute them! The

sailor will obey his captain and climb the masts and handle the sheets when the waves are rolling mountain high, and the great ship is being tossed, and those masts swing many feet back and forth and it would seem that they would throw him in the deep. But he climbs because he is told to do so. It is a matter of historical fact, and so said by military critics, that Gen. Grant was reckless and unsparing of the lives of his men. One time he lost 20,000 soldiers in an awful battle, trying in vain to take an objective point and ordering assault after assault, our men being driven back and mowed down to death, and there was an awful and useless loss of life. One time during that battle, I remember (I was then a clerk at Niagara Falls), Col. Peter A. Porter was colonel of a regiment that went from that point of Western New York. Gen. Grant gave a command to Col. Porter, and Porter looked him in the face and said: "You have ordered me to a needless death." He turned straight around, led the charge and was cut down! Blessed be God! our King, the Captain of our Salvation, never issues a needless command, nor orders to a needless death. He only asks us to die to self and the sin that damns us that we may live to God and righteousness forevermore. He never gave a command that wasn't sweeter than honey and the honeycomb, and in the doing of it there is great reward.

3. We ought to become holy because sin and every proclivity to sin is so dangerous. I am amazed as I think of the awful power of Satan, how he has covered this world with sin and shame and woe; how nation after nation has gone down into the awful mire, because of sin. The master stroke of Satan was made when he found that he could plant a germ of evil at the fountain stream of human life to be communicated through all ages. That was the germ

of carnality. Sin is awful. Sin has cursed individuals, wrecked families and made our great cities ungovernable. Sin has wrapped the world in a garment of sickness and shame. Sin has visited heaven and cast angels down from their high estate. Sin has filled the bosom of God with sorrow, and will roll a great gulf-stream of woe through the universe of God forever. If this proclivity is in me ready to be touched off, I pray "take the dynamite out of my soul!" ("Amen.") God can take that all out of you and you will have the blessed "I-know-so" salvation. If Jesus cannot do this, then the devil who injected this moral poison into the veins of our race is mightier than our Christ. He could inflict an evil which Jesus cannot cure. The very thought is almost an insult to our adorable God. This leads me to say:

4. We ought to be holy because holiness brings such blessedness. There is a world of joyless Christian living. There are multitudes of believers who go bowed down like bull-rushes, and hang their harps on the willows. If their souls sing at all it is in some minor key, like Windham. The poor hungry heart wails out the sad refrain—

> "'Tis a thing I long to know,
> Oft it causes anxious thought.
> Do I love the Lord or no?
> Am I his or am I not?"

Again, in some unsatisfied hour, it sobs its deep, pathetic want in the words,—

> "Look how we grovel here below,
> Fond of these earthly toys,
> Our souls, how heavily they go,
> To reach eternal joys."

What a sorry commendation this is of the religion of Jesus!—No exuberance of hope! no joy of assurance!

Fulness of life in Christ will bring "beauty for ashes, the oil of joy for mourning, and the garment of praise for the spirit of heaviness. The birds of gladness will sing in the heart, and the flowers of peace will bloom, and the hallelujahs of praise to our sanctifying and satisfying God will roll through the arches of the soul and rise as perpetual incense to our King. Glory!

5. Christ came for this purpose and died for this end. Jesus came to destroy the works of the devil and the greatest work of the devil was getting that carnality planted in the bosom of every child of Adam's race. I see Christ leaving his home in heaven, leaving the adoration of seraphim and cherubim, and taking his lonely way-down to suffer for this wicked world, which had no place for Him. I see him scourged and led out to be crucified. I hear the cruel mob cry "Crucify Him!" I see Him dying on Calvary's tree while God hides His face from Him, and my Saviour cries out "My God! Why hast Thou forsaken me?" And He is bearing all this, what for? That He might cure us of sin, and make us sanctified and holy.

When I meditate upon all this in solemn thought, my heart cries out: "O Jesus, if thou wert so anxious to have my heart cleansed and purified, it shall be cleansed. Thy soul shall be satisfied. I yield, I yield by dying love compelled. I can hold out no more. I'll say what you want me to say, dear Lord, I'll be what you want me to be."

We ought to want this blessing because God has set his heart upon it. The plan to restore man to holiness was planned by the Father. And he gave his Son that we might have it. For this Jesus poured out his cleansing blood. For this the sanctifying Spirit was given that we might be holy. For this the plan of redemption was instituted to restore man to holiness. It is the will, the desire, the longing, the command, of the triune God, that every moral being in the universe should be holy. All the work of the atonement for man, and all the promptings of the Holy Spirit move to this end. "Holiness! holiness needed, holiness required, holiness offered, holiness attainable, holiness a present duty, a present privilege, a present enjoyment, is the progress and completeness of its wondrous theme." This is the glorious truth that is seen in Bible history, and biography, and poetry, and prophecy, and precept, and promise, and prayer. "Be ye holy for I am holy."

III. I agreed to say something about how to get it, which I will try to do in five minutes.

1. In the first place, you must bring your will and lay it all at Jesus' feet. It is true what Bro. Nelson said the other day. No man can get justified that doesn't bow to the will of God. But we must live up to the light of the moment. And after you are a child of God, you get new light. Sometimes that old carnality draws you back and you shrink from it. You must lay your will on the altar afresh to know the will of God. You must hear God say "This is the will of God, even your sanctification," and you must say "amen" to the will of God. Beloved, do you pray our Lord's Prayer? Possibly 200,000 preachers prayed the Lord's Prayer yesterday in this country, and asked God to baptize them with the Holy Ghost; and yet the same men would turn around and fight holiness to the bitter end. You cannot get it in that spirit. He gives His Holy Spirit to those that obey Him. It seems to me I would either stop praying the Lord's Prayer, "Thy will be done," or I would seek sancification with all my heart.

BUD ROBINSON,
Greenville, Texas.

T. H. HATFIELD,
Cleveland, Ind.

JAMES HARRIS,
Guelph, Ont.

T. C. READE,
Upland, Ind.

DEACON GEO. M. MORSE,
Putnam, Conn.

W. T. LORING.
Knox, Ind.

PROF. D. A. HOYES.
Evanston, Ill.

J. R. ALLEN,
Waterloo, Iowa.

2. After you have brought everything to the altar, you have got to consecrate afresh for this blessing. You brought a dead offering. Now you bring a live sacrifice. You must lay your will down, giving your heart, your affections, reputation, time, and everything you have or may have for time and eternity,—laying all on the altar in sacrifice to God.

3. When you have done that, the last thing is to take God at His word and step on His promises. Say "Now I am on your hands for a clean heart. I believe you will do your part as I do mine." The last step is the step of faith. God always meets the truly consecrated and believing soul, and adds His blessing. As sure as God is God, the Holy Ghost will be given in cleansing power.

At the close of the sermon an altar service was held in which a goodly number of the congregation engaged and seekers for sanctification came forward.

AFTERNOON SESSION.

Bro. C. J. Fowler presiding.

Before the hour for preaching a few moments were given to testimony:

A Brother:—"He has forgiven my sins and taken the 'want-to' sin out of my heart."

A Sister:—"The blood cleanses my heart from all sin."

A Delegate:—"This experience of holiness is a reality in my heart. I received it five years ago. It has never left me a second." ("Amen!")

A Brother:—"Praise God for victory over the flesh, the devil and the world."

A Delegate:—"Salvation is the greatest thing in the world. I found this experience eight years ago. I was fifteen years in the wilderness. I know what it means to get salvation."

A Brother:—"I stepped out on the promises, and the blood cleansed me."

Singing, by congregation: "Trust and Obey," "The Open Fountain," and "Jesus has Lifted the Load."

Song, by Brother and Sister Harris: "Make me a Blessing To-day."

Prayer, by Rev. James Harris: "We are so glad, O Father, that we do not have to send to heaven to bring Thee down, but that Thou art present with us here. We find our sweetest hours on earth are when we talk to Thee. We like to say in our hearts: 'No price we bring, but simply to the cross we cling.' We rejoice that the Spirit maketh intercession with groanings that cannot be uttered. We want that groaning Spirit to-day. Many are happier at this time than ever before. As much as Thou hast cleansed these hearts, we have felt the cleansing blood coursing through our hearts again to-day. ("Amen!") O, how our hearts have gone up to Thee, to be more like Thee, to become like Thee. Grant to make us a little more like Thyself.

"How often the devil comes and tells us we can't preach, we can't testify or can't pray! We depend on Thee, and say, we can do all things. We like to have Thee in the right place, to be our 'All in all.' O, what is there we cannot do, if God is with us?

"We want Thee to crown this meeting with all the blessing Thou hast designed it to have. Be with him who shall address us this afternoon, and may we all go away from this meeting bolder to stand up for the cross of Jesus. We ask it all for Christ's sake. Amen."

Brother Fowler announced that Bros. T. K. Doty, L. B. Kent, E. F. Walker, W. T. Hogue, and Geo. M.

Morse were appointed a committee to nominate committees on Deliverances and Permanent Methods.

Bro. S. B. Shaw announced a special arrangement whereby cheap meals could be had at the restaurant in the Church Block, and that he had placed at the disposal of the restaurant a sufficient quantity of his Cocoa Cereal, that it might be served free of cost to the delegates of the Assembly. The amount up to five hundred pounds were donated for this purpose.

SERMON BY BRO. E. F. WALKER.

Text: "For this is the will of God, your sanctification."

The preacher of this morning preached holiness. I wish this afternoon to present sanctification. You will notice that in reading the text I omit a little word which is often rather emphazied—the word "even." "This is the will of God, even your sanctification," is the way it is usually quoted, and the word is in the English text, but in italics—the sign that it is not in the original—in the Bible proper—but supplied by the translator.

So Paul says to the Corinthians, "And this also we wish, your perfection," and the translator also put in there the word "even." We suppose the reason he put in this word is that he rated sanctification, or perfection, as extraordinary. Well, in modern times it certainly has not been the common experience of professing Christians. But as the Bible presents it, it ought to be the common experience of God's people. Christ gave His ministers for the perfecting of the saints; and the life into which sanctification brings His people is the normal life of the Christian.

This experience should not be regarded as the steeple to a church—not necessary, but proper to top-off. It is the temple itself, or rather the inner sanctuary of the temple, while justification is but the vestibule. Dr. Chas. Hodge says: "Justification is in order to sanctification;" and his son, A. A. Hodge: "We are justified that we may be sanctified." Sanctification is necessary to fully Christianize man. There were no Christians, in the proper sense of the word, till Pentecost, and there can be no true Christians without the Pentecostal experience. Sanctification is essential to make us "perfect and complete in all the will of God:" "For this is the will of God, your sanctification."

Habitually we pray, "Thy will be done." But what is God's will? Paul says to the Ephesians: "Understanding what the will of the Lord is." This sets us searching the Scriptures which reveal God's will. The margin refers us to our text. And this again to the next chapter, "For this is the will of God in Christ Jesus concerning you;" and a little farther down, "Faithful is he which calleth you, who also will do it." Do what? Sanctify you wholly. So Paul beseeches the Romans to consecrate, that they might "prove (by experience) what is that good, and acceptable and perfect will of God." Thus we find sanctification frequently presented as the will of God.

But what is sanctification? Strictly speaking, it is not the same as holiness. There is a distinction in the significance of the two words. Holiness is a moral quality, or state; sanctification is the experience by which we get that quality—by which we are brought into that state. Holiness is the life we live after we have been sanctified. The great German exegete, Delitzsch, says, "Sanctification is not holiness; but is the putting on of it —the becoming holy." The discriminating Dr. Godet explains thus: "In the cure of the soul, pardon is the crisis of convalescence, sanctification is the restoration to health, holiness is true life."

Now, I want to give you definitions of sanctification from three illustrious Johns.

First, John Fletcher: "It is the depth of evangelical repentance, the full assurance of faith, and the pure love of God and man shed abroad in a faithful believer's heart by the Holy Ghost given unto him, to cleanse him and to keep him clean from all the filthiness of the flesh and spirit, to enable him to fulfill the law of Christ according to the talents he is intrusted with and the circumstances in which he is placed in this world."

John Owen: "To be cleansed from the defilement of sin, whatever that be; to have a heart inclined, disposed, enabled, to fear the Lord always, and to walk in all His ways and statues accordingly, with an internal, habitual conformity of the whole soul unto the law of God, is to be sanctified, or to be holy."

John Wesley: "Sanctification, in the proper sense, is an instantaneous deliverance from all sin, and includes an instantaneous power, then given, always to cleave to God." How discriminating! Wesley recognized that the word is used in secondary and accommodated senses; but here he gives the proper meaning. Why does he say, "an instantaneous deliverance"? Because he knows that the instantaneous tense in the Greek is nearly always used with the verb to sanctify. Why does he say "from all sin"? Because the Greek aorist tense in the imperative mode—which Jesus used in His prayer for the sanctification of His disciples and Paul for the Thessalonians—always means instantly and completely. But sanctification is not only the elimination of all sin. Properly it includes a power given to cleave to God. And this power is not an after-experience. It belongs to sanctification—is then given.

My definition is this: "Sanctification is a work of grace wrought in a believer by the baptism with the Holy Ghost and fire, given by Jesus Christ, purifying him from all sin, and perfecting him in love."

Our second question is: For whom is this sanctification? "This is the will of God, the sanctification of you"—as it is in the original. What kind of people were the ones thus addressed? We find Paul's estimate of them from reading the epistle.

About the close of the letter he says: "Greet all the brethren with a holy kiss." Surely an unconverted preson could not do that. The kiss of Judas was unholy. These Thessalonians must have had the quality of holiness in some degree, to be able to give a holy kiss.

In the next verse Paul says: "I charge you by the Lord that this Epistle be read unto all the holy brethren." So those to whom the epistle was sent, and to whom our text applied, were in some sense already "holy."

Let me make a distinction here. Regeneration is a holy experience—an experience of holiness. When we are regenerated, we get holiness: when we are sanctified, we are made holy. ("Amen.") Regeneration is the impartation of holy life. In the regenerate the principle of holiness is implanted, and they are holy, but not all holy. ("Amen!" "That is it!") Sanctification is the gracious work of God by which all that is contrary to the new life given in regeneration is eliminated from the person, and he is actually and experimentally made holy. Because these Thessalonians were regenerated persons, partakers of His holiness, born of the Spirit, they were of the holy brotherhood.

But look farther. Turn to the first part of the Epistle. Here we see it was addressed to "the church;" and not simply a church organization but the church organism—"in God the Father, and in the Lord Jesus Christ" —vitally connected with God through Christ.

In the second verse Paul expresses his thanks for them.

In the next he declares that he unceasingly remembered their faith and love and hope. Here are the three Christian graces; and these were in lively exercise— "work of faith, labor of love, patience of hope."

Next he says that he knew their election of God. He entertained no doubt that they had been effectually called, and were numbered among the elect.

Next he tells them why he had this assurance concerning them. "For our gospel came not unto you in word only, but also in power, and in the Holy Ghost, and in much assurance." Very different this from many of the "conversions" (?) in these days, concerning which there is much doubt all around. The Thessalonians had been "powerfully converted."

Then they became followers, not only of the apostle, but of the Lord; and notwithstanding that they suffered much because of their adherence to Christ and His cause they knew the joy of the Holy Ghost—an essential part of the Kingdom.

They became ensamples to other believers in all that region round. Samples are always the best. So these Thessalonians were leading Christians. They were "the sample case" of that Gospel traveler, and were well-reputed for their good Christian work; so that it was known all around how they had "turned (literally, converted) to God from idols, to serve the living and true God."

And they were possessed of the blessed hope—the pole-star of the church in all ages—waiting for the return of Jesus from heaven.

Now, this is a good, long bill of particulars touching the Christian character of those for whom God willed sanctification. Much more might be said on this line, were it necessary. But certainly no more is needed to show that they were thoroughly converted to Jesus Christ.

But would some one suggest the possibility of their having backslidden? This point is well-guarded. In the third chapter the apostle confesses that he had entertained some fears "lest by some means the tempter have tempted you, and our labor be in vain." So, when he could no longer forbear, he sent Timothy to find out how it fared with them. But when this man of God returned with good tidings of their faith and love and good remembrance, the apostle was greatly comforted over them by their faith.

Still, they were the objects of the solicitude of Paul. He told them that he was praying night and day exceedingly in their behalf. Why? Because he wanted to go to them and perfect that which was lacking in their faith. Not to indoctrinate them more fully; but to bring them a fuller knowledge of the great salvation through faith—"to the end he may stablish your hearts unblameable in holiness before God." Here it is: Holiness;—heart holiness;—unblameable heart holiness;—establishment in unblameable heart holiness. Here is the will of God, and for this kind of persons.

Between the lids of the Bible nowhere will you find

that sanctification is promised to, prayed for, or urged upon any who are not the true children of God. It is an experience for those only who are already abiding and persevering in Christ—the elect of God. It is not God's will that anybody else should have it. God loved the world and gave His only begotten Son that the world should be saved. But Christ loved the Church and gave Himself for it that He might sanctify it.

Our next question is: What is the will of God?

(1) It is God's law. The briefest and most satisfactory definition of the divine law is, the will of God. Certainly that law which itself is holy, just and good, can demand nothing less than holiness in the subjects of the Kingdom of God. So it is the divine requirement that all His children who have not received the distinctive experience that makes holy, be sanctified.

Beloved! If we have due respect to the law of God, we surely must assent and consent to the doctrine and experience presented in the text of this afternoon. This is the demand of God, your sanctification. I appeal to you, as children of God—as obedient children—be ye yourselves also holy. Why? Because so it is written, "Ye shall be holy, for I am holy." What is written is for our guidance—the rule of our life. Even the devil himself acknowledged this in his temptation of Jesus. He appealed, "It is written;" and Jesus replied, "It is written again." This is the end of controversy with heaven and hell. And certainly there should be no question as to Christian duty, when it is plainly written. "Remember the Sabbath day, to keep it holy." Why? Many arguments in favor of the sanctification of the Sabbath might be presented; but this is sufficient: so it is written. The Holy Scriptures are the sufficient rule of faith and duty. Show me anything God requires in His word, and that is enough. That is a law for me. I am His subject and His child. If I am to be loyal and obedient, I must be sanctified, because my God and Father requires it. It is not a question concerning my desire or the desire of my fellows. It is: what does God demand?

We preachers have no preference in the matter of urging sanctification upon the church. We must preach the preaching He bids us preach. We must shun not to declare all His counsel. I declare that as a man of God and a minister of His Word I would not be loyal and faithful to my charge, did I fail to present this demand of His law—this requirement of His will—your sanctification. ("Amen.")

And as His child I must be obedient. He reveals to me His will concerning me. I want to obey. Adam fell by refusing to accept the will of God as the rule of his conduct, and I fear there are many persons to-day who have known God's justifying grace, who are fallen from favor and fellowship with God, because the duty to be sanctified—made plain by His word and Spirit—has been neglected. If we are going to continue to stand before Him in peace, we must say, "Not as I will, but as Thou wilt," and submit to His will, our sanctification.

Again: God's will for his children is His desire. He is not merely the Governor and Judge of all men. Let us not entertain the thought of Him as the supreme Sovereign who imposes the law, and is exacting and insistent that we shall be holy. He is our Father, and He desires for us the best He has. He wants to see His every son that was dead and lost, but who is now alive and found, clothed with the best robe from Heaven's wardrobe. As He Himself is clothed with light as with a garment, so He would have us to walk in the light as He is in the light. He wants us to be like Him in moral character in every particular. As He is light and in Him is no darkness at all, He would have His children to be made clean every whit, that with unsullied holiness they may show forth His praise, in His marvelous light.

And this just suits me. I want you to know, beloved, that I am on this line not merely from a feeling of obligation. If I didn't have to be holy, I would want to be. ("Amen!" "Glory!") If the Lord should say to me, "My Son, you don't have to be sanctified. I do not require it of you. You may go on trying to serve me in your own poor, weak way, and at last I will save you;" I would reply, "No; I thank you." It is a privilege that the angels of glory certainly must prize, and it is a privilege that every redeemed child of God on earth ought to covet and enjoy, to be made holy.

I want to say to you, friends, that I am in the enjoyment of this blessed experience. The catechism says that the effectually called do in this life partake of the several benefits which accompany and flow from sanctification. Well, I am one of them, praise the Lord! I am one of the beneficiaries. It is the fulness of the blessing of Christ. It is the table prepared for us in the presence of our enemies. ("Amen!") It is His desire that we all avail ourselves of this unspeakable blessing. He loves us. He yearns over us. He longs to bless us now. He wants to bring us to a place where we can enjoy religion. ("Amen!")

And again: God's will is His purpose to sanctify His children. What He demands and desires He decides for us. "Faithful is he which calleth you, who also will do it." Do what? That for which the apostle prays—sanctify you wholly, and preserve you blameless unto the coming of Jesus. He has taken oath that He will deliver us out of the hand of our enemies, that we might serve Him without fear in holiness and righteousness before Him all the days of our life.

How variously could this divine purpose be proved, illustrated and emphasized.

> He wills that I shall holy be:
> What can withstand His will?

Nothing—if we but pray with real meaning, "Thy will be done." ("Amen!")

And once again: God's will is His provision for our sanctification. That which is in the divine requirement, desire and purpose He provides. The children of God are His heirs. The Holy Ghost speaks of an inheritance among them that are sanctified. Certainly the New Testament in Christ's blood is for our full redemption and fullness of blessing. He devoted Himself that we might be sanctified. He suffered without the gate that He might sanctify us. He loved the church and gave Himself for it, that He might sanctify it. According to the riches of His grace and glory, abundant provision has been made. Nothing that He demands of us, nothing that He desires for us, nothing that He decides for us, but is found in His holy will, written in the blood of the everlasting covenant. Will you accept this statement? (Cries of "Yes!") Praise His name forever!

Yes; you assent to all this doctrine this far. But some may say, "It cannot be just now." But it can be, just now. This is what the text proposes: This is the will of God. Whenever the Greek word "is" is used it is always for emphasis. It is here, and sanctification is emphasized as a present experience. It is for you as much God's will—His law, His desire, His purpose. His provision—NOW, as it ever will or can be.

God's will. It is not simply the will of "the holiness people;" it is not simply the consummation which this preacher seeks—though we say to you as Paul did to the Corinthians, "And this we wish, your perfection." But man aside! It is the will of God!

It may not be the will of your sect. If not, I am sorry for it, and for you. But it is the will of God!

It may not be the will of your preacher. If not, I am sorry for him and for you. But it is the will of God!

It may not be the will of your earthly friends. If not, I am sorry for them and for you. But this is the will of God, the sanctification of you.

Is it your will? If so, just come now to the God of your salvation, and make an assignment of all to Him. Abandon yourself to the will of God, and as you so do, His holy will be wrought in you this very hour. Amen!

A number came forward at the altar call and proved the "good "good and acceptable and perfect will of God."

EVENING SESSION.

Bro. C. J. Fowler, presiding.

Singing by congregation: "Leaning on the Everlasting Arms," "Joy in the Soul," "The Half has Never yet Been Told."

Prayer by Col. E. Mayhew, (Christian Crusaders:) "Our Heavenly Father, as we come to Thee tonight, our hearts are overflowing with praise for Thy lovingkindness and tender mercy which Thou hast shown unto the children of men. We are glad that the showers are coming, and we pray that Thy blessings may be poured down to such an extent that we shall all sing: 'Praise God from whom all blessings flow.' We thank

Thee for a practical religion. While we love to hear people sing and clap their hands and shout loud hosannas, after all, the greatest thing is sanctification.

"We recognize that this has been a glorious day with us. God has been in our midst, and the Holy Ghost has been baptizing many hearts. We pray that it may not stop here, but reach out until multitudes may be brought to know Thee and many believers may be sanctified by the Holy Spirit.

"Bless him who shall speak. Give him power from on high. Bless, we pray Thee, those who hear. We pray Thee that many who are not clear in their experience, who are seeking the baptism of the Holy Ghost and fire, may surrender all to Thee to-night, and thus be gloriously endued with this baptism from on high. We ask it in the name of Jesus. Amen."

Song by Bro. and Sister Harris: "When I have Reached that Blest Home over Yonder."

SERMON BY BRO. G. W. RIDOUT.

Text: "And an highway shall be there, and a way, and it shall be called The Way of Holiness; the unclean shall not pass over it; but it shall be for those: the wayfaring men, though fools, shall not err therein." Isaiah 35:8.

The prophet Isaiah is speaking in relation to the blessedness and glories of the coming kingdom of Christ. Holiness is one of the characteristic features of this kingdom and its fundamental principle. Isaiah was prophesying about something you and I have the privilege of seeing and enjoying. Thank God we see that which prophets and kings desired to see and know, but never did. The Kingdom of Christ is on the earth to-day and Holiness is its chief glory and its mightiest factor.

Holiness is one of the most conspicuous features of the Church of God. It may with safety be said that every branch of the church evangelical, believes in and teaches Holiness in a theological and theoretical sense. I am a Methodist. I was born a Methodist. My father was an old fashioned Methodist. I was brought up in it and am a member of one of the M. E. Conferences. It is hardly necessary for me to say that Holiness is one of the great tenets and the cardinal doctrine of Methodism. John Wesley said: "This doctrine is the grand depositum which God has lodged with the people called Methodists; and for the sake of propagating this, chiefly, He appears to have raised us up." Holiness should not only have a conspicuous place in our church doctrine and creed, it should likewise have a prominent place in the life. The subscribing to a creed or doctrine, or the assenting to a formula is one thing and living it is another. I have often thought of this when as a Methodist preacher I have seen young men stand before the Bishop to be received into full connection. The question is asked them "Are you going on to perfection?" and they have all answered in the affirmative. "Do you expect to be made perfect in love in this life?" likewise answered in the affirmative. "Are you earnestly striving after it?" again replied to affirmatively. I have never heard these questions answered in the negative yet, but it is a matter to be deeply deplored that too many of these same young men privately and publicly fight and oppose and antagonize this very thing they professed faith in and confessed they were seeking. This state of affairs however, does not discourage me or make me feel like quitting Methodism. I love the church and Methodist ministers none the less. I want to confess to you that I am having a delightful time in the Methodist Episcopal Church. Being a pastor I am glad to say that the same kind of preaching that I give at camp meetings and holiness gatherings I give from my home pulpit and thank God not a year of my pastorate goes by without many souls finding God—backsliders seeking restoration, sinners seeking pardoning love and believers finding holiness of heart.

Holiness, being in the creed and doctrines of the church ought to have as aforesaid a prominent place in the life and I am thoroughly convinced that it should characterize the preacher. There are too many in the pulpits to-day who are afraid if they preach holiness that they are going to offend the weak ones, they will upset the young converts and lose the friendship of some of their "dear people." I am glad that God has taught me in my brief ministry that the most successful and the happiest way to run a pastorate is along Holiness lines. I have seen brother pastors always in hot water, having a quarrel, contention or strife always on hand and have thanked God that the man who conducts his chuch on holiness lines has not a tithe of the worry or strife or trouble others have. I believe the happiest preacher, the happiest man, the happiest believer is he who is on the blessed way of Holiness.

The text has the word "highway" in it. Let me emphasize that word for a moment in order to suggest to you that Holiness is no low experience but eminently high. It is an experience never intended for people who are living away down in a low plane of religious life. When God would have me seek holiness of heart He first brought me into the highest state of regeneration. Holiness is not for a man who is backslidden in heart. It is not for a person who has lost touch with God. It is not for people who have no communion or fellowship with the Father, the Son and the Holy Ghost. I have often been afraid

L. L. PICKETT,
Wilmore, Ky.

A. W. MILLER,
Gladbrook, Iowa.

S. P. JACOBS,
Bedford, Mich.

O. L. SNOW,
Peiro, Iowa.

BISHOP WM. TAYLOR,
Palo Alto, Calif.

DANIEL STEELE,
Milton, Mass.

GRACE WEISER DAVIS,
Jersey City, N. J.

ELIZABETH RIDER WHEATON,
Tabor, Iowa.

that at Camp meetings and other gatherings we have set the thing too low, that we have brought it down to meet the backslidden in heart. Alas! How many people in our churches continue to live in the very lowest plane of religious life. How many like Lot of old when he separated from Abram pitched his tent towards Sodom. Many are doing this to-day pitching their tents towards Sodom, getting out of fellowship with God, losing their grip on spiritual things. I have been deeply impressed with a passage of Scripture found in Numbers 20: 17. It is in connection with Israel on their journey towards Canaan. They come to the borders of the country of the Amorities and Moses sends a deputation to the king bearing a request that the Israelites be permitted to pass through his land unmolested. Moses makes this agreement with the king if he will grant the desired permission, "We will not turn into the fields or into the vineyards, we will not drink of the waters of the wells: we will go by the kings highway." What a delightful resolution for the Christian who whilst passing through this world on his way to glory determines by the grace of God not to partake of worldly fruit or drink at worldly cisterns! This world is no friend to grace. Happy the man who goes through it by means of the king's high way!

Another word in the text which we desire to bring into prominence here is the word "unclean." "The unclean shall not pass over it." This would teach us that Purity is an important constituent of Holiness. Purity must come before power. It is at this point I think that many make serious mistakes. This was the great mistake Simon the Sorcerer made when he saw those young converts of Samaria getting the baptism of the Holy Ghost and fire; he coveted the same gift but not from a becoming motive. Simon wanted the power that he himself might become some great one. He offered to buy it with money but what a rebuke he suffered at the hands of Spirit filled Peter. "Thou hast neither part nor lot in this matter: for thy heart is not right in the sight of God." One of the first things necessary to get this blessing is a right state of heart. There are many who come to the altar in our holiness meetings with the idea that if they get this power it will make something out of them. So it will truly, but they must first get knocked out. The work of purification must precede the power. We must put the emphasis on here. Purity, cleanness and then Holiness is the result. On this point hear the word of God: Ezekiel 36: 25. "Then will I sprinkle clean water upon you and ye shall be clean from all your filthiness and from all your idols will I cleanse you." 2 Corinthians 7: 1. "Having therefore these promises dearly beloved let us cleanse ourselves from all filthiness of the flesh and Spirit perfecting holiness in the fear of God," John 13: 8, "Peter saith unto him Thou shalt never wash my feet. Jesus answered him, If I wash thee not thou hast no part with me," 1 John 1: 7. "If we walk in the light as He is in the light we have fellowship one with another and the blood of Jesus Christ his Son cleanseth us from all sin."

Thank God there is perfect cleansing in the blood; There is perfect purity, and no one is permitted on this blessed old way of holiness who has not come to it by way of the cleansing fountain. A brother in Massachusetts was seeking sanctification. He came to a holiness meeting in Boston and there at the altar was directed to trust the cleansing blood. Without any change of feeling he took hold by faith and confessed that "the blood cleanseth." His home was several miles out of Boston and in order to exercise his faith the more, he decided to walk home and as he proceeded homeward he would say to himself, "The blood cleanseth—the blood cleanseth." It was a lonely walk that night. He stepped up to a policeman and exclaimed, "the blood cleanseth." The policeman thought him crazy and locked him up. Word was sent to his residence that he was at the lock up, crazy. When his friends arrived to take care of him, his first ejaculation was, "The blood cleanseth." He got through. The blood had cleansed and sanctified him wholly.

Now, the next thing brought out in the text is the plainness of the way of Holiness. How easy it is of access—"The wayfaring men, though fools shall not err therein." Oh that we could get the people to believe that the way of holiness is not so hard to find when sought from the right motives. I am sorry that so many preachers and teachers befog and becloud the people at this point. They confuse and mystify the whole subject of holiness to the people—making it appear as a something to be looked upon and thought of only as an ideal and not as a reality and an actually obtainable experience and blessing. The idea that holiness is so far removed from the realm of the obtainable has kept many out of the blessing for a long while. Alfred Cookman when seeking it said: "Frequently I felt to yield myself to God and pray for the grace of entire sanctification, but then this experience would lift itself in my view as a mountain of glory, and I would say it is not for me, I could not possibly scale that shining summit; and if I could my besetments and trials are such I could not successfully maintain so lofty a position." James Brainerd Taylor wrote "My mind loves to dwell upon ths delightful theme, Holiness. It is a blessed doctrine.

O why did I not come to possess it before? **Why?** because like many other professors of religion I looked for a death purgatory—not believing that the blood of Christ, and not purgatory—cleanseth from all sin. This is in the present tense. It is efficacious now and the Lord has proven to me a full, a complete Savior." Rev. Mark Guy Pearse in his Thoughts on Holiness gives expression to the truth I am now trying to convey, in a very beautiful parable. Hear it: "Once I went forth to look for Repentance. I sought her one day and night in the City of Mansoul. I asked many if they knew where she dwelt, and they said they had never seen her. I met one grave and scholarly, who told me what she was like and bade me seek her earnestly; but he did not tell me where she was to be found. Then all sad at heart and wearied with my search, I went forth without the city walls and climbed a lonely hill and up a steep and rugged way, until I came in sight of the cross and of Him who hung thereon. And lo, as I looked upon Him, there came one and touched me. Then instantly my heart was melted, and all the great deeps of my soul were broken up. 'Ah, Repentance I have been looking everywhere for you,' I said. 'Thou wilt always find me here,' said Repentance, 'here in sight of my crucified Lord. I tarry at His feet.' "

Again I went forth to look for Forgiveness. I knocked at many a door in the city of Mansoul and asked for her. And some said they thought she did live there sometimes: and some said she used to, once; and some said she came there occasionally when the weather was fine to spend a Sabbath. So I came forth wearied and sad; and as I reached the city gate I met again the grave scholar, and he gave me much account of her birth and parentage, and he showed me her portrait and told me of her gracious works and he bade me seek her earnestly but he did not tell me where I could find it. So I went along my way and I found myself again upon the high hill, climbing again the steep and rugged path. And I lifted my eyes and saw once more the Cross and Him who hung thereon and lo, at the first sight of my dear Lord, Forgiveness met me and filled my soul with holy peace and a rest like heaven itself. "O I have had a weary search for you," I said. "I am always here," said Foregiveness, "here at my Master's feet." Long afterwards I wondered within myself where Holiness dwelt, but I feared to go in search of her. I knew she would never be at home in the low lands and busy streets of Mansoul. All whom I asked about her answered doubtfully. One said she had died long ago. One said that she lived away at the end of the Valley of the Shadow of Death, on the brink of the river, and that I must hope to meet her just before I crossed over. "Nay" said another "she lives farther still; search as thou wilt, thou shalt never find her till thou art safely across the river and landed on the shores of the Celestial City." Then I remembered how well I had fared aforetime on the Holy Hill and went forth again. So up the lonely way I went and reached the top of it and looked once more upon my blessed Savior. And lo! there was Holiness sitting at the Master's feet. I feared to say that I had been looking for her, but, as I gazed upon the Crucified, Holiness rose up and came to me all graciously and said, "I have been waiting for thee ever since thy first coming." "Waiting where?" I asked. "At His feet" said Holiness. "I am always there." Repentance at the Cross! Forgiveness at the Cross! Holiness at the Cross!

Our Text also indicates that Holiness is a safe way,

"No lion shall be there, nor any ravenous beast shall go up thereon." This however is not intended to convey the meaning that those who walk the way of holiness are free from temptation, trials or enemies. Whilst in the body we shall suffer temptation and pass through trials and tribulation. None of God's children upon the earth are exempt from these. We believe however that there is a difference in the way the devil manifests himself to the Christian. In the early stages of Christian experience Satan presents himself as a lion. "Your adversary the devil as a roaring lion walketh about seeking whom he may devour." I believe in the more advanced Christian life the devil comes as a serpent to beguile and to deceive. The devil seeing he cannot prevail against the believer as a lion, comes in the form of a serpent. Thus he came to our first parents in their time of holy innocence. Many, alas, of God's dear children who have successfully fought the devil as a lion have been deceived by him and led astray into side tracks and fanaticism and some times into cursed sinfulness when he made his visits to them in the serpent form. We need take care at this point. The holiness people meet with some perils here. The first holiness couple fell, through allowing the old serpent a chance at their intellects.

The way of Holiness is the "Happy Way." "The redeemed shall walk there, and the ransomed of the Lord shall return and come to Zion with songs and everlasting joy upon their heads; they shall obtain joy and gladness, and sorrow and sighing shall flee away."

EXHORTATION BY COL. F. E. PECK.

I am glad that we have a Saviour that is able to save from the very uttermost to the very uttermost. He is not only able to save us from great sin, He is not only able to save us from the gutter, He is not only able to be with us in great trials and great afflictions, but He is able to save us from the very torments and troubles of daily life that have hindered us. ("Amen!")

I heard one brother, a minister at a certain place, testify in a meeting like this: (I wasn't going to say that it was a minister, but I guess it is all right.) The minister rose up and said by way of confession: "When my house burned and everything was lost, we praised God and rejoiced. When our little one was taken away, we could rejoice and say, 'The Lord gave, and the Lord hath taken away; blessed be the name of the Lord!'" But he said Sunday morning, when he was getting ready for meeting and couldn't find his collar and sleeve buttons he had been in the habit of scolding his wife, and he sad, "I want to confess it." The cleansing power of Jesus' blood will take this out. It will also take out all the fret and worry and save to the very uttermost. I have found these things so. It will remove all the enemies from within. It is better to have a hundred foes on the outside where they can be seen and reached than one on the inside the lines in disguise. Get the enemy removed from your heart. ("Amen!") I am glad He is able to deliver us from our enemies. Have you any of these enemies to Christian life?

Paul says for us to lay aside the sin that so easily besets us. It may not be great things, but the "little foxes that spoil the vines." In Colossians it says: "But now ye also put off all these; anger, wrath, malice, blasphemy, filthy communications out of your mouth." Such things as these are fruits of the flesh. He says: "Know ye not that the unrighteous shall not inherit the Kingdom of God? Be not deceived: neither fornicators, nor idolaters, nor adulterers, nor effemiate, nor abusers of themselves with mankind, nor thieves, nor covetous, nor drunkards, nor revilers, nor extortioners shall inherit the Kingdom of God."

Have we let malice or unkind feelings enter our hearts? People call that thing "temper" which rises up when things don't go right. How many there are in the church, who are Christians, who have this kind of feeling when somebody don't do as they think they ought! This blessing we are talking about makes us humble. It makes us free. ("Amen!") I praise God that He is able to take these unclean things out of the heart.

Some six months ago, I was called to speak at a place. I went and the Lord gave me a message to deliver, and when I got through I asked: "Do you believe Jesus is coming?" It was a country place, and we had a nice large congregation. I said: "How many in this congregation can say: 'Come Lord Jesus. Come quickly?' Or would you want about 15 minutes for prayer, or to ask somebody's forgiveness?"

You cannot enter the Kingdom of Heaven with anger, or malice, or any of these things in your heart. You cannot get in. I asked that congregation how many were prepared, and only four were ready. I want to ask how many of you are ready. How many of you can say: "I am ready any time he calls me?" Stand up. Be careful! You who talk about your neighbors, don't stand up.

Quite a large number came to the altar for pardon and purity and some found glorious victory.

Tuesday, May 7.
MORNING SESSION.

8:00 A. M., Prayer and Praise Service, in charge of Bro. T. H. Agnew.

9:40 A. M., Business session, Bro. C. J. Fowler presiding.

Minutes of Monday's session read and approved.

The report of the Committee on Credentials being called for, the chairman of that committee gave the names of delegates, acted upon up to that time, which had the approval of the Assembly.

On motion, G. A. McLaughlin and S. B. Shaw were made a committee to wait upon the Chief of Police, and obtain a permit to conduct street meetings.

The President announced the loss, by Bro. Thomas Nelson, of a satchel containing about $3.00 in cash and clergyman's railroad permits which would cost $15.00 to replace. By common consent, an offering was taken to make good the loss. On motion, the Railroad Secretary was authorized to report this loss to the proper railroad authorities, and, if possible, secure a renewal of the permits without the usual fees ($5.00 for each permit lost.)

The committee to nominate members of the committees on Deliverances and Permanent Methods, reported the following nominations:

For Committee on Permanent Methods: Alex. McLean of Brooklyn, N. Y., Chairman, T. K. Doty, Cleveland, O., A. L. Whitcomb, Evanston, Ill., T. H. Agnew, Virginia, Ill., G. A. McLaughlin Evanston, Ill., J. R. Allen, Waterloo, Ia., J. B. Foote, Syracuse, N. Y.

For Committee on Deliverances: W. T. Hogue, Chicago, Chairman; L. B. Kent, Jacksonville, Ill., E. F. Walker, Greencastle, Ind., Hiram Ackers, Big Prairie, O., A. M. Hills, Greenville, Tex., M. L. Haney, Normal, Ill., W. E. Shepard, Los Angeles, Cal.

On motion the report of the nominating committee was accepted.

By vote of the Assembly the nominations of the committee for members of the Committee on Permanent Methods and Committee on Deliverances, respectively, were confirmed.

Bro. G. A. McLaughlin moved, and the motion prevailed, that Wednesday be set apart as a day of fasting and prayer, excluding all matters of business pertaining to the Assembly.

By a vote of the Assembly, it was decided to listen to representations of the state of the work on the part of the delegates, and that each delegate be limited to five minutes, the president to call for reports from the various sections at his discretion. The following named brethren and sisters were called upon, and addressed the Assembly:

Bro. B. S. Taylor, of Iowa: "I bless God for a full and free salvation. The Lord called me out into evangelistic work soon after I was called to preach. I was converted when seventeen years of age. There came to me like an audible voice, the words: "Preach the Gospel." While yet a boy, I used to attend holiness meetings and get down and pray and cry, but I didn't understand what it consisted of. I attended college at Middletown, Conn., and in 1875 went to Nebraska, where I took charge of my first circuit. I attended holiness meetings there, got the blessing, and God has been with me ever since. I felt that the Lord had given me a special call to go to North Dakota. I said, 'Lord, I will not go until the call is made very definite.' It was a time of tremendous heart-searching on my part. Some of the brethren said: 'We feel that you ought to go out as an evangelist.' So, I went and took up my work in North Dakota, and I have been in the evangelistic work now for thirteen years. God has wonderfully blessed me. In the fields where I was the most persecuted, I got the greatest victories. I am still connected with the old Methodist Church. I have never been a 'Come-outer.' I love the Church of God next to Jesus, and I want to praise God for the privilege of being a Methodist preacher, as my father was. I could have a charge, but I am still holding on in evangelistic work."

Bro. E. C. De Jernett of Texas: "I am glad indeed to represent this big state. I came from the Holiness Association in Texas to represent them in this Assembly. I want to say that we praise God for what He has wrought for the holiness cause. We have some fifty holiness camp meetings in different parts of Texas, and God has marvelously blessed us and many are getting sanctified. While there seems to be some falling away in certain sections, we do not believe the work in Texas is going to pieces. We didn't get organized until last year. We merely had praying bands, but in order to get them more closely allied together, we organized the Holiness Association of Texas. We found another need: We found that many people came into this holiness experience, whom the Lord called to be workers. They felt unprepared for that, and the Lord laid it on our hearts to arrange for a school, where they could get the proper instruction to fit them for carrying the Gospel and spreading holiness among the people. We felt that we could not get this in the existing religious schools of the state, and, in one of the foremost schools of this character, where the students wanted to hold holiness meetings, they were told that they could not hold them from room to room among themselves, and they were brought up before the authorities. God gave us, two years ago the Texas Holiness University, and there have been 212 students enrolled during that time. What we need particularly now is financial aid in behalf of this institution."

Sister Hattie Livingston, of Iowa:—"God has made this one of the most wonderful winters of my life. Most of my work has been in Kansas the past season. There are many people in Kansas that want to get this salvation. ("Amen!") I have seen many converted and sanctified, and there is one young man now studying for the ministry, as a result of our labors in Kansas this year. I praise God that He is working in the midst of the people. There are many holiness people in Kansas. We have had forty or fifty calls from churches of different denominations that we have not been able to fill. Holiness is what the people want. ("Amen!") They are saying, that, in the large city churches, God will not bless the people. God saved two hundred and fifty sinners inside of five weeks in one church in Council Bluffs. They came in from the different denominations, and got converted and sanctified. I am glad I have a part in this battle. God is leading me, and I praise Him for my own experience. I can say that 'I live yet not I, but Christ liveth in me.' I haven't any home in this world, but I am willing to be homeless for His sake. I am willing to go alone for Jesus." ("Amen!")

Deacon George M. Morse of Connecticut:—"I am here, Brethren, because I love you. God has identified me with you. I have been a Baptist for forty-three years. My mother was a Baptist and brought me up in that church. I walked three miles, four months before I was 'born' (again) to talk with an old lady on the subject of the salvation of her own soul; when I got converted, I walked back again. ("Amen!") I sat up with my mother evenings for many years preaching holiness, before I experienced holiness in my heart. She went down to a camp meeting and got sanctified two or three months before her son got the experience. It was through Wm. T. Harrow (now in glory) at New Bedford, that I was led into the faith more perfectly and God sanctified me wholly. I know it! ('Praise the Lord!') I started a mission after God sanctified me, and set up in business. I bought a 'second-hand' Episcopalian Church and paid so much for it that they built another and had a little to spare! A great many souls have been sanctified through this mission.

I love the holiness brethren, and the holiness element better than anything on this round earth to-day!" ("Amen!")

Bro. H. C. McBride of New York: "I became a minister when I was seventeen years of age, starting in at a school house on the corner of my father's farm, and had one hundred and fifty souls converted in nine weeks. Praise God! A number of them entered the ministry, and a good many have gone to heaven. Soon after that, I entered the Philadelphia Conference, and Alfred Cookman took me under his wing. In Spring Garden St. Church I was gloriously sanctified, and I am going through on that line. ("Amen!") I have no family but my wife, and she being in sympathy with my work, sings with me, as Sister Harris does with her husband. For twelve years I have been doing evangelistic work from Canada to Chicago, and God has wonderfully blessed me in this work. I am glad to be here. I have enjoyed this convention very much. Pray for me that the Lord will keep me humble, and make me more useful in His cause."

Bro. H. L. Jones, of Arkansas: "I trust you don't think that no good thing can come out of Arkansas! (Laughter.) I tell you there are some good things in Arkansas. There are other holiness camp meetings in the state, but I will speak particularly concerning the Fulton County Holiness Association. It is not a year old yet. We tried to get the Methodist Camp Grounds, but couldn't come to an arrangement, so this Association was organized. We drew up a constitution, and I referred the matter to Bro. McLaughlin, and he indorsed it. There are eighty members in our Association. We own 3 1-2 acres of land, and have a plain shed 38x50 feet. We have only had one camp meeting, but we had between forty and fifty sanctified. ("Amen!") We want to be connected with the National Holiness Association, or in some way connected with you, that you may be a blessing to us. God is with us in Arkansas." ("Amen!")

Bro. W. E. Shepard of California: "I had a call last winter while I was in California, to come to a town in the East. California folks don't like to come East in the winter time. I wrote them that I did not expect to come East then. I was walking along the street in Los Angeles, about two months afterwards and the Lord spoke to me and said: 'You better send a telegram and tell them that you will come.' This was the 21st of January. I prayed about it half an hour or so, and it deepened on me. I telegraphed them that I could come, and got their reply to come quick. When I got there the pastor said: 'This is a case of Cornelius and Peter.' It seemed that two of the pastors had an arrangement as to evangelists, and this one had been disappointed, and right in the midst of it, he got my telegram. I believe the Lord sometimes gives me an appointment. I spent a great deal of the winter in Los Angeles, with our home church of about 1,000 members. Never a week passes by but what we have sinners converted and believers sanctified."

Rev. A. L. Whitcomb of Illinois:—"I was converted

when I was fifteen years of age; sanctified wholly when I was twenty-three. During the seventeen years I have been a pastor, I have had more or less to do with the subject of holiness:—I might perhaps say 'more.' I was at the head of a Theological Seminary at Evansville three years, and, now, in addition to my duties as pastor, I have seven camp meetings on my hands for this summer, all on holiness lines." ("Bless God!" "That's enough for one pastor!")

Bro. John Norberry of Connecticut: "I was fourteen years of age, when the Lord and Saviour came into my life. He regenerated me, transformed the whole tenor of my being, and gave me a 'title clear to mansions in the skies.' ("Amen!") I have got the blessing of perfect love. I am in the experience. ("Amen!") My wife is over there, and she will tell you that I have it in the home. I thank God, I am in love with holiness people." ("Amen!")

Sister C. B. Boyce of Chicago:—"I rejoice, in my heart, for the Kansas work Sister Livingston has been telling about. I have been putting in about three years, most of the time in the great state of Kansas, and there is room enough there for others. There is a great, hungry call for full salvation. I have seen multitudes of souls come into the experience. One pastor said, just as I got into town, 'Let me tell you something: Don't say anything about holiness for awhile. Wait until you get the hearts of the people, before you talk about holiness.' I said: 'Why didn't you send for somebody else? I will pack my grip and go.' He said: 'That will not do. Just be careful how you speak of holiness.' I tell you I talked sactification and holiness as I never did before in my life. The result was we had eighty sanctified and one hundred and fifteen conversions. I love the holy people, the Holy Son, the Holy Ghost and the Holy Father. I am in for all there is in salvation." ("Amen!")

Bro. James Harris of Canada:—"I thank God that I was wholly sanctified nearly fifty years ago in a little village in Canada. I had no idea I would meet with any opposition, but sometimes during that time, I have had to stand almost alone along these lines.

"You have given me a big territory about which to speak, everything above your Northern boundary, except Alaska. I want to tell you that holiness is there. We are spreading holiness throughout that country, and God is blessing us."

Bro. Thomas Nelson of Indiana:—"I love the holiness brethren. God drew me to the holiness people when my folks were very anxious to make me a Roman Catholic years ago. I haven't any people except holiness people, and I have been giving my life to that cause for a long while. I am not here to congratulate people on the success of their work. I believe we are here more for humiliation than for congratulation. ("Amen!") If I would give vent to my feelings at this moment, I would break down and sob like a baby. God wants us to get on our faces and pray. I don't believe we ought to come like the great bankers and aristocracy, and boast of what our fathers and grandfathers used to do. I believe God has as much power to-day as He has ever shown through His people in the past. I praise God that He sanctified me wholly, and I am glad for what He is doing along the line of holiness among the people. I am here to take on a deeper type of holiness, if possible." ("Amen!")

Sister Kent White of Colorado:—"I assure you that it affords me much pleasure to look into the faces of

DAVID B. UPDEGRAPH,
(Deceased).

H. F. KLETZING,
Naperville, Ill.

C. M. DURYEA,
Holland, Mich.

J. L. GLASCOCK,
Cincinnati, Ohio.

W. B. OSBORN,
New York, N. Y.

MRS. L. D. OSBORN,
New York, N. Y.

HATTIE LIVINGSTON,
Des Moines, Iowa.

MISS ANNA DOWNEY,
Evanston, Ill.

the people of this convention. It is wonderfully comforting to sit down by somebody's else fire-side, and I am glad to be with you. It is a glorious thing to know that you are saved and sanctified. The Lord led me into the experience eight years ago. It is the biggest thing in this world. I couldn't contain it all. ("Amen. Glory") I extend the invitation for you all to come to Colorado. We have been called to establish a mission at Butte, Montana, which has been the means of saving two or three hundred souls. In Wyoming, we have another mission. You would be surprised at the number of letters that come in from those parts of the country, from young people who want to go into the work. I praise God victory is coming our way."

Song by congregation: "Make me a Blessing Today."

Bro. A. C. Morehouse:—"I move that Bro. Alex. McLean be appointed to despatch greetings to the Tuesday Afternoon Holiness Meeting in New York, accompanied with our prayers for the conversion of sinners and the entire sanctification of believers. These meetings began Feb. 9th, 1866, and have continued without a break every Tuesday afternoon. We ought to encourage Sister Van Cott and Bro. Howland." ("Amen!")

The motion prevailed and greetings were sent.

Bro. Aura Smith of Indiana:—"I assure you that I am glad to be here, but I had a hard time getting here. I was converted thirty years ago. I was sanctified twenty-three years ago. God immediately called me out into this holiness work, and I have been in the work ever since God sanctified me. I have had the privilege of seeing Mormons get down on their knees and get this blessed religion. ("Amen!") I saw one of the most beautiful sights within the last two weeks I ever witnessed. A Mormon woman came to the meetings. She had a baby in her arms, and she would come to the altar with it, and it would cry. She would get up and take it away, then she would be right back again. She got gloriously converted. ("Amen!") I just had to tear myself away from the work. Utah is opening up to holiness. ("Glory!") Since I left there, I had a letter from another minister. He says: "We want holiness all over Utah." Praise God for the spreading of holiness all over the land. I want to see a great, sweeping revival move over the whole country. ("Amen!") It has not often been my privilege to be in large meetings of holiness people. I am glad when I have the opportunity."

Bro. J. T. Hatfield of Indiana:—"I was sanctified twenty-one years ago. Since that time, I have been going to and fro over the earth, preaching holiness and praising God. ("Amen!") I have been in every county of our state from the Michigan line to the Ohio River. The Lord has been giving me the victory. When God gives us the Holy Ghost in our souls, He will give us the right of way. ("Amen!") All we need is to get the Holy Ghost and keep sweet. I am dead to everything else except God. I don't care for men, or money or anything else. ("Amen!") I tell you I have gone right up in the pulpit and taken the meeting out of the minister's hands, and got him to seek sanctification. Five of our presiding elders tried to keep me out of the work down there, but one told me if I would stay, he would give me work three hundred and sixty five days in the year. Bless God! During that year we had 3,500 conversions in his district, while all the five others combined only had 2,000. I am looking for great things." ("Amen!")

Bro. Wm. R. Benkert of Iowa:—"I belong to Jesus Christ. I am one of the new born. The world may call us crazy, but it is not on new wine, brethren. I am acquainted with this Jesus, and I came about it honestly. When I was but a child, I was crippled. Three doctors, after treating me for thirteen years, said I would always be a cripple. My Christian mother read to me out of the Word of God, how Jesus healed, and how he was still the same healer. I went out on the farm, and, although I have not been there for forty years, I believe I could find the exact spot. I knelt down and made a vow to God and said: 'If you will heal me, I will be Thine forever.' I got up from my knees and was instantly healed. ("Bless God!") So you see the God of Daniel still lives."

(Bro. Fowler: "Everybody that is willing to praise God for that healing say, Amen."—Cries of "Amen!")

"I was only thirteen years old when I was healed. I once was a Methodist; I once was a United Brethren; I once was a Republican; I once was a Prohibitionist, but now I have become a Christian." ("Amen!")

On motion, it was decided to invite Bro. Seth C. Rees to hold his noonday meetings in the audience room (occupied by the Assembly), during the week days of the Assembly. The invitation was extended by Brother Fowler but declined.

Bro. A. L. Whitcomb tendered his resignation as member of the Committee on Permanent Methods, on account of his duties as secretary, and Bro. Aura Smith was chosen to succeed him on said committee.

It was announced that Wednesday forenoon would

be devoted to prayer and supplication, and that Bro. A. L. Whitcomb would preach at 2:30 P. M. and Bro. B. S. Taylor at 7:30.

The meeting was brought to a close by the congregation singing the Doxology.

AFTERNOON SESSION.

2:00 p. m. Bro. C. J. Fowler, presiding. Sister S. B. Shaw: "I want to say a few words about that Prayer Roll. (This stretched twice across the church from gallery to gallery.) Could you all have had the privilege I have had of reading those letters I am sure your hearts would cry out to God for an answer to those many petitions. Many are from those who are either themselves afflicted in body or who have friends whom they long to see healed. Many represent the cry of a mother's heart for the salvation of her children. Some ask you to pray for a wandering boy far away from God. Some tell the story of the yearning of a heart-broken wife who has long prayed for the salvation of her husband and whose heart has almost grown faint because of answer long delayed. Some of those letters are from hearts longing for pardon—others ask you to pray that they may be made whiter than snow and filled with the Holy Ghost. Pastors and Sunday-school teachers and other workers ask you to pray that God may baptize them with the Holy Ghost and help them to win souls.

The Spirit will help us to bear these petitions to the throne. ("Amen!") God knows them all: ("Amen") and as we pray, let us remember that every letter represents some heart that is crying out to God and let us unite with them, and God will hear and answer prayer. ("Amen" "Amen.")

Earnest united prayer followed in which all requests represented by the Prayer Roll were remembered.

Singing by the congregation: "He Brought me Out," "There's Power in the Blood," and "Walking with Jesus My Lord."

Bro. S. B. Shaw called attention to the holiness literature, for sale at the book table, and to the fact that all proceeds from the sale of his works, during the Assembly, would be donated to the expenses of the Assembly.

Prayer by Sister Jennie Smith: "Our Father, Thou knowest just why each of us has come to this convention. Thou knowest our needs. We bless Thee, Lord, that we have come here for a general house-cleaning. ("God Grant it!") We ask, for Jesus' sake, that the work may be so definite, and Thy will so fully accomplished, that every one of us shall receive a fresh anointing from heaven, that we may be better fruit bearing branches. ("Amen!") Help us to get where our influence will be felt by everyone with whom we come in contact both inside and outside of the churches. Help us to get to a place where, by word of mouth and every act of life, our influence that goes out, whether conscious or unconscious, may touch the hearts of those about us. Our Father, we want just such a baptism of the Holy Ghost sanctifying power to come upon us that we will honor and glorify Thee in every avenue of life, and then we shall not be a stumbling block for the criticising world. O, let salvation come to souls and sanctification to believers, through this Assembly!

Our Father, bless each one of the leaders, and each member of the committees, and let such as shall be saved, be saved through and through, sanctified and made meet for the Master's use. Be with him who shall address us this afternoon, and may we all be so faithful to our trust, that, when the final call comes, we may have thousands of trophies laid at the Master's feet. We ask it all for Jesus' sake. Amen.

Song by Sister Aura Smith: "The Old Fountain."

SERMON BY BRO. AURA SMITH.

Text: Ezekiel 36:25-29. "Then will I sprinkle clean water upon you, and ye shall be clean from all your filthiness, and from all your idols, will I cleanse you."

That is the kind of sprinkling I believe in! ("Good!" "Glory.") It would be a big thing if we even stopped there, but He tells us in the next verses the process by which this is brought about: "A new heart also will I give you, and a new spirit will I put within you." That would be glorious, wouldn't it, if you just stopped there. I will never forget the day when that took place with me, when I found that a new heart had come into me, when I found a new spirit possessed me. But I soon found out there was something else in me and then my trouble began. I shouted in a quiet way, because I was a quiet person at that time. I praised the Lord all that day. But I soon found I had something in me contrary to this new heart and trouble began and kept up for about seven years. Then I found the experience of this text: "And I will take away the stony heart out of your flesh, and I will give you an heart of flesh. And I will put my Spirit within you, and cause you to walk in my statutes, and ye shall keep my judgments, and do them. And ye shall dwell in the land that I gave to your fathers; and ye shall be my people and I will be your God. I will also save you from all your uncleannesses; and I will call for the corn, and will increase it, and lay no famine upon you." "And I will multiply the fruit of the tree and the increase of the field, that ye shall re-receive no more reproach of famine among the heathen. Then shall ye remember your own evil ways, and your doings that were not good, and shall loathe yourselves in your own sight for your iniquities and for your abominations."

The first thing I call your attention to in the text is that water and fire are used as symbols of the work of the Holy Ghost. Or, let me put it in another simple way: Water and fire are used as symbols of the work of salvation.

Turn now to the 3rd chapter of Matthew, 11, 12 verses. "I indeed baptize you with water unto repentance: but He that cometh after me is mightier than I, whose shoes I am not worthy to bear: He shall baptize you with the Holy Ghost, and with fire: Whose fan is in His hand, and He will thoroughly purge His floor, and gather His wheat into the garner; but He will burn up the chaff with unquenchable fire." (I hope that you who are in the experience are all praying—("We are.") that somebody that hasn't this experience of holiness will get it and I am going to preach to that particular person.) ("Amen!") What does He mean by "you" here? In my early days, I heard this used as a proof text for hell fire. John says the very people whom he had baptized with water unto repentance, Jesus was to baptize with the Holy Ghost and fire. Some preacher in Indiana put a question on the board and asked if anybody could prove that there was any other baptism than the baptism of water. A drayman walked right to the front and wrote under the question Matthew 3: 11, 12, and the preacher read the verses I have quoted. It only took a sanctified drayman to answer that question. Here He promises the baptism of the Holy Ghost and fire to those whom he has baptized with water unto repentance.

Notice again: "Whose fan is in His hand, and He will throughly purge His floor, and gather His wheat into the garner, but He will burn up the chaff with unquenchable fire." Who is the floor of Jesus Christ? Not sinners. Recently a man said to me "I believe in the great universal fatherhood of God." "But," I said, "If you mean that every man and woman are children of God, you are mistaken. We are not children of God nor the 'floors' of Christ until we are regenerated and born into the family of God." God promises to baptize those that have received the baptism of water unto repentance, with the Holy Ghost and fire, and this fire is to burn up the chaff of our evil natures.

Turn to the 3rd Chapter of Malachi. Keep in mind that water and fire are used as symbols of salvation. "Who shall stand when He appeareth? for He is like a refiner's fire, and like fuller's soap: And He shall sit as a refiner and purifier of silver: and He shall purify the sons of Levi, and purge them as gold and silver, that they may offer unto the Lord an offering in righteousness."

Next take Isaiah 4: 3: "And it shall come to pass that he that is left in Zion, and he that remaineth in Jerusalem, shall be called holy." Please note the qualification: "Even every one that is written among the living in Jerusalem." It does not stop yet. "When the Lord shall have washed away the filth of the daughters of Zion, and shall have purged the blood of Jerusalem from the midst thereof by the spirit of judgment, and by the spirit of burning."

Now, he says these are to be called holy when this

washing takes place that is to wash away the filth of the daughters of Zion.

I had been converted seven years, but never during that time applied the term "holy" to myself, but the moment I went to the fountain, from the moment I received the baptism of the Holy Ghost and fire, people have introduced me as a holiness man, and my denomination have spoken of me as such. I happened to be in a strange town. I went to the depot to take the train. There was a lady and her husband waiting there, and as I came by she said to her husband: "There is one of them now! There is one of those holiness fellows." I said, "I am. You are correct. I would like to tell you a little of my experience. I told them how God had sanctified me. She turned to her husband and said, "I want that washing," and he said he did too. I didn't get this until I got the second experience. You will notice all of these verses indicate cleanness and purity of the very highest type. The first verse of my text expresses simply the result promised. There are passages that simply give the results of salvation, without especially noting the process. For instance: Matt. 1:21: "Thou shalt call His name Jesus, for He shall save His people from their sins." There is nothing said in that about the process, but the simple fact that Jesus was to save us from our sins. Then Romans 6: 22: "But how being accounted (?) free from sin."—("No, sir. That isn't accounted.") But some people quote it that way. "But now being made free from sin, and become servants to God, ye have your fruit unto holiness, and the end everlasting life." It doesn't say "you will be," but now being actually made free from sin, you have your fruit unto holiness. Some people talk about having everlasting life now, and, when they die, they are going to be made free from sin, then they are going to have their fruit unto holiness. The freedom from sin, the fruit unto holiness is an experience we get here, and the crowning thing of everlasting life, we get hereafter. This is the divine order. Jeremiah 33: 8: "And I will cleanse them from all their iniquity, whereby they have sinned against me; and I will pardon all their iniquities whereby they have sinned, and whereby they have transgressed against me." I read that for this purpose: to show that He promises to cleanse away the very thing that causes us to commit iniquity. God promises to save every man up to the place where he can live a holy life. In order to do that, he promises to take out the very root of the matter that causes us to commit sin. To illustrate: In a meeting at Aspen, Colo., I stepped up to a man at the altar and asked him if he was there for pardon or purity. He looked up and said: "I am here because my wife told me to come." "Don't you want to be a Christian?" "I can't be a Christian." "What do you mean by that?" "Brother, lots of nights I lay awake all night and promise I will never touch another drop of liquor, but the next morning I am in the saloon before breakfast and drunk before nine o'clock. I can't be a Christian. I can't let rum alone, and there is no use of my trying." "Brother, Jesus Christ can deliver you from rum so that you will not want it any more than the man who is speaking to you to-night." "Then I can be a Christian." The thing he needed was deliverance. I went to his home, and he said: "I will never touch another drop of liquor, so help me God! if I die for the want of it." I drew up a pledge and he put his signature to it, and we got down and prayed until he was gloriously converted. A few days after that, I met him on the street. I said, "how is it?" He answered, "I am the happiest man you ever saw. I can walk right by the saloon, and smell the liquor without a particle of longing for it. I don't want it. I am a free man." "I want you to stay free." "Have you any doubt?" "Yes." "Why?" "On account of that thing you have in your mouth. I have doubts of every fellow that indulges in tobacco. (Cries of "That's so!") Brother, that cigar will feed the appetite for liquor, and, as sure as you hold to that you will be back to the saloon in a little while." "Do you want to kill me outright? the appetite for liquor was a mere plaything to this." There is so much said by some about getting drunk on liquor, and nothing about tobacco. As I said to a temperance lecturer, who wanted to use my pulpit, "Do you get up and scalp the drunkard and hold him up as a horrible example, and leave the tobacco devil alone? Do you come with a cigar or quid in your mouth and lecture on temperance? If you do you can't speak in my pulpit on temperance." ("Amen!") He said, "I don't know what liquor tastes like. I don't know what tobacco tastes like. I never touched tea or coffee in my life." ("Amen!") That brother who had discarded drinking said: "I don't smoke but thirty cigars a day." No wonder he was in bondage! I said: "Do just as you did with the liquor. Throw it away." He did so. We knelt down on the pavement, ("Glory to God.") and God rid him from tobacco. ("Amen!") I saw his wife some years after, and she said he never touched tobacco or liquor after that day. Just as God delivers a man from rum and tobacco, He can deliver us from that thing which keeps us from living a holy life, I do not care what it is. ("Amen!")

Beloved, we are a little Assembly of holiness people here, and, we should spread the glad tidings of deliverance wherever we go. There are men and women that will never be saved in the world until somebody brings to them the gospel of full salvation. ("Amen!")

I was holding a meeting a few years ago when I said to a judge: "Judge, are you a Christian?" "No, sir. I am not. I am a long ways from being a Christian. My judgment approves the logic of your preaching, but I don't live it. I cannot live it, and I don't try." "I know you can't, judge." "Then why do you want me to try?" "I don't want you to try." He looked at me, astonished. "Judge, why can't you live it?" "It is the old Adam in me, that is the reason." "Suppose the Lord takes that out?" "If He should I could live as you preach." "I am going to ask you to come to God to get rid of the old Adam." The next night he staid at home with the children. He said, "I don't see why God can't convert me here as well as in the meeting." When his wife came home he asked: "Who was converted?" She asked why he was so much interested. "The Lord converted me while you were in the meeting." When the next night came, he again said that he would stay home. He said: "Smith says after you are converted, the next step is to get sanctified and get rid of the old Adam. God converted me here last night, why can't he sanctify me?" He got down and plead with God, and his wife came home and found him shouting. She said: "What has happened?" "The Lord has sanctified me!" There are multitudes of men and women like that. They don't want to start until they can make a success of it. They have their minds on holiness, and, if you can make them see that they will begin a Christian life.

The next thing for consideration is the process by which we come to this result. He says: "A new heart also will I give you and a new spirit will I put within you." God always begins the work of salvation by giving men a new heart. God never intends to improve the old nature. Never! Never! ("Amen!") God gives you something you never had before ("Amen!")—a new spirit, regeneration not reformation. That is the trouble with so many. They try reformation. They do not get to the bottom, and the result is, they get nothing. God begins by regeneration—giving a new heart and a new spirit. Puts something in your heart that was never there before. And it is this that gives you control of yourself, causing you to hate the things you formerly loved, and love the things you formerly hated. I never went to a prayer meeting until I was converted. I had nothing in me that wanted me to go there. When God put a new spirit within me, I went right to prayer meeting, because I loved the prayer meeting. This thing settles the card and dance business.

The very fact that some do not see any harm in these questionable things shows that they haven't the genuine grace in the heart, or they would turn away from them. Regeneration settles this by giving us a new heart.

"I will take away your stony heart and give you a heart of flesh." There must be a time then when there are two hearts, or two sets of motives in man. Paul speaks of the old man. You don't talk about a new and an old bonnet until you get a new one. The Indian said after conversion: "There is a good Indian and a bad Indian in me. The good Indian wants me to be good. The bad Indian wants me to be bad." That Indian noticed this dual nature. He never heard of holiness! You do not need a sermon on holiness to get you to see that. ("Amen!")

But we need not remain in that state. God says He will take the stony heart out, that is, He will deliver us from that "old man," "body of sin," from which ugliness, man fearing, passion, covetousness, and these unholy things spring that you find in your life after you became a Christian. He promises to take this away, and leave only the single nature. But He doesn't propose to stop there. "And I will put my Spirit within you."

The crowning thought here is the enthronement of the Holy Ghost in our heart—to be filled and possessed of the Holy Ghost, and we ought never to stop short of that culmination. Hold on long enough to receive the baptism of the Holy Ghost. Hold on by your faith until this comes upon you. Stick to it, if it does take a few nights, or some midnight praying. Press through until you touch rock-bottom, until the Holy Ghost comes in with all His fulness, and leaves no chance for you to doubt the fact that God sanctifies you. There was a time when I was baptized with water. Not all the people in the world could make me believe I wasn't baptized. I want to say to you that, seven years after that, I was fully as conscious that I was baptized with the Holy Ghost. ("Amen.")

The next thought in the text is: "I will cause you to walk in my statutes and ye shall keep my judgments and do them." The question is, how can a man keep the commandments? Get the commandment inspirer in His fullness in your heart, and He will cause you to keep them. A woman had been reading in her catechism that "no merely mortal man can, by all the grace that is given him, keep the commandments of God." She said: "O, my! Can't God give us the power?" You will note it says "no merely mortal man" can do it. When you get converted you are not a "merely mortal man." You have a divine nature. I am glad to say that this is something that makes it easy for one to be a Christian. God can make it as easy to serve Him as any sinner finds it to serve the devil.

"Ye shall dwell in the land that I gave to your fathers." God is to put us in a place where there is stability. This will take the back-sliding tendency away. It will get you so you will not have cold spells and backslide between meetings. You get lukewarm. You don't abide. You don't stay. The text promises to place you where you will stay; where you will abide and dwell in the land of your fathers.

"I will call for the corn, and will increase it." God has put growth in its place after cleansing. That is the divine order. First cleansed, then grow. "And lay no famine upon you." God has a salvation that never has any droughts—that never gets parched up. ("Amen!") It will keep you perennially green. That is what the church needs. ("Amen!") We need an experience that will make us all feel like we are just converted. When I get into meetings, and the blessing comes on my soul, I feel like I am right from the fountain myself! ("Glory!") I haven't backslidden either. When I get to feeling that way, I talk just like a young convert. Often one just converted can lead a sinner to the altar, when older ones in the experience cannot do anything with him. He can put you where there is no drought or famine. ("Amen.")

"I will multiply the fruit of the tree, and the increase

of the field, that ye shall receive no more reproach of famine among the heathen." This verse teaches satisfaction.

I have never been so grieved as during this past winter over one thing, that so many good men and women have allowed themselves to be united with other societies than the church of Jesus Christ. ("Amen!" "God help them!") Sinners get to saying that the lodge is as good as the church, and give out the idea that there is a lack in the religion of to-day. I say that every man that is a Christian, who is connected with secret orders, is helping people outside of the church to believe that there is a failure in the religion of Jesus Christ. ("Amen!") Saying nothing about the good there is in them, we ought to consider that, by connecting ourselves with them, we are deceiving the world. ("Amen!") I don't need them. I bless God, religion gives me all I need. ("Amen!" "Glory to God!") It satisfies me. You ministers of God, who are associated with the lodge, you go, and that man of the world points to you and says the reason you attend the lodge is that the church doesn't satisfy you. If we do not do anything else, let us have the world see that Jesus Christ is all that any man needs,—all the society he needs; all the victory he needs. ("Amen!" "Glory!") I know one man that goes up and down this world, who is satisfied, and don't need any man to pity him! ("Amen!") I ask you to see that in the text it is God who does the work. He says: "I will sprinkle water upon you and ye shall be clean. I will give you a new heart. I will take away your stony heart." The same being that converted you, regenerated you, is to sanctify you. It is not a growth. It is not a development. It is the work of God. A woman once said to me: "When I think about my

MRS. PHEBE EPPERSON,
Boone, Iowa.

FANNIE BIRDSALL,
Indianapolis, Ind.

AMANDA SMITH,
Harvey, Ill.

MARY E. EDINGER,
Demotte, Ind.

J. P. BRUSHINGHAM,
Chicago, Ill.

S. C. TODD,
Atlanta, Ga.

JOHN S. INSKIP,
(Deceased).

L. B. KENT,
Jacksonville, Ill.

heart and carnality and sins, I believe it will take God 40 years to sanctify me." What is time to God?

> "In the twinkling of an eye,
> God, my Lord, can sanctify."

("Glory!") One thousand years is as but a day with God. You do not have to work yourself up by a growth in grace. Bless your soul! When in God's order you are growing when you don't know it. ("Amen!")

He says, "I will multiply the fruit of the tree and the increase of the field, that ye shall receive no more reproach of famine among the heathen." When you get it, you do not have to get up and advertise that you are satisfied. ("Glory!") You can tell a man that is sanctified by the company he keeps; by the shine in his face; by the language of his mouth. ("Amen!") God can sanctify you. He can do it right now. ("Glory!")

At the altar service at the conclusion of the sermon, fourteen seekers presented themselves, and a large part of the congregation moved forward and engaged in this after service.

EVENING SESSION.

7:30 p. m., Bro. C. J. Fowler, presiding.

Singing by Congregation: "Calvary's Stream is Flowing," "He Touched Me and Made me Whole," "Love Found Me," "The Open Fountain," and "We Have an Anchor."

Prayer by Sister Lilian Smith: "O, God, Thine ear is open to us. Thou hast promised to hear us. We praise Thee for the power of Jesus' blood.

O, God, wilt Thou honor Thy Word? Give Sister Livingston just such a message as Thou wouldst have her deliver. Help us to understand it as God sends it to us. We pray Thee that we may go out from this place equipped for Thy work better than ever before.

We never could have saved ourselves; all the glory is Thine. We are so grateful that Thou ever hadst anything to do with us. We want to praise Thee forever, world without end. Amen."

Prayer by Sister Sarah A. Cooke:

"O, Lord, Thou hast said in Thy Word, that whatsoever we ask in Thy name, believing we shall receive. O, Lord, we ask Thy special blessing on these services tonight. Touch the lips of her who shall speak to us. We know that she has brought many souls unto the precious Lamb of God. Thou didst speak to Lazarus, and he came forth and lived. Thou hast said: 'I am the resurrection and the life. He that liveth and believeth on me shall not die.' We thank Thee for eternal life. O, Praise the Lord! May the glad tidings of great joy reach many a heart to-night, and, through this meeting, may Thy people not only get a fresh unction, but let many be led to God. We ask it all in the all-prevailing name of our Lord and Savior Jesus Christ. Amen."

SERMON BY SISTER HATTIE LIVINGSTONE.

I wish to call your attention to the 20th chapter of Revelation beginning with the 11th verse: "And I saw a great white throne, and Him that sat on it, from whose face the earth and the heavens fled away; and there was found no place for them. And I saw the dead, small and great, stand before God; and the books were opened: and another book was opened, which is the book of life: and the dead were judged out of those things which were written in the books, according to their works. And the sea gave up the dead which were in it; and death and hell gave up the dead which were in them: and they were judged every man according to their works. And death and hell were cast into the lake of fire. This is the second death. And whosoever was not found written in the book of life was cast into the lake of fire."

We shall meet again the record of our lives that we have lived so carelessly here. God hath said, for every idle word we shall give account thereof at the day of Judgment.

In the closing scenes of earth, the angel will set his right foot upon the sea and his left foot on the earth, and swear by Him that liveth forever and forever that time shall be no more.

The Son of God will leave the Mediatorial Throne and take His seat upon the Judgment throne, with His eyes as a flame of fire, His voice as the sound of many waters, His countenance as the sun shining in his strength. Every receptacle of mortality will be thrown open and all will gather at the throne. Adam and Eve and their descendants all down the ages; Sodom and Gomorrah will be there. God hath said, they are now suffering the vengeance of eternal fire, but it will be more tolerable for them at the day of Judgment than for us who live under the Holy Ghost dispensation, under the light of the Gospel, and reject Christ.

On they come of every kindred, tongue, tribe and nation; the good with their glorified bodies and radiant faces reflecting the very glory of the Triune God. The wicked shall come forth with a damned body for a damned soul; their mouths distorted with blasphemy, impure, unholy, unclean, loathsome and vile. The fallen angels will be there and we shall be there. The Judgment will be set and the books will be opened. There are many books, but one is the book of life. In the many books are written the record of our lives. We are also keeping a corresponding record, day by day, upon the tablets of our hearts. We are writing that which will never be erased, in time or eternity. We are treading upon chords which will vibrate at the Great White Throne. The record written in the tablets of our memory will meet the angel's record at that day.

A young lady who came nigh unto death's door by drowning said: "At a certain descent phosphoric radiance sprang to my eyeballs and a mighty theater expanded in my brain and I saw as part of co-existence, every thought, word, act and deed of my life." So will it be at the throne.

There will be diversities of judgment commensurate with knowledge. Those under the Mosaic dispensation will be judged by the Old Testament. Those living under the Holy Ghost dispensation will be judged by both the Old and the New Testament. The heathen, by the law of nature. The measure of light will be the measure of guilt. There never was a day when people sinned against so great light as they do to-day. I would rather come up from dark Africa, a sinner, and stand before the throne, having never heard of Christ, than to come from our Christian land, having heard and rejected the call of the Gospel. The rich and poor, the great and small, shall stand upon a common level. Then shall we know, even as also we are known. The secrets of the heart will there be made manifest; the secrets of lust, ambition, covetousness, sins known only to your heart and God. Sins committed in the dark; that which has been hidden from the eyes of man will there be brought to the light under the searching eye of God, and before the universe. Sinner, what will be your answer and what will be your plea at that day when the record of your life is opened up before God? In view of the family altar, the calls of the Spirit, the rejection of God, will you plead, "Lord I am innocent"? Because you did not understand, will you plead ignorance with an open Bible—while the Spirit plead with your heart for years? What will you answer, brother, and what will be your plea? Will you plead hypocrisy in the church? t will not be what other people did, but we will stand an l answer for ourselves. ("Amen") Sinner, what will you plead, when you see the saints on the right hand and the glory that might have been yours? Beloved what will you answer who are building upon the foundation, wood, hay and stubble, with no family altar, with your cold, formal, empty prayers, when you might have been on fire for God and won souls, had you let the Holy Ghost come in and let Christ Jesus have His way with you?

My heart has been made to bleed as I go over the land to find among God's professed people so many who have no interest in the salvation of souls, not even their own loved ones. Some who profess holiness have no family altar, and no power in their prayers or life. Perhaps there are those here to-night who can look back to a time when their testimonies and prayers and life were on fire. To-day they are powerless. Time speeds away. These golden opportunities will face us again at the Judgment. I have asked myself the question many times, Will I be held responsible for the power I might have had, if I had been more prayerful and more fully abandoned to God? And because of the lack of power will souls I might have reached, and hearts I might have won, be lost? I can afford to do without the things of the world; I can afford to be misunderstood and misrepresented; I can afford any heartache and suffering; but I can not afford to lose God's best and be without the Holy Spirit. ("Amen.") My soul must meet the record of these days and years before God. I must meet my influence with my loved ones. How my heart has cried to God that I might touch the deepest depths of the highest power! I want to get more of God that I may win more souls for Jesus my Lord. I feel like catching on to the fleeting moments as they pass. They will never return. Many times I have stood before the people and thought, I shall never touch all these souls again but I shall meet them at the Judgment. I have prayed, My God, give me the right message and the power to present it to help them to Thee. ("Amen") Beloved, some of you used to plead with souls, but some way you have lost the power and joy of salvation. You are saying, "I walk by faith." Yes: God has called us to walk by faith, but faith brings joy, and God's power will come into your lives and you will be anxious for the lost. Souls are going into eternity all about us. What we do must be done quickly. Touch us workers. The last angel will be judged and the last sentence pronounced. "Then shall the king say unto them on the right hand, Come, ye blessed of my Father, inherit the kingdom prepared for you from the foundation of the world. Then shall he say to them on the left hand, Depart from me, ye cursed into everlasting fire, prepared for the devil and his angels." And whosoever was not found written in the book of life was cast into the lake of fire."

Here when we lose a case in court we may carry it to the supreme, or United States court; but when we lose our case at the Judgment throne, there will be no higher tribunal; but the sentence received there will burn and flash in the tablets of an endless eternity. ("Oh Jesus!") Then comes the separation at the throne—the last good-bye. Here in this world the mother looks upon the cold remains of her darling child whom God has taken from her bosom and transplanted into the paradise above, and, amid her tears and agony, she says, "I'll meet my precious one again." We carry our dead and commit their bodies to mother earth. Although we may be unsaved there springs up a hope of a meeting beyond. Beloved, there is coming a time when we shall say good-bye forever. Mother and child, husband and wife will part never to meet again. The redeemed will go to inherit mansions as numberless as the sands of the seashore; domains of never-ending power, love and glory.

The damned will turn from the God they have spurned, the Saviour who shed His blood to redeem them. And they will take the last look upon the faces of loved ones who prayed for them. Ah, it will be good-bye to all hope and gladness; good-bye to all peace and happiness; good-bye to the songs of joy. Only from henceforth to hear the awful wails and shrieks of the damned. Good-bye to light. No ray of light will ever pierce the dungeon darkness. Hell is to be their doom; banished and separated from God forever; homesick, and no home; away from all love and friendship; never to hear another kind word; they are hopeless forever.

Sinner, the devil is promising you something else tonight. He is holding before you the pleasures of the world, wealth and position. He is promising you happiness, but he will give you something else. He will give you a Christless death bed, the companionship of damned souls, with the unclean, unholy, impious, loathsome and abandoned, and, with the demons of darkness your poor soul will spend an endless eternity.

Mother, are your girls and boys going to wail there? Do you wonder God says He wipes away the tears from the eyes of His people? We would weep forever over the loss of loved ones, and over lost opportunities. Don't let us wait to weep over yonder—let us weep for the lost here. ("Amen") Let us weep and pray for our loved ones here. Pray that God may reach and save them here at any cost or sacrifice.

At the close of the sermon, the invitation was extended and a number of seekers came forward, the altar and front seats being crowded with those engaged in prayer and supplication.

Wednesday, May 8.

MORNING SESSION.

8:00 a. m. Prayer and Praise Service.

9:00 a. m., Bro. C. J. Fowler presiding.

Bro. Fowler: "None of us would have been here in this Christian gathering, had it not been for united prayer. Somebody prayed for you and for me. God thrust conviction upon us, and we hurried to Jesus. What has been done for us can be done for others. This is a day of fasting and prayer. Not so much a day for song, possibly, as a united crying to God. We must not forget to pray with thanksgiving. Just see this prayer roll! Everywhere, they are praying for the success of these meetings, and for these requests. God is looking upon the names on that roll. I think, perhaps, not many of us appreciate the value of the moments before us."

After a season of earnest prayers, in which the congregation participated very generally, the intensity of prayer being very marked, a letter of greeting was presented to the Assembly from Bro. C. B. Ward of India, and Bro. S. B. Shaw stated the contents of a letter received from an inmate of the Wisconsin State Prison, showing that, while he was imprisoned behind the bars, he was no longer a prisoner to sin. He asked the prayers of the Assembly.

Bro. J. B. Foote, led in prayer in behalf of Bro. Ward of India and the brother at the Wisconsin State Prison.

Another long, continuous season of prayer was engaged in. Perhaps some idea of this service can be conveyed to the reader, from the description given by a party who was present to record the meeting. He says: "Imagine a vast assemblage of God's people under the spirit and inspiration of prayer upon prayer, and long waiting upon God. Have you ever witnessed a great frontier prairie fire rise in intensity of blaze, then die down momentarily to break forth with renewed power? It was just so that the prayer waves rose on this occasion, until it seemed that every soul in divine presence was petitioning, from its very depths, the throne on high. Then would come a lull, and, while there was an absence of the sound of supplicating voices, one seemed to be overwhelmed with a mighty, indescribable Presence. Following this brief pause would come again the voice of prayer, gradually increasing in volume and intensity, on every hand, until it exceeded every previous bound and it seemed that each individual soul was vying with every other to prevail the more mightily with the Eternal Father. With brethren and sisters prostrate before God, with fervid petitions, with agonizing groans and tearful appeals to the Throne of Grace, it was truly an awe-inspiring spectacle, and one never to be forgotten by any who witnessed it."

The closing words of the session, by President C. J. Fowler, are a fitting expression of the presence of the Spirit on that occasion. Bro. Fowler said: "You may not have felt the pressure that is on some hearts here; you may not have had upon your hearts the burden that is on some hearts here now—it does not necessarily follow that you are not right with God, because you haven't it. You are not necessarily out of harmony with God. Do not let the accuser take advantage of you there. But, if you have not been in sympathy with what you have witnessed here, and have looked upon it as creature activity, as human manifestation; if you have been nervous in the presence of this thing, you want to look out.

What meaneth this? That question will come up in the intermission. Let us be careful and walk with bated breath. When the gathering comes together in the afternoon, we may see the whole thing either enhanced or lowered. During the intermission, at dinner, or fasting, or whatever engaged in, let us hold steady before God, and every heart that has the least suggestion that you are not where God wants you, don't fail to get there the very second God shows you the way.

We are going out from here this morning with a widening, deepening and strengthening experience, or else we go with a narrowed experience. We have seen our poorest day, or our best day. If we are filled with the Spirit and awake to the full meaning of this hour, this is the poorest day we will ever have, and we are at the smallest end of our experience. If there is a hesitation on our part, we are seeing the best day we may ever expect. God does not give us light to play with. He wants us to go forward in His cause with the swing of victory, and with the tread of a conqueror. ("Amen!")

Brother, if you have been betrayed into coming here merely to look on, I say to you, look out. It is an awful peril, let me repeat it, if a heart here has not been in sympathy with this thing.

O, what a revelation God gives my soul! How my affections go out to God! ("Amen!" "Glory!" "Hallelujah!")

AFTERNOON SESSION.

2:00 p. m., Bro. C. J. Fowler presiding.

Singing by congregation: "Power Divine," "Jesus Has Lifted my Load," and "Love Everlasting."

Sister Amanda Smith, upon request, came to the platform and described how she had been inspired to write four additional verses to the song "He Rolled the Sea Away," which original adaptation she sang before the Assembly.

Song by Sister Aura Smith: "I cannot Tell Why."

Bro. C. W. Ruth took charge of the collections, and made a special plea to the Assembly.

Prayer, led by Sister Kent White: "O God, our Father, we praise Thee for the Pentecost Thou hast been giving us all day. We ask, while the saints are getting blessed and unified, that the unsaved may be converted and believers sanctified in this meeting. May it be a "red-letter" day in somebody's life. May many plunge into the fountain and be made whiter than snow. May Thy servant's lips be touched with a live coal from off Thine altar.

We pray that the Holy Ghost may abide in this place in mighty power. We ask Thee, Holy Spirit, to have the right of way here, and may all of our plans not in the Lord be smashed up, and, as we leave this place, may we be able to look back and feel, indeed, that we have been in Thine upper room. We know Thou art present with us, and we would ask Thee to show us the particular niche we are to fill, and help us to fill it. We ask it in Jesus' name, Amen."

SERMON BY BRO. A. L. WHITCOMB.

Text: "The arrows are beyond thee." (1 Samuel 20-22.)

About 2,900 years ago, two armies faced each other in the Valley of Elah in South-western Palestine. The issues of the contest were to be settled in single combat by the representatives of the contending armies. David, the shepherd lad from Bethlehem, met Goliath, the Giant of Gath, smote him with a sling-stone and cut off his head with his own sword. On the return of the armies to Gibeon, the daughters of Israel came out to meet them with tabrets and songs. They sang, "Saul hath slain his thousands and David his ten thousands." Immediately, Saul was jealous and cried what more could they do than to give him the kingdom. From that time forth, he looked upon David with an evil eye and sought to slay him. Thrice, he attempted to smite him to the wall with his javelin, but as often, David fled out of his presence, finally fleeing to Raamah, the home of Samuel. Saul pursued him thither, and David returned to Gibeon and met Jonathan in the open field, according to appointment. He inquired: "What have I done that your father seeks to slay me? If I am guilty of any crime, slay me with your own hand." Jonathan replied: "My father will do nothing either great or small, but that he will shew it me." David replied: "Your father knoweth that I have found favor in thine eyes, so he has said to the young men, 'Tell it not to Jonathan,' but truly as the Lord liveth, and as thy soul liveth, there is but a step between me and death." Jonathan then made an oath to David and said to him: "Go to your father's house and return in three days. Meanwhile, I will prove my father, and, on the third day come and hide in the field behind a rock that I will show thee, and I will come out with my artillery and a lad. When I shoot an arrow, if I say: 'Behold the arrows are this side of thee,' come, for no evil is intended you; but, if I say: 'Behold the arrows are beyond thee,' depart, for the Lord hath sent thee away." "Behold the arrows are beyond thee," to David meant flight. Arrows suggest flight, circuit, life, character. Arrow heads were formerly made of Beryl, often called "Arrow Stones." In the vision of Daniel, the body of the person who came before the Ancient of days, was like unto beryl; and we should remember that as the material body veils the character here, in the celestial world the character pervades, inswathes and covers the spiritual body, as in the body of Christ on the Mount of Transfiguration. Again, one of the most prominent stones in the breast-plate of the Jewish high priest was beryl. That breast-plate typifies Christ's righteousness, and is spoken of by Paul as the "Breast-plate of Righteousness." Man's righteousness is all from God. In the beginning, God said: "Let us make man in our image," that is, in righteousness and true holiness. Hence, Paul, in Ephesians, says: Let us put off the old man (the first Adam—the carnal), and let us put on the new man (the second Adam,) which, after God, that is, like God, is created in righteousness and true holiness. Accordingly, the spiritual putting of the text is: Righteousness and true holiness including all spiritual treasures, are beyond thee.

I. Righteousness and true holiness are beyond and out of us naturally. God's method of salvation is revealed in the gospel. For this reason, Paul was not ashamed of the gospel of Christ. Men often substitute other methods. These substitutes are usually of two classes: Ritualism and naturalism. The former rests in a form of godliness; the latter in something called nature. This naturalism divides into two branches. One denies the supernatural in toto; the other admits the operation of the supernatural in the beginning of the saving process, after which the chief part of the work is to be done by self effort, by works of righteousness. According to this method a sinner is expected to do what he can to build up a manly character and then trust death, or something else to do the rest, either just before, or, somehow, just after death. Of all false doctrines this is the most dangerous, because it wears sheep's clothing. It begins with the gospel, but ends in a false Gospel. Those who adopt this scheme descend quickly to the position of the naturalist who sees no need of supernaturalism in the way to heaven,—if there is a heaven, which he may doubt. This naturalism was the creed of the church when Methodism began to proclaim to a dead church and an infidel world the forgotten Gospel of a supernatural life, by the Holy Ghost overshadowing the soul, producing successively conviction of sin, justification and entire sanctification, and imparting the divine evidence and conviction of the same to the soul of the believer. This is God's method of salvation, as unfolded by Christ and His apostles. Christ exposed the falseness of His time and ours in the pungent question: "Do men gather grapes of thorns, or figs of thistles?" and by the declaration: "A corrupt tree bringeth forth evil fruit." Cultivate it as you may, its fruit is evil. Make the tree good, and thus its fruit will be good, was Christ's plan. The Scripture declares "The whole head is sick and the whole heart faint. From the sole of the foot even unto the head there is no soundness in it." And David exclaims: "Behold I was shapen in iniquity: and in sin did my mother conceive me." "For, though thou wash thee with nitre, and take thee much soap, yet thine iniquity is marked before me, saith the Lord God." And Job says: "If I wash myself with snow water, and make my hands never so clean, yet shalt thou plunge me in the ditch, and mine own clothes shall abhor me."

If man were in harmony with God and His law, he would be at his best, for God's law is the simplest statement of the condition of best existence. (Cries of Amen!) But man is far from his best for even the "whole creation groaneth and travaileth in pain together until now." Hence, man's fallen state is evidenced first, by the abnormal condition of nature. Earthquakes, tempests, weeds, thistles, scorpion fangs, wild beasts' venom,—all declare the same tale that man has fallen. Secondly, it is evidenced by the abnormal condition of our earthly body in sickness, pain and death,—man's own body striving to throw off a fallen lord. Thirdly, evidenced by the sinful condition of the world. There are one thousand million heathen on earth to-day, most of whom know nothing of the wisdom and power of the gospel; two hundred millions of Mohammedans, enslaved by their harems, slave traffic, and belief in iron fate; one hundred and fifty millions of Protestants, and according to the estimate of the most liberal judges, not more than one million of these know anything about the power of the gospel of Jesus Christ. ("God Help us!")

Fourth—evidenced by man's efforts to reconcile deity to himself, as seen in the sacrifice of all nations. But human religions cannot save man from the mire of sin. Even Socrates, the best of the Greeks confessed himself guilty of the worst of vices. What the depths exclaim concerning wisdom, man must admit concerning holiness: "It is not in me," and, when honest, will cry out with St. Paul: "O wretched man that I am! Who shall deliver me from the body of this death?" Yet such

> "Men homage pay to men
> Thoughtless beneath whose dreadful age they bow,
> In mutual awe profound of clay to clay,
> Of guilt to guilt; and turn their back on Thee,
> Great Sire! whom thrones celestial ceaseless sing
> To prostrate angels, an amazing scene!"

II. All spiritual and god-like character is beyond us; that is, above us as the celestial is above the earthly and the supernatural is above the natural. Christ said to Nicodemus: "Ye must be born again" to enter the Kingdom of Heaven. His lack was not in culture, not in education, for he was thoroughly trained. It was not in disobedience to church laws, for he was a ruler among his people. But he was dead spiritually and must needs become a new **creature.**

Drummond has said: "The kingdoms of this world are all hermetically sealed to each other on the lower side." A rock cannot become a tree by its own power, but the roots of the tree may take up the substance of the rock, and, by their own process of assimilation change the mineral to vegetable. A tree cannot become an ox, by its own power, but the ox may feed upon the grass and the leaves, and by its own process of digestion and assimilation change green grass and oak leaves to red ox flesh. So, natural man cannot become godlike by his own power. He must be born from above. When the disciples inquired, "Who then can be saved?" Jesus replied, "With man it is impossible, but with God, all things are possible." None who trust in anything earthly (failing to open their hearts and thus commit their case into God's hands,) can be saved, no matter what that earthly thing trusted in may be, whether health, wealth, morality, good works, benevolence self-sacrifice or pharisaical strictness. ("Amen.") Yea, they may do many mighty works, cast out devils, even give their bodies to be burned and their goods to feed the poor, and yet be lost, but when we turn to Jesus Christ by penitence and faith, the supernatural comes to us, and we are lifted up into the heavenly kingdom. "For as many as received Him, to them gave He power to become the sons of God, even to them that believe on His name."

In every church there are two classes. The first class might be called Ishmaelites. Their origin is natural; their life is "of the earth, earthly," and their hopes partake of a worldly cast. The second class might be called Isaacs. They are children of promise, born not by natural generation, but by supernatural power. Their life is spiritual. Their hopes are heavenly. Paste gems may look like true gems, hence our only safety lies in the sealing of the

W. B. GODBEY,
Perryville, Ky.

JOHN M. PIKE,
Atlanta, Ga.

WM. A. F. ARMOUR,
Oakland, Calif.

MRS. WM. A. F. ARMOUR,
Oakland, Calif.

C. N. CRITTENTON,
New York, N. Y.

P. F. BRESEE,
Los Angeles, Calif.

LUCIUS HAWKINS,
(Deceased).

O. M. BROWN,
Cleveland, Ohio.

Holy Ghost. It is easier for a camel to go through a needle's eye, than for a man to enter the Kingdom of God by his own efforts. But what is impossible with man is possible with God. No matter what you are, or where, by faith and repentance make connection with God, and God will stream his life through and through you. ("Amen!" "Glory!")

There is something, we admit, in cultivation, in development, in bringing out the inherent qualities in a thing, itself, but this is not all. There must be the incoming of a new life to bring about his regeneration. There is a truth here in regard to experimental religion which is lost sight of by many, and that is, that cultivation and refinement can only develop the inherent qualities already in the creature. ("Amen!") This is the real firing line between the world and true religion to-day. The doctrine of evolution is largely being preached. Men do not say, "I repudiate your religion; I am a skeptic, I am a deist, or a naturalist," but they preach that all that is required to bring man up to his highest condition is simply that which comes from education and culture, or the development of that which is already inherent in him. They say educate, cultivate, develop, and thus you will bring man up to his highest attainment. Well, educate, cultivate and you will bring out all that is inherent in him. And what have you? A gentleman, a scholar, a polished man, it may be. But you have the man with all the good natural qualities and all his evil ones besides. You have added nothing; you have extracted nothing. You can make a "whited sepulcher," but you cannot make a saint by this process. ("Amen!") The savages in the heart of Ethiopia do not know by any means how to be as wicked as we Americans. "Why?" you ask. Because they have not gone through the process of developing all that is in them. There are deeper crimes and far more damning sins in enlightened America to-day than in Africa. Read the records of your daily press, and compare them with all the wickedness of the savages if they do eat a man occasionally! We dispose of him if we don't eat him.

If ever a man is brought from this lower and sinful condition, he must be born from above, for "that which is born of the flesh is flesh." Cultivate it as you please, it is but flesh at last, and "that which is born of the Spirit is spirit." "Marvel not that I say unto you, ye must be born again." What is it to be born again? It is the incoming of a new, divine life at the very beginning of the change from a creature to a son of God.

Salvation by Jesus Christ is supernatural. We may pride ourselves as we will on cultivation, education and evolution, but, after all, we have an impassable gulf to bridge between the natural and the supernatural. Evolve as you please, and you are still on the under side of that gulf. But be born from above, and everlasting joy will strike you, and you will come up from the dead level of the natural, the earthly and sensual, to the high plane of the supernatural, the spiritual and the God-like. ("Amen." "Glory!")

III. "The arrows are beyond thee," in that the richest spiritual treasures are found by pressing toward the mark of the highest Scriptural perfection, and all is lost by resting in any attainment, no matter how high. Hence, Paul exclaims: "Therefore leaving the principles of the doctrine of Christ, let us go on unto perfection; not laying again the foundation of repentance from dead works and of faith toward God."

With Israel at Kadesh-barnea, it was advance or defeat and death. With Israel in Canaan, it was possession of the land or captivity in Babylon. With the human body, it is growth or death. Where growth ceases, death always begins. This is true spiritually. ("Amen.") Vegetables grow to a climax and then decline. The earth moves out to its farthest arc from the sun, then wheels back to its perihelion. All natural strength rises, matures and declines; but spiritual strength will ever increase if normal. ("Amen.") "They go from strength to strength; every one of them in Zion appeareth before God." "The path of the just is as the shining light that shineth more and more unto the perfect day." "But we all with open face beholding as in a glass the glory of the Lord, are changed into the same image, from glory to glory, even as by the Spirit of the Lord."

When a boy in Northern Michigan, I used often to visit the blast furnaces. With interest, I watched the workmen as they dumped common brown colored ore, with charcoal and a little lime into the furnace. A little later, I would go down into the blasting room. The workmen would open up a small place at the lower part of the furnace, and out flowed a red-hot liquid iron, filling all the gutters. Thus, the crude brown stone ore, through fire was brought up to a condition of wrought iron, in which shape it is of great value to mankind, whereas, in its lower state it is comparatively, if not altogether useless. I understand that this same wrought iron may be put into a furnace where the fire is heated seven times hotter than in the former case and the moulds will be filled, not with wrought iron, but with steel. In its changed, or transformed state, it is so wonderful in comparison with crude ore that it seems entirely like another substance. You can polish it until it will reflect your image. You may turn it into elastic watch-springs or the finest cambric needles. This double process of transformation clearly illustrates the divine plan of salvation. Hence, the apostle declares that we are saved by the washing of regeneration and the renewing of the Holy Ghost,—a baptism of water and a baptism of fire. The baptism of water is not simply actual water (which is a figure), but it is the washing of regeneration, or the washing by the water of the word. But there is another baptism. John says: "He shall baptize you with the Holy Ghost and with fire." Hence we often sing:

> "Refining fire go through my heart,
> Illuminate my soul,
> Scatter thy life through every part,
> And sanctify the whole."

We have now scaled two mountain ranges—Regeneration and Entire Sanctification. You ask is there no more beyond? He who stands at the base of the first range may imagine that there is nothing beyond his own vision, but let him reach its summit and peak beyond peak looms up before him. From the summit of Regeneration we behold the higher range called Entire Sanctification. From that peak, we behold mountains piled on mountains!

It is said that Jesus took three of His disciples and ascended into an exceeding high mountain and that He was transfigured before them, and His face shone as the sun, and His garments were white and glistening, whiter than any fuller could make them. Is not this a type of the ideal character for which the ardent Christian soul aspires when he sings:

> "Changed from glory unto glory,
> Till in heaven we take our place;
> Till we cast our crown before Thee,
> Lost in wonder, love and praise."

IV. "The arrows are beyond thee." In that final consummation lies beyond. This world is not our home. We seek a better country. "He builds too low who builds beneath the stars," is not only poetical, but true. Hence, Paul's exhortation: "Set your affections on things above," and Christ's command, "Lay up for yourselves treasures in heaven." This is but our training school. We ought to submit to the discipline, and endure as seeing the invisible that awaits us; for God designs making kings and priests of us to reign hereafter. We should submit to being perfected even through suffering. ("Amen.") We should labor, suffer and overcome, for these light afflictions are but for a moment, and work out for us a far more exceeding and eternal weight of glory.

A locomotive is not built to rust out in the work shop, but to thunder o'er the plain carrying its wealth of human life and blessings to thousands. So the human soul, valued above worlds, was not built to grovel here and cease to live at the close of this life, but to take on wisdom, power and spiritual capacities utterly incomprehensible.

John Angell James has well said: "Our notions are the opinions of children; our discourses are the lispings of children. The prodigious attainments of Bacon, Locke and Newton are but the productions of children, written for the instruction of others less taught than themselves." Richard Baxter has said: "The more perfect the sight, the more delightful the object. The more perfect the appetite, the sweeter the food. The more musical the ear, the more prefect the melody, and the more perfect the soul the more joyous those joys, and the more glorious that glory." "We have latent powers," says Dr. Price, "which it may be the business of eternity to evolve."

There will come a time in the distant future when the least zealous disciple will overtake the zeal of the burning Paul, and the poorest singer will sing sweeter than the sweetest archangel that burns beneath the throne!

We find water in various conditions. First, as cold water, which fairly represents the state of many in the Christian church to-day. Then we have water at boiling temperature,—a good illustration of the fervent love of the regenerate child of God. Later, under greater heat, water may be raised to steam,—dynamic force,—a fair illustration of the sanctified soul under the baptism and power of the Holy Ghost. I understand this same steam can be raised to a condition called super-heated steam. We have no boiler to-day that would endure the pressure of super-heated steam. So, "It doth not yet appear, what we shall be, but we know that when He shall appear, we shall be like Him, for we shall see Him as He is."

During the Fourteenth Century, Spanish coins had the Pillar of Hercules upon one side and the motto "Ne Plus Ultra" upon the other. The latter part of the century a faithful sailor struck out the "Ne," leaving it "Plus Ultra," (More Beyond), and boldly sailed westward into the Atlantic. After a time, the sailors mutinied and threatened to throw Columbus overboard and return to their home, but Columbus prevailed upon them to continue for a few days. On the morning of the third day, branches with fruit floated by upon the waters. Land birds appeared in the rigging, and the perfume of flowers scented the air. They shouted, "Land ahead!" So, I exclaim. There is land ahead! for I have seen the branch of healing. I have heard the songsters in the arbor. I have scented the aromatic atmosphere by the power of the Holy Ghost. So we catch glimpses of eternal glory in Prophecy and in Apocalypse. We have seen it flashed out as a city with foundations, a kingdom, mansions, a better country, an inheritance, a temple. Its accidents have flashed out—no pain, no sickness, curse, death nor tears, for God shall wipe all tears away; but life; transparent seas; palaces of light; thrones of fire; streets of gold; walls of jasper; gates of pearl; gates of praise; walls of salvation; cavalcades of victory; led by the King of Kings; songs of triumph; shoutings and hallelujahs like mighty thunderings, and like the waves of the sea; angels and archangels, seraphim and cherubim; living creatures; the Lamb as slain; throne of God! Amen! Hallelujah!

Columbus supposed he had discovered an island in front of Asia, nor did he dream that in front of him lay two mighty continents. So the light of revelation is not the morning sun reflection of a small spiritual kingdom; but the light from the front lands of a mighty continent, in excellence and splendor infinite.

> "Far from these scenes of night,
> Unbounded glories rise,
> And realms of joy and pure delight,
> Unknown to mortal eyes.
>
> Fair land! could mortal eyes
> But half thy charms explore,
> How would our spirits long to rise,
> And dwell on earth no more.
>
> No clouds those regions know,
> Realms ever bright and fair;
> For sin, the source of mortal woe,
> Can never enter there.
>
> Oh may the prospect fire
> Our hearts with ardent love,
> Till wings of faith, and strong desire
> Bear every thought above.
>
> Prepared, by grace divine,
> For thy bright courts on high,
> Lord, bid our spirits rise and join
> The chorus of the sky."

Thus, we often sing and delight to speak of heaven and loved ones gone on before, of fathers, of mothers and many other friends and kindred. But this vision is not to us, except we obtain the character necessary to admission there. Then we can cry: "All hail, heaven!" "All hail, father!" "All hail, mother!" "All hail, loved ones gone on before!" Oh! brethren, we cannot afford to miss the unclouded vision of God's face, but we should remember that God is not only love, by His loved embrace destroying the body of sin, but a consuming fire, taking vengeance on them that know Him not, and obey not the gospel of our Lord Jesus Christ.

EVENING SESSION.

7:30 P. M., C. J. Fowler, presiding. Prayer, led by several in succession. Singing, by congregation, "The Comforter has Come."

Repeating of Scripture texts, in which about forty took part in rapid succession. The quotations given were remarkably appropriate and this exercise was very evidently in the Spirit, and used of the Spirit; as evidenced by the hearty responses given and the spiritual uplift resulting. Lack of space only hinders us from quoting in full.

Singing, by congregation: "The Walls are falling Down," and "The Sword of The Lord and Gideon."

Prayer, led by Bro. J. B. Foote: "O God, our Father, let Thy clear light shine upon us; let the fire burn in every heart in Thy presence, and we ask that the light of the Holy Spirit be distinctly recognized by every soul tonight. Give us spiritual perception. We pray Thee that we may be well equipped for the battle before us, and that we may not shrink from the enemy. We trust in God to conquer the enemy, and expect him to be utterly routed. May we not flinch before the foe. Give us understanding minds, so as not to be ignorant of his devices. Give us clear heads and clean hearts. Bless and strengthen Bro. Taylor in head and heart and hand, and may Thy word, as presented, perform its work to the conversion of sinners, and the sanctification of believers, and Thine shall be all the glory, forever. Amen."

Scripture Reading, by Bro. B. S. Taylor, from Matthew 5: 43-48; Matthew 7: 6 and Matthew 6: 24-27.

Singing by Bro. and Sister Harris: "He Came for Me."

SERMON BY BRO. B. S. TAYLOR.

Text: "For I say unto you, That except your righteousness shall exceed the righteousness of the scribes and Pharisees, ye shall in no case enter into the Kingdom of heaven." Matthew 5:20.

(Introduction.) This text is found in the Sermon on the Mount. I like the Sermon on the Mount. I believe in it. I believe it is real, genuine Christianity. It is the platform of Christ. When political parties meet in convention, they proclaim their principles by a platform, and each doctrine is called a plank. And, as Jesus launched His Gospel into the world, He laid down the Sermon on the Mount as a platform of principles. There are nineteen planks in this platform. It is a kind of barb-wire fence, and I am going to pray the Lord that, as we proceed, some of you may get caught on this barb-wire fence. ("Amen!") This is not my sermon. It is the Sermon on the Mount. It is Jesus' doctrine; His teaching. It was here before I came. It will be here after I am gone. I didn't steal this sermon. I found it already here, and I say: "Lord, rub it in!" (Laughter.) If any of you don't want it rubbed in, now is the time to get out. But don't run,—you may get hit in the back! ("Amen!")

We are not here on dress-parade or show. God says that His word is sharper than a two-edged sword. It cuts you and me when we get hold of it. ("Amen!") It is a mighty poor sermon that doesn't cut me up! This is a grand sermon. Nobody has any business to go away and say they don't like this sermon. If you do, I am sorry for you. ("Amen!")

The Pharisees taught morality: Jesus preached holiness. Morality will keep you out of jail, it will take holiness to keep you out of hell. The Sermon on the Mount teaches Holiness. Let us see if we can stand on these nineteen planks, or pass these barb-wires, without some one getting caught before we get through. Nineteen strands to this wire fence around the Kingdom of God! See if we can get through every barb-wire, without getting stuck somewhere. It takes a read good Christian to get through. ("Amen!") It is the doctrine of this convention. I suppose this Assembly is going to enunciate its principles. We have already got them. ("Amen!") We cannot improve on this. We may "resolute," but this fills the bill. This convention believes in the Sermon on the Mount. ("Amen!") It is holiness of heart and life.

I am going to present the truth as the Holy Ghost shows it to me, not as Bro. Taylor applies it. I am not going to be personal in the pulpit. I don't believe in preaching sermons to hit a person or a class, but I do believe in preaching the whole truth, letting it hit where it will. ("Amen!") God blesses His word. He has blessed it for years. I am going to stand by it whether men hear, or forbear.

"And they, whether they will hear, or whether they will forbear (for they are a rebellious house) yet shall they know there hath been a prophet among them." (Ezekiel 2:5.) This was concerning the House of Israel.

Men ought to know we have spoken. We ought not to be in town a week without the devil, or a hypocrite, or a Pharisee, or a lost sinner knowing that we have struck town. ("Amen!")

The subject of the text runs through the whole Sermon on the Mount. It is a series of parallels. It is the Law, spiritualized. It does not destroy the Law, but by grace fulfils it. It is the New Testament in a nutshell: "Blessed are ye when men revile you." "Leap for joy."

We that jump for joy are obeying Christ. You have no right to criticise. He says "Jump," and I expect to jump before I get through. I shall, if I feel like it. ("Glory to God!")

This is a holiness sermon, preached to the disciples, those that were obeying Him, hanging to Him, listening to His words. He said: "Ye are the light of the world. A city that is set on a hill cannot be hid." Setting us up on a hill, they can't hide us with smoke or fog, or in any other sense. Hear the text again!

"For I say unto you, That except your righteousness shall exceed the righteousness of the scribes and Pharisees, ye shall in no case enter the kingdom of heaven." There are multitudes of people who call themselves Christians, but there are really very few Christians. There are just a few sanctified Christians. Wesley says no man has a right to be called a Christian, until cleansed from all sin. The disciples were not Christians, until they had Pentecost. "Christo" means to anoint. To be a Christian means to be anointed by the Spirit. No one can measure up to the Sermon on the Mount, without being anointed with the Holy Ghost. This passage-way seems too high, too sharp, too deep, too narrow, altogether to be filled by sinner, by philosopher, by Pharisee, by a self-righteous man, moral man or even any disciples of Jesus Christ not yet baptized by the Holy Ghost. Now who does measure up to this? Who are the holy people? Who are the real Christians? The Sermon on the Mount is a holiness sermon.

Let us go down in prayer at any point where we

do not measure up to any plank in the Sermon on the Mount. People say we are cranks. Well Brother we are standing here for primitive Christianity. ("Amen!") We are standing on these nineteen planks, and living it, which is the best light God has given to man. I have had men come and say no mortal man could live up to this standard. I didn't say they could. But get baptized with the Holy Ghost, and you can. Jesus announced the divine principle of inward heart purity. I am not ashamed of heart holiness. ("Amen!") This reference to purity in the Sermon on the Mount is not "morality." It is heart purity. No man can be pure in heart, except through the cleansing of the blood and baptism of the Holy Ghost. Morality admits you to good society on earth; Holiness admits you to heaven. Jesus says: "Love your enemies; pray for them that persecute you and hate you. So shall ye be perfect." No one is a Christian that does not love his enemies.

That is Christian perfection. That is what this convention is teaching. Jesus draws a parallel to compare his teaching with the Pharisees' doctrines. They taught some good doctrine. They were not altogether wrong. He said they professed, but didn't possess. He said they were fair outwardly, and their inward part full of deceitfulness and sin,—full of all manner of evil, like a whitewashed sepulcher! He denounces them as hypocrites and vain deceivers to be calling God "Abba! Father!" and do not the things I command you. Morality is no substitue for Holiness. Every holiness man is a moral man, but no moral man is holy, until grace sanctifies him. Jesus gathered His disciples together and taught them the nine Blesseds saying: "Blessed are the poor in spirit," and so on. He carefully draws the line of distinction between outward morality and inward purity of heart. He takes up the ten commandments: "Ye have heard that it hath been said by them of old time thou shalt not kill." But I say unto you whosoever is angry with his brother is a murderer.

This platform of nineteen planks is exactly the same as the United States or Illinois Statutes or the Common Law platform. That is only an outward standard. Men cannot read your hearts, your emotions and intentions, or your ambitions. They can only read the outside and judge you. God looketh on the heart—the motives.

Let us look at Plank No. 1. Jesus said: "Whosoever is angry with his brother shall be in danger of the judgment: and whosoever shall say to his brother, Raca! shall be in danger of the council: but whosoever shall say, Thou fool! shall be in danger of hell fire." Angry terms expressing hate in the heart. "Agree with thine adversary quickly while thou art in the way with him,"—be reconciled to your brother. All common law recognizes that we should not take life. The Bible lays it down: "That whosoever sheddeth man's blood, by man his blood shall be shed." Our common laws require the fact of the killing, merely, the "Corpus Delecti." The body of the victim is laying around somewhere; that has to be recovered. But Jesus teaches that whosoever has murder in his heart, and wishes he dared to carry out that purpose, is guilty of murder, in motive, in the sight of God. A man may lie in wait and the gun don't go off, or the victim goes by another way. That man is a murderer according to Christ, although he may never be caught or hung. The record on high has him entered as a murderer. In this plank Jesus teaches holiness of heart.

This rankling, this anger in the heart, if allowed to

grow, causes murder, insanity; and the lunatic asylum finally, if not saved and sanctified out of a man. Nothing took it out of me, except the blood of Jesus Christ. You get up with an attack of "spells," and get into a rebellion with your collar button, as many a minister does. His wife said: "It was a spell." He has some guncotton in his heart that shoots off, when some little thing comes up to jar him. At 11 o'clock he is in the pulpit. He doesn't feel just exactly right in his heart. He gets down to pray: "O, God! Forgive us for all the manifold sins which we have so grievously committed in thought, word and deed. Have mercy upon us!" And then that collar button looms up like a new moon. (Laughter.) There are many preachers that a collar button will down, that have spells of "unholy anger!"

In Mark IX Jesus met a child, who was possessed of a dumb devil, and often cast into the fire to destroy him. In those days He purged the hearts of children who had spells on the floor before they were six months old. He called it a "dumb devil," inbred anger. You can't grow out of these spells. You send your children to Sunday School, and they have spells. They get married and have spells. They grow old and have spells,—they have spells in the presence of their grandchildren! Nothing but the blood of Jesus will take them out. ("Amen!")

Plank No. 2. Again, he takes up the ninth commandment "Thou shalt not commit adultery." The Pharisees taught, there is no adultery until the act is committed. But Jesus says "Whosoever looketh on a woman to lust after her hath committed adultery with her already in his heart."

The rake that plots to seduce; the young scoundrel that seeks to destroy the fair, sweet chastity of your daughter, may not succeed in his nefarious devilment, but the lust in his heart condemns him already before Almighty God. He needs a clean heart, or He will never see God. I don't apologize for taking up this subject. There are more whore-mongers and pimps than ever before, and this country is rotten to the core with licentiousness. You say: "Tut, tut! Don't talk this way." Well, Brother, we have it in the Sermon on the Mount. Jesus talked this way. Some people get very mealy mouthed about matters of this kind, but if you pick up the newspapers you will read about specifics for nameless diseases, and you will find the same thing displayed on the bill-boards on every hand. Let the pulpit be as bold for God as these quack advertisers, for money. This plank also teaches holiness of heart and life. All other "Christianity" is a sham. "Whosoever shall put away his wife, let him give her a writing of divorcement," said the Pharisees. There is no end of that going on.

Now hear the King: Read Plank No. 3. "But I say unto you, That whosoever shall put away his wife, save for the cause of fornication, causeth her to commit adultery: and whosoever shall marry her that is divorced committeth adultery." And yet, we have divorces for desertion and drunkenness, divorces for total depravity and incompatibility of temper, and a dozen more. There would never be any divorce cases, if all differences were made the subject of prayer at the family altar. All the friction and troubles can be met and gloriously overcome around the family altar. ("Amen!") Jesus in the home cures all that. The most appalling failure in the church to-day is the decline of the family altar.

After you get sanctification in your soul, you will not buy three-fourths of the literature that is offered for sale, and as you pass along the streets you will not allow your eyes to rest upon the obscene posters on the bill boards. ("That's so!") You will not buy obscene or suggestive pictures or photographs, or sculpture, or stereopticon views to distill lust in the minds and hearts of those who gaze at them. When you are sanctified, you will cut those "gilded Venuses" out of your frames and dump them into the coal fire. Clean up your photograph albums! Cast out the Sunday papers. If you have a holy heart, you will not have a thing around you that suggests immorality or lewdness. I had five divorces in one of my charges, and I said to these parties: Don't you marry again, if you have faith and hope in Jesus and His glorious salvation. He says, if you put away your wife and marry another, you cannot enter the kingdom of heaven, (save you do it for one cause only.) ("Amen!") If you put your wife away for any other than a scriptural cause, there is nothing this side of hell for you! ("Amen!")

Fourth Plank. "Again, ye have heard that it hath been said by them of old time, Thou shalt not forswear thyself, but shalt perform unto the Lord thine oaths." "Thou shall not take the name of the Lord thy God in vain." That is God's commandment. That is a blessed commandment. And there is many a moral man that never curses or swears. They say "We are as good as you are. We are as well off as any sanctified Christian." But that is not enough! Jesus says "Let your communication be, Yea, yea; Nay, Nay: for whatsoever is more than these cometh of evil;" literally: from the devil! We have by-words and expressions coming up in our hearts until we are converted and sanctified. "Let your communication be: Yea, yea; Nay, nay." "But I say unto you, Swear not at all: neither by heaven; for that is God's throne: Nor by earth; for it is His footstool." You say "As sure as I live." You ought not to swear by your life for you cannot turn one hair white

W. E. SHEPARD,
Wilmore, Ky.

MRS. W. E. SHEPARD,
Wilmore, Ky.

J. A. DOOLEY,
Omaha, Neb.

MRS. J. A. DOOLEY,
Omaha, Neb.

O. WENDEL,
Peiro, Iowa.

A. E. BURLISON,
Chicago, Ill.

W. T. EVANS,
Concord, Ill.

I. N. McHOSE,
Chicago, Ill.

or black; you may be dead in an hour. Let us say if the Lord will, we will do this or that.

Again, Plank 5. "Ye have heard that it hath been said, An eye for an eye, and tooth for a tooth." That is, if a man puts out your eye, you have a right to put out his eye. That is not Christianity. It is the old Lex Talionis of the Romans. "But I say unto you, That ye resist not evil; but whosoever shall smite thee on thy right cheek, turn to him the other also." You say, "I don't see how I can stand this." But this is what we are taught by the Christ to do, and this is perfect love, this is the doctrine of this Assembly. This plank also teaches holiness of heart and life!

About three years ago, I went to Texas, and preached holiness, where they are turning out of the churches so many holiness people now. A great big, two-fisted fellow came up to me, grabbed me by the throat and knocked me! When I came to, I was on my knees praying for him. ("Amen!") You can't make that to order, but the Holy Ghost can do it. You don't know what you have to resist, until you are tried, then Grace is sufficient.

Can't a Christian go to law? ("No!") Why, if a man is owing you, can't you collect it by law? No. You have no business to bring suit on a claim. If you can't afford to lose it, don't trust it. If the credit system were abolished it would be a blessing. Not that you haven't a right to bring a bill to settle a matter in probate, chancery or something of that kind. If sinners try to "do you" out of anything, let them have it. But do not go around selling goods on monthly installments, and then distress those who cannot pay. God forgives only as we forgive. Somehow, the Old Testament is rather played out these days. We say we don't need it. We have got Christianity. Yes, brother, but hear this: "Thou shalt not harden thine heart, nor shut thine hand from thy poor brother; but thou shalt open thine hand wide unto him, and shalt surely lend him sufficient for his need, in that which he wanteth. Beware that there be not a thought in thy wicked heart, saying, The seventh year, the year of release, is at hand; and thine eye be evil against thy poor brother, and thou givest him nought; and he cry unto the Lord against thee, and it be sin unto thee." The Old Testament says it is sin to refuse, when your brother asks for aid. You are to do this out of pure love, not grudgingly: "because that for this thing the Lord thy God shall bless thee in all thy works, and in all that thou puttest thine hand unto." You have got to trust to Jesus that nobody shall demand of you that which he ought not. If anyone is so bad off that he ask, give it him, and turn him not away. That is the Sermon on the Mount.

We don't have to sue men at law. Of course it is necessary to do a little chancery business. The point is, the man with a corrupt and carnal heart is glad to use the courts for extortion; to oppress his victim.

Hear him again "Love your enemies, bless them that curse you, do good to them that hate you," etc. What the Pharisees taught was: "Be good to them that are good to you." But Jesus said, "Bless them that hate you." You hear men say: "I like a good hater." Jesus Christ doesn't. A man that has a "good hate" in him is going to hell. ("That is so.")

Have you this baptism of the Holy Spirit? or do you say mean things about others? Do these untoward things well up in your heart? Do you go to bed at night and dream bad things? Jesus Christ can keep nights as well as days. ("Amen!")

"If ye love them which love you, what reward have ye? do not even the publicans the same?" Let us be filled with love. Lord! make this convention a mighty baptism of love! ("Amen!") Here are some more barbed wires!

Here is 6th Plank. "Take heed that ye do not your alms before men." What a contrast!

What are they doing nowadays? Building churches, putting in stained glass memorials for Brown, Jones and Snicklefritz. I was holding a meeting out in Colorado. An old sinner had put a good deal of money into the building and had it named after him. He couldn't stand holiness preaching, and the third day I was put out. They pulled the knob off and stayed inside so that I couldn't get in. I got up on a pile of brick, and had the whole town there to hear me. ("Amen!") Well, when Sunday came, we had a deliverance. The pastor came and said to us that the church and brethren had misunderstood, and that he would have the church opened up. We went back, and fourteen fell at the altar for prayers. You never have victory without a fight! ("Amen!") The bigger the fight, the greater the victory. ("Praise God!") Well, here we are again in the track of the Pharisees! How do they get up weddings these days? Old Brown marries off his girl, and invites the Smiths, and they bring in sofa pillows and tidies and china and silverware. Then old Smith marries off his girl and invites the Browns, and they say, "Well, what did the Browns bring us? We've got to get them something just as good." And so they make out a list, and Smith goes off to town to get something for Brown's daughter, equal to what the Brown's gave their daughter. It's qiud pro quo!

Some speak of a lodge being a charitable institution. There is no charity in it. If you belong to the

Odd Fellows or the Even fellows, or to the Free Masons or the Hod Carriers,—that is not charity at all! The lodge is no better than any hose company or base-ball club, as far as charity is concerned. Jesus says "When thou makest a feast call not thy rich relations, lest they repay thee!" Do you say: "I went and called on the old woman that takes in washing, poor old Widow Brown, and I brought her a basket with turkey and cranberry sauce? I did'nt advertise it. Nobody found it out." Well Brother that pleased Jesus! We say we will go to see Mary this year; next year we will invite her to our place, and so on. Who is there here tonight made a feast Christmas or New Years or Thanksgiving as Jesus directs? "It's me and my wife, my son John and his wife; we four and no more."

Seventh Plank. Jesus says, "let not your left hand know what your right hand doeth." Where are the churches that follow that? Are not the most of them Pharisees?

Hear the Text: "Except your righteousness shall exceed the righteousness of the scribes and Pharisees, ye shall, in no case, enter the kingdom of heaven." Pray in secret. Give alms in a modest way. Sound no trumpet, rush into no newspaper, in order to have praise of men. God help us, but this is searching.

This applies to the men who pray to be seen of men; this applies to the pastor that prays to show off. ("Amen!") People that do not pray in secret, never pray in truth. People that pray in secret, God hears them. This plank teaches holiness of heart and life.

Plank No. 8. "Lay not up for yourselves treasures upon earth * * * But lay up for yourselves treasures in heaven, where neither moth nor rust doth corrupt, and where thieves do not break through nor steal." Oh, what a place for heart searching! ("Amen!") Is your money devoted to the cause of God and the salvation of souls? Is it given in such a way as to please Jesus? Are you employing every dollar that comes in honestly to the glory of God? John Wesley says: "Call me a hypocrite if I die worth a hundred pounds."

No. 9. Again, He says, "when thou fastest, thou shouldst not do as the hypocrites," for they used to daub black streaks under their eyes, so they would look as if they were all worn out by fasting. Don't go with long melancholy faces, showing off, so people will say, "O, isn't he pious?"

And how is the mercenary, money lover to pass through this barb wire? "No man can serve two masters: for either he will hate the one, and love the other; or else he will hold to the one, and despise the other."

•Plank No. 10. "Give not that which is holy unto the dogs, neither cast ye your pearls before swine, lest they trample them under their feet, and turn again and rend you. Ask and it shall be given you; seek and ye shall find; knock and it shall be opened unto you." You can have this grace! You can live up to the Sermon on the Mount. Get yourself right down on bed-rock, where Jesus can keep you. ("Amen!") Steal away to Jesus. Weep and cry: "Lord, strengthen me in the points where I fail!" May we be perfect, as our Father in heaven is perfect, in love, in holiness and in a pure heart. I haven't an enemy on earth. I don't mean that some one might not be an enemy to me, but I am not an enemy to them. ("Amen!") I am at peace in my soul. I tell you the blessing of holiness raises one up and delivers him from the snares of the devil. I would rather die than to fail to preach holiness anywhere and at any time.

O God! Send us out from this place to have a greater victory than ever before, is my prayer. You need this blessing to help you keep sweet with your family; you need it in your trials and tribulations. I want you to have the baptism of the Spirit tonight.

At the close of the sermon, twelve seekers came forward at the invitation, and about twenty-five of God's people gathered with them around the altar.

Thursday, May 9.

MORNING SESSION.

8:00 A. M., Praise and Prayer Service.

9:30 A. M., Business session, Bro. C. J. Fowler presiding.

Bro. H. F. Kletzing led with a brief prayer that the blessing of God might rest upon the meeting.

Minutes of previous session, read, corrected and approved.

The Committee on Credentials reported further names of delegates, which, on motion were added to the roll.

On motion, it was decided to devote the hour between eleven and twelve to reports from delegates on the state of the work, if the business of the Assembly would allow, and the hour between two and three P. M. was set apart for editors and agents of holiness periodicals to represent their publications.

A letter was read by the Secretary from Bro. Seth C. Rees, in which he and the brethren laboring with him declined the invitation of the Assembly to conduct their noonday meetings in the Assembly Hall.

A fraternal letter from Pres. T. C. Reade of Taylor University, Upland, Ind., was read by the Secretary, containing the greetings and prayers of Pres. Reade for God's blessing upon the Assembly.

The Committee on Permanent Methods, through its Secretary, Bro. T. H. Agnew, presented the report of this committee, the entire report being adopted with slight changes in the wording. The report as adopted is published elsewhere.

Acting on motion of the Assembly, the President appointed five persons to nominate the members of the Committee on Preparation and Permanent Work, as follows: Bro. G. W. Ridout, Sister S. B. Shaw, Bros. George Hughes, C. W. Ruth and B. S. Taylor.

Bro. J. P. Brushingham moved and the motion prevailed, that those who were out of relationship with their respective churches through no fault of theirs, be upheld in every way possible, and that their cases be referred to the committee on Permanent Methods.

Owing to press of work, Bro. Geo. A. McLaughlin tendered his resignation, as a member of the Committee on Permanent Methods, which was accepted, and Bro. C. B. Whitaker was appointed in his stead.

The Assembly then listened to reports from different sections as follows:

Bro. Isaiah Reid of Iowa: "I am glad to report an increased interest in the holiness work in my state, accompanied with great confidence and expectations. Bless the Lord.

Bro. C. W. Ruth of Indiana: "Since the first of November, it has been my privilege to labor in thirteen states, beginning with a meeting in Maine and extending to the Pacific Coast, so I have covered the field rather widely. The ministers in general are conscious that a deeper type of piety is the need of to-day. The people are hungering for holiness everywhere. I think we are coming to be better understood as holiness people. I am delighted to have had a part in the work. The Lord has been pleased to put His blessing on my labors, and I am encouraged to push forward. I am glad the Lord permitted me to unfurl the banner of holiness." ("Amen.")

Bro. C. B. Jernigan of Texas: "I am glad to be here. I am here in direct answer to prayer. I have been in this work only six years. When the Lord sanctified me, the last question was: Will you preach holiness? I said, 'Yes.' I have seen thousands of people converted and sanctified the past six years. God is honoring the work. ("Amen!") I am praying that God will melt the whole thing down, until all the holiness forces will run together. I want a Pentecostal blessing from the sky. We have fifteen or twenty bands of holiness people, each band consisting of from fifty-five to sixty members. Some of these have pastors and other places have none.

"I am going back from this place a wiser man, and I am going to get down deeper before God. It has been a benediction to my soul. I feel that we are nearer in oneness than ever before. I want that this Assembly should be permanent, and that it shall take in all the other holiness associations and bands throughout the country." (Applause.)

Bro. Jonas Brooks of Iowa:—"I bless the Lord for the secret of a happy life. I was 'born' twice in one town in old New York state, and sanctified in the bargain. ("Amen!") Soon after the blessed Lord touched my heart with holy fire, He set me going, and called me out into Christian work, and, by the grace of God, I have been at it over thirty years. I have had a good time in the service of the Lord. ("Amen!") They call me a scout, peddling holiness literature. I have visited fifteen different states, carrying my grip-sack on my back, walking thousands of miles and scattering thousands of dollars' worth of holiness literature. I have seen in this work many conversions, and many led into entire sanctification. I love the Lord with all my heart, and, by the grace of God, I am going through on this line." ("Amen!")

Bro. Daniel D. Lyon of Iowa:—"I want to say that I love the Lord. I have been connected with the Methodist Church for thirty-three years. The Lord is wonderfully helping us in Woodbine. We have an association there of perhaps fifty members. The Lord is opening the way, I believe, for the spread of Christian holiness all through the country.

"I can say personally, that I am standing on the Rock. ("Amen!") I want your prayers. I am only a layman, but I have been privileged to see quite a stirring lately among the people, on holiness lines. The Bible says that holiness shall be put upon the bridles of the horses."

Bro. H. Grentzenberg of Ohio:—"I want to let you know that we have some German holiness people. In 1867, in the spring, during a series of meetings held by Dr. and Mrs. Palmer, in Union Church, St. Louis, I touched the blood that cleansed me from all sin. ("Amen!") I felt, from that moment that the Lord wanted me to spread that knowledge of full salvation. I was then a member of an English church. A year afterwards, the Lord sent me out into the German M. E. Church, as a preacher, and I preached full salvation, entire sanctification, perfect love, and I cannot preach without bringing holiness into my sermon. I suffered a great deal of persecution at first. I was brought up before a committee of investigation on the charge of unscriptural teaching, but the Lord stood by me and I came out clear.

"I hope to go back from this Assembly like a flame of fire." ("Amen!")

Bro. S. T. Entorf of Naperville, Ill: "I am very glad to be here this morning. I love your fellowship. I feel very much at home in this place. I trust God will still more wonderfully pour His Spirit out upon us all. ("Amen!")

"I was converted in 1877, and soon after I felt called of God to go into the ministry. I want to say that soon after my conversion, I was led to think upon the personality, office, work and indwelling of the Holy Spirit. I felt that there was much more in store for me. I had heard no holiness sermons. I am sorry to say I sought seven years before finding what my heart was longing for, as I might have had it at once, had I known the way.

"Let us keep humble. May the Lord bless and fill you all." ("Amen!")

Bro. J. B. Foote of Syracuse, N. Y.:—"I was converted when thirteen years old. At twenty-two, I was entirely sanctified at a camp meeting. I had set my heart upon being a college professor, or some big man, not simply a preacher, but when the Lord asked me if I would be a missionary, I said 'yes,' and I was wonderfully and entirely sanctified.

"In 1867, I think it was, when I was Presiding Elder, we got a new camp ground. We bought the property, and they asked me to present the opening sermon. They insisted that I should. At the close of the sermon, I said: "I fling out the banner of entire sanctification for every believer, and conversion for every sinner that comes upon these grounds.' I invited all who would to enlist under that banner. Many did. Three days afterwards, one of the men said he wanted to apologize for not raising his hand on that invitation. He said he could then raise both hands. ("Amen!") He had experienced the blessing the evening before. A hundred thousand, two hundred thousand,—nobody knows how much that man has given for benevolent purposes. I am leader of a holiness meeting in Syracuse, which has a history of thirty years. ("Bless the Lord!")

"Five years ago, my health became such that I could not continue as pastor. I have been chaplain in a penitentiary for three or four years. I preach strongly, holiness of heart by the indwelling of the Holy Ghost to those men and women, and I am convinced that that kind of preaching is the best for them." ("Amen!")

Bro. T. M. McClung, of Spring Green, Wis.:—"I like to look into the faces of holiness people. I got this blessing the first year of my ministry, and I didn't have any better sense than to try to spread it around! ("Amen!") I find it makes lots of trouble. ("Hallelujah!") I made lots of mistakes, but I made it go through. This thing has had its effect on me. I haven't preached a scorching sermon for some time. I do love God, and I love his people. I believe in honoring the Holy Ghost. ("Amen!") I love to hear you talk of your experiences. I am with you heart and soul for holiness." ("Amen!")

By vote of the Assembly, the hour from 7:00 to 8:00 P. M., was set aside for the hearing of report of Committee on Deliverances.

AFTERNOON SESSION.

2:00 P. M., Bro. C. J. Fowler, presiding.

This being the appointed hour, reports on holiness literature were called for.

Bro. Hiram Ackers depicted the prevailing power of a mother's love as portrayed in his booklet entitled "Saved by Grace Through Faith."

Bro. Thomas K. Doty represented "The Christian Harvester," (8 pp., Cleveland, O.,) established in 1872. Bro. Doty called attention to the fact that the "Harvester" was the oldest holiness paper of consecutive issue, mainly made up from original contributions. He mentioned, briefly, his works: "The Two-fold Gift of the Holy Ghost," and "Lessons in Holiness."

Bro. Joseph S. Dempster, called attention briefly to his paper, "The Interior Advance," (8 pp., Washington, D. C.,) but recently established, and his two works entitled: "Bread from Heaven," and "From Romanism to Pentecost."

Bro. A. M. Hills represented "The Texas Holiness Advocate," (8 pp., Greenville, Texas,) edited by Bros. C. M. Keith and C. O. McConnell, now in its fourth year.

Bro. Hills also called attention to the Texas Holiness University at Greenville, Tex., to the head of which institution he was called, in part, through the reputation of his books: "Life and Labors of Mary A. Woodbridge," "Holiness and Power," "Pentecostal Light," "Whosoever Will, Gospel," etc. Bro. B. A. Cordell donated forty-two acres of ground, and the work of founding and equipping the University started less than two years ago. The first day's enrollment was 27, but before the close of the college year, the number was increased to 108, and there are at present over 200 students.

Bro. Hills also represented Bro. M. L. Haney's book, "Inheritance Restored," pronouncing it the best among some ninety holiness works he had read.

Bro. W. T. Hogue, Editor of "The Free Methodist," represented that paper (16 pp., Chicago, Ill.,) the official organ of the denomination, which he stated was a clean journal, adapted to the family, and for holiness throughout.

Bro. George Hughes represented "The Guide to Holiness, (magazine form, 36 pp. and upwards, New York,) established under the name of "Guide to Christian Perfection." Bro. Hughes said: "Some tell me that they have read this paper for forty years. ("Amen!") They placed me in as editor, and I have been in that work for twenty years. We are trying to run this periodical on Pentecostal lines."

Bro. J. McD. Kerr, Editor, represented "The Holiness Berean," (8 pp. Toronto,) established twelve years ago to meet the demand for something distinctive along holiness lines, in Canada. Without enumerating, Bro. Kerr stated that their press was given to the publication of books and tracts wholly along the full salvation line.

Bro. Geo. A. McLaughlin represented "The Christian Witness," (16 pp., Chicago and Boston,) one of the organs of The National Holiness Association. It was founded in 1870, originally as the "Advocate of Bible Holiness," and merged into this paper nineteen years ago, Bros. G. A. McLaughlin and C. J. Fowler being present Editors, and Bros. B. Carradine and Isaiah Reid, on its staff of writers.

Bro. Benson H. Roberts represented "The Earnest

Christian," established in 1860, and continuing until the death of his father, when he assumed the editorship. Bro. Roberts said: "It stands for true, Scriptural holiness, and God has made it a blessing to many thousands."

Prayer, led by Sister E. R. Wheaton, (Prison Evangelist.): "O God, our Father, we are glad we have One that will stick closer than a brother, One that will not turn us away, if we let everything in our lives be in harmony and subjection to His will.

Bless, we pray Thee, the delegates, the editors, the ministers and the leaders. Bless all in attendance. Help us, we pray Thee, to go forth full of the Holy Spirit's power. Keep us from all false doctrine, and lead us in the true religion of Jesus Christ.

Bless Brother and Sister Shaw, while they speak. Remember the poor prisoners in the jails and penitentiaries all over the land, and, finally, may we all meet in that other and better land, we ask it for Jesus' sake. Amen."

Singing by the congregation, "Wondrously Redeemed."

SERMON BY SISTER S. B. SHAW.

Dearly Beloved! If there be any reason in the providence of God why I should be here to-day, you know as well as I, that it is not the mere preaching of a sermon. There are too many here that can do that better than I. If there be any reason, it is that I might bring to you something of the lesson that I believe, in my inmost soul, God has been writing on my heart by the power of His blessed Spirit, during the last three months.

I invite your attention this afternoon to part of the thirty-seventh verse of the thirty-sixth Chapter of Ezekiel: "Thus saith the Lord God: I will yet for this be enquired of by the house of Israel, to do it for them."

The "this" referred to in the text was a deep, thorough, wide-spread, searching revival—a glorious revival in Israel, promised and described in the chapter from which the text is taken. I invite your attention to a study of this revival for God is an unchangeable God and if we can learn what He did for His professed church and His professed people under certain circumstances and conditions in the olden time, then we may know what He is willing and able and waiting to do for His professed church to-day. I say His professed church for I ask you to notice that Israel in this chapter and in this connection meant not Israelites indeed in whom there was no guile, but the professed people of God—those who had been known and were called by His name. Here I believe as Holiness people we have sometimes made a mistake. We have sometimes seemed to think that God cared nothing for His professed church as such, but I believe that this is a sad mistake and that the Scriptures abundantly confirm me in this. All of God's dealings with His Israel of old show that in spite of their rebellion and hardness of heart they were precious in His sight. When they were disobedient and rebellious He chastened them and if they returned not, He suffered them even to be carried away captive into the land of their enemies—yet because they were called by His name, He was jealous over them and when their enemies rejoiced in their downfall He visited them in awful vengeance because they rejoiced over the calamity of Israel. Nor did He give Israel up because of their sin—nor has He given them up for Paul plainly tells us that they are to be grafted in again and both the Old and the New Testaments promise that Israel shall be restored. So I believe God cares for His professed church to-day and as it was His will to grant a **sweeping revival** in Israel in the olden-time, so it is His will and He wants us to ask for and expect a sweeping revival to-day not outside of the church but in the church and that for this end in spite of difficulties we should labor and pray and believe.

In studying this revival promised by the prophet I call your attention first to the

Prevailing Conditions. It was a time of desolation— a time when the church seemed to have no cause to expect favor at the hands of God. For disobedience God had chastened her and because of her continued disobedience and terrible idolatry she had been carried away captive into Babylon. From the human standpoint, she had no claim on the mercy of God—no right to expect His favor or a gracious outpouring of His Spirit. Yet in spite of her unworthiness God declared that He was for her and would turn unto her and that He would take her from among the heathen and bring her unto her own land. I ask you then next to notice

God's Reason for Promising a Revival. What moved God then to make this vow? What moved God to declare He would send to them the heathen round about, and bring them back, and that He would build the waste places, and the land of Canaan should no longer be desolate of souls? Not the worthiness of the church; not the spirituality of the church, but the glory of His own name. ("Amen!") God values us for His own name's sake. This is plainly stated in the twenty-first and twenty-second verses of this same chapter. "But I had pity for mine holy name, which the house of Israel had profaned among the heathen, whither they went. Therefore say unto the house of Israel, Thus saith the Lord God;

A. C. MOREHOUSE,
New York, N. Y.

AURA SMITH,
Seymour, Ind.

JAMES WASHBURN,
Los Angeles, Cal.

JONAS BROOKS,
Des Moines, Ia.

C. W. RUTH,
Indianapolis, Ind.

MRS. C. W. RUTH,
Indianapolis, Ind.

A. L. WHITCOMB,
Evanston, Ill.

CAPT. HENRY BUNDAY,
Chicago, Ill.

I do not this for your sakes, O house of Israel but for mine holy name's sake, which ye have profaned among the heathen, whither ye went." God promised, then, a revival not because of the worthiness or the faithfulness of the church, but for the glory of His own name. Notice also in the third place that the

Source and Beginning of This Revival—was not in Israel but in the mind and purpose and plan of God. God saw not the worthiness of His people but the reproach brought upon His own name by their unworthiness—even the profaning of His own name among the heathen. In other words He saw the terrible need and declared that He had lifted up His hand in behalf of Israel and against her enemies. Notice also

The Thoroughness of This Promised Revival. This thoroughness was to be shown, first, in deep repentance and humility. "Then shall ye remember your own evil ways and your doings which were not good, and shall loathe yourselves in your own sight for your iniquities and for your abominations. (Verse 31.) Moreover this revival was to be a holiness revival. Its thoroughness was shown in the second place by the thorough cleansing of their hearts and their restoration to their own land, the land of Canaan. "For I will take you from among the heathen, and gather you out of all countries, and will bring you into your own land. Then will I sprinkle clean water upon you and ye shall be clean: from all your filthiness and from all your idols will I cleanse you. A new heart also will I give you and a new spirit will I put within you: and I will take away the stony heart out of your flesh and I will give you a heart of flesh." (Verses 24-26). Its thoroughness was also to be shown by its permanent results.

"And I will put my spirit within you, and cause you to walk in my statues, and ye shall keep my commandments, and do them. And ye shall dwell in the land that I gave to your fathers; and I will call for the corn, and will increase it, and lay no famine upon you. And I will multiply the fruit of the tree and the increase of the field, that ye shall receive no more reproach of famine among the heathen." (Verses 27-30.) And in the fifth place I ask you to notice.

The Conditions Upon Which This Revival Was Promised—as shown in the text itself. "I will yet for this be enquired of by the house of Israel to do it for them." Prayer, then, was the only condition named on the human side in the accomplishment of the will of God in the revival of Israel.

Now, beloved, in harmony with these points to which I have called your attention, I would bring to you the lesson that God has, as I said before, been deeply impressing upon my own heart, during these last few months.

We noticed first that it was a time of great desolation in Israel, and her faith had no claim to the mercy of God. She had gone away from His service. She was cold and indifferent, bowing down to false gods. By the chastening of God, all her lands were laid waste and her people were carried away captive into Babylon. We read that the prophet was to speak to the mountains of Israel, as if they alone were left to hear the word that was spoken.

O beloved, you may draw the picture as dark as you choose of the need of the professed church to-day—of her coldness, her indifference her worldliness, her idolatry. Still, the word of God gives you ground for confidence in a revival,—a sweeping revival in Israel. ("Lord help us!")

I say it was a time of desolation. God always has chastened His people, when disobedient. I presume He always will. When the church grows cold and careless and indifferent to any degree; when to any degree she loses sight of the glory of God and His salvation—her one object and cause of existence,—just to that degree God withholds His blessing from her. This was a time of famine—a famine of souls. Beloved! What is this cry we hear to-day? What is the message we read in nearly every Christian paper? It is the cry that we need a revival. This cry comes from the Episcopalians, the Presbyterians, the Baptists, the Methodists, the Congregationalists. We read this message in denominational and undenominational papers. Ministers in their conferences and their presbyteries are asking, "Why is the church with all its power and all its wealth and all its carefully laid plans and all its multiplied organization making so little real progress? Why is her membership not increased? Why is she not accomplishing greater results? Why are her members being carried away in captivity to worldliness and sin? Why are the thousands round about us unmoved? Why will they not attend our services? Why can the Christian church not accomplish in the evangelization of the world what she accomplished in the first two or three centuries of her existence? Beloved, what is all this but an acknowledgment that God has laid a famine upon us? And there is a cause! God has not laid a famine upon the church without cause! ("God help us!"). Loving her, the church, as we do, we are compelled to acknowledge to some extent—and may I not say to a large extent, she has her eyes off of one thing: God demands the salvation of those about her at every hazard, at every cost! ("Amen!")

I would not ignore the good that is being done. I would not question the faith of the weakest of God's children, nor fail to encourage every spark of grace in a human heart. I believe there never was a time when I was disposed to break the bruised reed or quench the smoking flax. But are we to be satisfied with weakness? Are we in our love for the church to overlook her worldliness, her backslidings? By no means! But on the other hand let us remember God's love for His people of old, and that God has said that He is married to the backslider. Let us remember God's infinite tenderness and patience with us and let us bear in mind that it was at such a time as this—yea, truly at a worse time than this, that God declared by His prophet, moved by the Holy Ghost, that He would send a revival. So I believe to-day that God has given to those who are taught of the Spirit a promise of glorious and sweeping revival in the professed church of God.

And that our faith may be strengthened, let us look in the right direction. Let us remember that this revival had its beginning, not in the mind of the church; not in the minds of God's people; not in the minds of those sanctified and true, but in the mind and purpose of God, Himself. Let us remember, too, that God's purpose to grant a revival was not brought about by the faithfulness and spirituality of the church but for the glory of His own name and because of the great need. God had laid a famine upon Israel but that famine did not bring glory to God! On the other hand, the heathen only profaned His name the more because of it. They did not comprehend that God was able and willing to bless and prosper His people as of old and was only chastening them for their disobedience: They only mocked and said, The God of Israel is not able to deliver them out of our hand.

So all around us to-day the name of our God is profaned and souls are hindered from yielding their hearts to Him by the spiritual famine that is upon us. They do not see that we are being punished for our sin and unbelief but they say, "There is nothing in the religion of the Bible." "Christian experience is nothing but imagination." "God has no power to save and keep from sin and build up His people." "Our lives are as good as theirs ("God help us"). Why should we seek after their God?"

O, beloved, this is the saddest part of all! For the church to suffer is only just; but through this famine the very name of our God is reproached. The name of our mighty Redeemer is profaned in all the heathen world 'round about us, because of our sin and need, and because of the famine God has placed upon us. ("God, help us!")

O, Beloved! There is too much excuse, there is too much cause, there is too much reason; when the men of the world 'round about us say, "I do not believe there is a man that lives without sin." ("Amen!") The church of the living God ought to be a living contradiction to such a statement as that! Surely the same motive which led God to make His declaration to Israel, will lead Him to declare in this day that He will send a revival. It is the glory of His own blessed name that is to be accomplished in such a revival in the church of the living God! ("Amen!") And if we ask for it and plead for it and believe for it on this ground, we shall find our faith increasing and God will answer our prayers. I remember at one time being greatly burdened for a poor, proud, wilful backslider—a man whom God had once called to preach the gospel and had used in the salvation of souls; yet he had wandered so far from God that he had gone into spiritualism and sin of almost every kind. For about two weeks a great burden of prayer was upon me; but as I saw his awful pride and rebellion and hardness of heart my faith would have utterly failed had not the Holy Spirit prompted the cry in my heart, "O Lord, for Thine own name's sake, save that precious soul." I saw the evil he was doing—the awful reproach he was bringing upon the cause of God and how God might be glorified in his salvation and with that cry—"For Thine own name's sake" I was enabled to prevail and that poor hardened, sin-bound soul was brought in deepest humility to the foot of the cross; every sin was confessed and abandoned and deliverance and salvation came. And was not God glorified in his salvation more than in his bondage and condemnation? O brother, if you cannot prevail for the salvation of souls and for a revival in any other way, plead the name of God Himself—that His name may be glorified.

We noticed also that while this revival was to begin in the mind and purpose of God, it was to bring, what every true revival always brings, heart transformation. We have been saying, "If the people will only repent, God will have mercy; if people would come to the fountain, God would send His blessing." God proposes to bring His people to repentance! I believe in the free-will of every soul that God has created; but I believe this revival is to come to Israel not because she is worthy, but because God purposes and wills it. He says, "They shall be willing in the day of my power." Sometimes you preachers say God can't do anything until people are willing. I say, if God had done nothing for me until I had of myself come to a point of voluntary and unconditional surrender, I would never have been saved. But God for His own mercy's sake wrought in my heart to bring me to heart-felt repentance and submission to Himself.

God can and will, in answer to prayer, work mightily upon human hearts and hear and answer the weakest longing of a human soul after Himself. My case is but the experience of every soul that is converted. God will not forgive you until you repent. But, if you haven't grace enough in your heart to-day to repent, you have a right to call upon God to move your soul to repentance, and God is willing to answer that prayer. ("Amen!") I know I prayed that prayer and He answered it mightily. I remember when my heart went out after God. I knew I ought to realize my lost condition. I knew I ought to come, above everything else, to seek the salvation of my soul, yet I was still cold and careless, until, from the depths of my soul there came a prayer prompted by the Holy Spirit that God would help me, and He, in some way, humbled my proud heart and brought me where I could seek Him from my very inmost soul. He answered the prayer and even the very longing of my soul. When a revival comes to Israel, the depths of hearts will be broken up and they will be moved to repentance.

God doesn't visit Israel with His chastenings, and leave her in that condition. That is not God's way. He says, after He comes and brings her back into her own land, then she shall remember her own evil ways and her doings that were not good and shall loathe herself in her own sight for her iniquities and for her abominations. Let us not say then that when the church, as a whole, repents, God will revive his work but that when, in answer to the prayer of those whom God can use, God pours out His Spirit and revives His work, the church will repent. Then repentance will come. God will see that it does come. God alone is able to break up the deep of hearts and bring them down in the very depths of humility and sorrow for their coldness and their indifference and their lack of faith and love and devotion.

As we have seen, this heart transformation included heart cleansing and restoration to Canaan. As of old, the rightful inheritance of the church is purity and prosperity. He wills that His people should dwell in the

"Land of corn and wine and oil,
With every blessing, blessed,"

and in working and praying for the revival God promises, we must be satisfied with nothing less!

A result of that promised revival that we did not particularly mention was that the waste places should be built up. O my brother, my sister, are there any waste, any desolate places in our land to-day—places that ought to be built up and occupied by the church of the living God? Have we any waste places in Chicago? Are there any churches in Chicago, where on Sunday morning there is a congregation occupying a few seats and thousands all around them going down to an eternal hell? These waste places are not only in Chicago, but all over this land we find them—the waste places, the desolate places. God says these waste places shall be builded up.

We have been limiting the power of our God! We have been looking the wrong way. God says, "I will build up the waste places." There are none so waste but that God is able to build them up again. There is no wilderness so desolate, but that, under God's blessing, it will blossom as the rose.

God help us, and send us down in confusion to-day, because of our little faith and love! ("Amen!") O, beloved, if your faith is small, is it not because your love is so small?

Some of you may have heart-aches because of loved ones out of Christ. For many years my heart has never ceased to go out for a loved one back-slidden from God. I have cried from the very depths of my soul for God to bring him back. I never think of him without praying for him and I have never given him up. I have never let go of my hold on the throne of God in his behalf. I know he is fighting against God. I know he is (so far as I can see) going farther and farther away, in the rebellion of his soul, from the God that once saved him. But I have only pled for him the more earnestly, "For Thine own mercy's sake! For Thine own name's sake," spare that blood-bought soul! I cannot give him up! I will never, never give him up so long as God in His mercy does not utterly withdraw the Spirit's aid in intercession. I don't expect to give him up, until God brings him back, —a broken and a contrite soul, to Jesus Christ. What has given me that faith? It is the love back of it! We have given up people too easily. We have given up pastors, when they fought holiness. We have given up brothers and sisters here and there. Why? Because we didn't have faith; because we didn't love them as we should, had we gone down in humility at the feet of Jesus, and cried to God as Christ did when He said: "Father forgive them, for they know not what they do." But some of you say that those cold-hearted men knew what they were doing, and that they had had the light, but they drove in the nails, and crucified him. In a sense they did; and if Jesus could say what he did in behalf of that mob, the Holy Spirit can come to our heart and say it in behalf of such as those we have mentioned that seem to fight against the truth. Then before you cease to pray for any soul be sure that that soul is worse than the members of that cruel mob that rejected the Savior and cried out, "Crucify him, crucify him," for doubtless many of them were afterward converted in answer to the prayer of Jesus.

But there is a condition. I said that this revival started in the mind and purpose of God. Glory to God! I believe God speaks, some times, to the hearts of the Children of Israel, as He spoke in olden times to the prophets. I believe He has been telling his children up and down our land in places of prayer that He will build up the waste places and send a revival to the church; but he says: "I will yet for this be inquired of by the house of Israel, to do it for them." The very first thing God does in bringing about a revival is to grant an especial spirit of intercession for such a revival to souls that are moved by the burning love of Jesus. I said to you, beloved, I believed that God had promised it. I can't tell you how God has moved my soul the last few months. I have been just a little worker in His vineyard for a number of years. I love the holiness movement, and holiness people. I want to live and die with them, but while I am praying for the holiness work and the holiness people I am praying for more than that. For months an agony of prayer has taken possession of my inmost being. I have been praying for this assembly but not for this alone. I have been praying for the denomination of which I am a member but not for that alone. I am praying for a revival in Israel a revival like that described in our lesson that shall begin in the church and sweep through the church and reach out to the uttermost parts of the earth.

God has brought us together for a purpose. We are here in obedience to the calling of God and the leading of His Spirit. We are here, many of us at least, because our hearts have been led out in prayer for a mighty out-pouring of the Holy Spirit,—not for our own sakes but that we might be better fitted to be used of God in bringing about such a revival as we have been talking about, and prayer is the condition God has given. If God has sanctified our hearts, it is not because He wanted to do us some special favor. Jesus said that it was written that His Father's house should be called a house of prayer. If our hearts have been made temples of the Holy Ghost it is that the Holy Ghost might find in us a place to pray,—might find in us instruments that He might use in interceding with groanings that cannot be uttered for the accomplishment of God's will and purpose in the salvation of others.

God will hold us responsible for this opportunity! The very heart of our God is going to be grieved if we do not get down lower before Him than we have ever been in the past! Great responsibility rests upon us as holiness workers—as those that know the power of the blood of Jesus and the baptism of the Holy Ghost, and God will require much at our hands! God wants to use the holiness movement and to use it gloriously in bringing about a revival that shall take away the reproach that is upon the church and bring eternal glory to our Redeemer. O beloved! God commands us to go down! down!! down!!! in the unsearchable love of God, until God shall lift us up and move us out and carry a revival of pure and undefiled religion all over this land of ours. ("Amen!") May God help us for His name's sake!

EXHORTATION BY BRO. S. B. SHAW.

I want everyone to look at that Prayer Roll yonder. Somebody has faith in our prayers. Thousands of people are looking in the direction of this Assembly. We are here to consider the most important subject this side of heaven. There is nothing on earth better than holiness; there is nothing better in heaven. If there was ever a time of need in the holiness movement, it is now; and we ought to be burdened for it in the very travail of our souls. God is laying this conviction and burden on many hearts. ("Amen!") This travail of soul is becoming common among holiness people, and there is a conviction throughout the land that we are on the eve of the greatest revival of holiness the world has ever known. ("Amen!") I believe it is the plan and purpose of God to use holiness people with all their faults, failures and weaknesses, because they are the best representatives He has. ("Amen!") God wants to bring them together as He brought His disciples together on the day of Pentecost, until they are all of one mind, one heart, and one accord, in one place. ("Amen!") Then He will open the windows of heaven and send down another Pentecost. One of our brothers has a book "Back to Pentecost." That is what we want. I am a candidate for the altar. I believe that, instead of going on, we need to go back, back to Pentecost. ("Amen!") I believe we can in answer to prevailing prayer, have a repetition of the power they had at Pentecost. Before God delivered the people from Egyptian bondage, they had been praying and crying to God for deliverance. They had been hoping to get back to the Promised Land, and in their affliction they cried with an unearthly cry and unearthly groanings. God raised up a man to lead them whose faith enabled them to withstand the Egyptian army, and the combined forces of earth and hell. I tell you, friends, the holiness movement lacks leadership. There is more for me. I am going to the altar. If we get near enough to God we shall agree touching the vital points of this work. We need to get where God can indicate His own chosen leaders. Do you know, no man could interfere with Moses without being smitten of God? When they did, we know how God afflicted them. With all this talk about splits and divisions in the church and among holiness people, we never were in a better condition for a revival in Israel.

See how God revealed Himself and manifested Himself not only to Moses but to the elders of Israel, and all the elders of Israel saw the will of God in the choice of that man as their great leader. When they got to the Red Sea, they found mountains on either side, the Egyptian army behind them and the Red Sea before them; and their faith wavered. They doubted God's ability or willingness to lead them through the difficulty. They found fault with Moses and reproached him and talked out their doubts and unbelief. Was Moses discouraged? No!—but in agony of spirit he fell on his face and cried to God all night. He never got off his face until God said to him: "Why criest thou to me?" Some of us speak before we get through crying to God. ("That is so.") The trouble is, we don't stay on our face long enough, or until we hear from God. There is some room for that here. We need to get down with one mind, one heart and one accord, before God; and wait until we get an answer. ("Amen!") We need to get on our faces and stay there until we hear from God. O, that God would bring us down in order that He might bring us up! ("Amen!")

"And the Lord said unto Moses, Wherefore criest thou unto me? speak unto the children of Israel, that they go forward." You know the result. There was no power that could stand before the Israelites. No power can stand before the church of God, when He says: "Go forward." When we get low enough before Him, and close enough to Him with our cries and prayers, He will tell us to go forward. ("Amen!") How many have faith in Him and bless Him for it? How many say: "I am going down! down!! down!!!" until God answers, 'It is enough.' After God sent His angel to Daniel, he cried, with weeping, unto the Lord for the fulfillment of the covenant revealed to him. He saw that the time had arrived when God was to bring his people out of bondage. He cried, wept and prayed for not only one week, but three weeks. He afflicted himself for twenty-one days. He confessed the weakness of his people and their iniquity, bewailing their sins with deep humility of spirit, until God sent an angel to tell him his prayer was heard. Has God sent us an angel to tell us that our prayers are heard?

The Lord wants us to go down on our faces and cry with an unearthly cry until His work shall go through. He wants to give a revival of pure and undefiled religion that shall spread all over this land. ("Amen!")

At the close of this exhortation, all joined in singing "When Israel out of Bondage Came" and a large portion of the congregation fell on their knees. Seekers of pardon and purity wept and prayed for themselves andl in answer to the united cry of many hearts, heaven opened and the glory of God was revealed. Then followed a blessed season of joyous testimony and rousing exhortations given in the power of the Holy Ghost.

EVENING SESSION.

7:00 P. M., President C. J. Fowler in the chair.

Sisters Fannie Ross and M. E. Palmer of Lincoln, Neb., (en route to the Afro-American Holiness Convention at Pittsburg, Pa.,) visited the Assembly, and Sister Ross made a brief address. Bro. S. B. Shaw moved that the Assembly send greetings to the Afro-American Convention in session. The motion was carried unanimously and greetings sent.

Singing by the congregation, "Am I a Soldier of the Cross?"

Prayer, led by Bro. Fowler.

TESTIMONIES.

Bro. James Harris:—"I praise God for the wonderful blessing He is showering down in my soul. I thank God that His full salvation satisfies."

A Sister: "The fire is burning on the altar of my heart. The song of my heart is: 'Nearer my God to Thee.'"

Sister Aura Smith: "I praise the Lord for this holiness experience. The Lord led me into it 15 years ago. I found it was just the thing for the home girl and just the thing for the school girl. The Lord has given me a chance to test it under a variety of circumstances. It fits everything."

A Delegate: "I praise the Lord, not only for a negative salvation that saves from sin, but a positive salvation that fills my heart with love for God and love for man."

A Delegate: "I find the days precious and the way clear and glorious as I walk with God."

Bro. Brushingham: "I said when the Assembly came to us that this church and pastor would not be the same after having this privilege. We will not be the same, but Christ will be the same and more too, as far as we are concerned. I thank God for that 'more too' in Jesus Christ. Remember us here, one one of the worst streets in Christendom, right down in the midst of iniquity. Pray for us here."

Song, by Brother and Sister Harris: "Clinging and Resting."

Bro. H. Hunt: "I was converted in 1887, during the great Murphy campaign, but it was only five years ago this month, in Western Ave. Church that I experienced the blessing of entire sanctification. It was through the preaching of Bro. Carradine that I first had this definitely placed before me, and I found that there was a remedy for this inbred sin. It has brought peace and comfort to my soul." ("Amen!")

The report of the Committee on Deliverances was read, accepted, and ordered taken up for discussion immediately after the opening exercises on Friday morning.

8:00 P. M., Bro. C. J. Fowler presiding.

Singing, by Bro. and Sister Harris: "They Tell Us of a City Far Up in the Sky," and " I Want to be There, don't You?"

SERMON BY BRO. C. W. RUTH.

Text: "There is therefore now no condemnation to them which are in Christ Jesus, who walk not after the flesh, but after the Spirit. For the law of the Spirit of life in Christ Jesus hath made me free from the law of sin and death. For what the law could not do, in that it was weak through the flesh, God, sending His own Son in the likeness of sinful flesh and for sin, condemned sin in the flesh." (Rom. 8:1-3.)

Sin and condemnation are inseparable. Whoever commits sin is, necessarily, under condemnation. The soul may not be conscious of that fact all the while, but the truth remains. We all have sinned; hence, all, in our unrenewed condition, are under condemnation.

Some have supposed that condemnation would set in with the judgment; that is, if they come down to death and judgment overtake them in their sinfulness, then condemnation would set in. We read in the third chapter and eighteenth verse of St. John: "He that believeth on Him is not condemned: but he that believeth not is condemned already." Every individual under the sound of my voice is either saved now, or lost now; a child of God now, or a child of the devil now; pardoned and delivered from guilt now, or under condemnation and the sentence

G. A. McLAUGHLIN,
Evanston, Ill.

MRS. G. A. McLAUGHLIN,
Evanston, Ill.

COL. F. E. PECK,
Dutton, Mich.

MRS. COL. F. E. PECK,
Dutton, Mich.

C. J. FOWLER,
Haverhill, Mass.

E. F. WALKER,
Greencastle, Ind.

T. B. ARNOLD,
Chicago, Ill.

R. M. GUY,
Meridian, Miss.

of death now. Death can only make this final. I mean to say that all death has to do with our eternal destiny is that of making it final in our state and relationship toward God. If any man here,—yea, if any say they have not sinned, they make God a liar. God says "All have sinned and come short of the glory of God." Hence, I insist that all, by nature, in our unrenewed state, are under condemnation. But the text makes mention of a relationship where there is freedom from condemnation. It is found in that beautifully chosen and select phrase of the Apostle: "In Christ Jesus." And that means more than assenting to the truth. That means more than subscribing to some credal statement. That means more than simple observance of rituals and ceremonies. It means a personal contact, a vital union with Christ, even as the branch is united to the vine. The question arises: How may I know I am in Christ Jesus? I shall give a proof text: (2 Cor. 5: 17) "Therefore if any man be in Christ, he is a new creature: old things are passed away; behold, all things are become new." Men are inclined to modify that statement. They will admit that persons coming from the lower walks of life should experience a change of this nature, but you people who are morally good, all you need to do is to join the church, pay your dues, do a little better and not expect much change. But I insist that you should know when this radical transformation takes place, by the grace of God. Any man, whether he be a big or little sinner (if there be a distinction), if he be in Christ, he should know when such a radical change was wrought. "Old things are passed away; behold, all things are become new." Glory to God! I contend that the change is so distinct and radical that the soul will come to the consciousness of the fact. You will know when that takes place. ("Amen!")

I am glad of a distinct experience along this line. A little girl applied to a church, where it was not counted the proper thing for children to unite and be taken into church fellowship and membership. They questioned the little thing, because she was of such a tender age. They said: "Why do you want to join the church?" She said: "Because I am a Christian." "How do you know you are a Christian?" "Because I am changed. My heart has been changed." But they said: "How do you know your heart has been changed?" That was pretty close cross-questioning for a child. "Well," she said, "If my heart wasn't changed, the world was; there was something new; there was something changed." ("Amen!") It was even so in my life, blessed be God! If any man be in Christ, this change has taken place. This is not simply reformation. It is something far beyond that. You can see the importance of maintaining this relation, in John 15: 6: where the Saviour says: "If a man abide not in me, he is cast forth as a branch, and is withered; and men gather them and cast them into the fire, and they are burned." Some one will say: "Yes, I knew of that change, of that transformation, many years ago." Let us bring it to the present tense. Do you still maintain that union at this hour of the ninth day of May, 1901? We read (?) in 1 John, 3: 6, "Whosoever abideth in Him sinneth every day in thought, word and deed" ("No, sir! No, sir!")—Excuse me, that is according to the unauthorized version. (Laughter). The correct reading is: "Whosoever abideth in Him sinneth not." ("Amen!") Do you see the connection? "There is therefore now no condemnation to them that are in Christ," being saved from sin. Blessed be God! ("Amen!")

The man who contends and insists that he is a Christian and yet is sinning every day in thought, word and deed, as we frequently hear it stated and openly confessed, — is either woefully deceived, or an abominable hypocrite. No man can be a Christian and a sinner at the same time. ("Amen!") A sinner is one who sins, be he in the church or out of the church. ("Amen!") Whosoever is born of God does not commit sin. He that committeth sin is of the devil. "For this purpose the Son of God was manifested, that He might destroy the works of the devil." "Thou shalt call His name Jesus, for He shall save his people from their sins."

Friends, if a man is not saved from sin, from what is he saved? ("Sure enough!") What is his religion good for? He could do that without a spark of religion! The truth is, the lowest plane on which a man can be saved at all, is deliverance from all outer sin. ("Yes. That is right!") We are frequently misunderstood and misrepresented here. It is urged that these holiness people are preaching sanctification in order to have people cease from sinning. Good old-fashioned repentance will bring you to the abandonment of sin. A repentance that does not carry with it the abandonment of sin is a farce, a delusion and a humbug. You may sign your name to a creed, join a meeting house, train with the gang, and call it religion, but you don't know the a, b, c's of religion, unless you know what it is to forsake sin.

The emphatic word in the text is the word "Therefore." "There is therefore now no condemnation." You see the text is the summing up. It is the conclusion of a line of thought that has gone before. The question naturally presents itself: What are the premises? How does he arrive at this conclusion?—"There is therefore now no condemnation." This couples the text to the preceding chapter. In viewing the preceding chapters we may better understand the line of thought. The first.

chapter, reveals God's hatred of and attitude towards sin. Take the second chapter, and you find it says sin is "inexcusable." You see God allows no excuse for sin. The third chapter teaches the universality of sin. The fourth chapter teaches justification by faith, showing how Abraham was justified and saved through faith. Faith was accounted to him for righteousness. We have the summing up of the fourth chapter in the first verse of the next chapter: "Therefore being justified by faith, we have peace with God through our Lord Jesus Christ." The fifth chapter shows the result of the disobedience of Adam and Eve in the Garden of Eden, the entailment of sin and death upon the race through the disobedience of Adam. In the concluding verse of this chapter He speaks of abounding grace. In the sixth chapter, as though he would anticipate the repression theory, he says: "What shall we say then? Shall we continue in sin?" Is that the idea of the abounding grace of God? "God forbid. How shall we that are dead to sin live any longer therein?"

He calls attention to God's method of dealing with inbred sin in the sixth verse: "Knowng this that our old man is crucified with him, that the body of sin might be destroyed," not suppressed, "that henceforth we should not serve sin." In the twenty-second verse, he sums up by saying: "But now being made free from sin, and become servants to God, ye have your fruit unto holiness, and the end everlasting life." Did you ever discover that passage in your Bible? I admit that my Bible is one of those holiness Bibles! ("Amen!") It is so announced on the outside of my Bible. This verse I have quoted says "now," not in death or in purgatory, but "now being made free from sin." ("Amen!")

Then we come to the seventh chapter, which precedes

the verses of the text. I do not propose to interpret this chapter for everyone here, but I do propose to tell you what I believe about that chapter—the seventh of Romans. God never intended that you and I should live in the seventh chapter of Romans. ("Amen!") I believe if you would take your testament and turn to that chapter, you would find the key to the chapter in the first verse: "Know ye not, brethren, (for I speak to them that know the law)," ("That's it!") "How that the law hath dominion over a man as long as he liveth. For the woman which hath an husband is bound by the law to her husband so long as he liveth: but if the husband be dead, she is loosed from the law of her husband." "Wherefore, my brethren, ye also are become dead to the law by the body of Christ; that ye should be married to another." What is the import of this? What is the thought? You will note that he is speaking of law. He calls attention to the power of the law, and, second, to the duration of the law. Then he preaches the second blessing. He says they are to be married to another. Marriage cannot be construed to symbolize the new birth. There must be birth before matrimony ensues. Some insist that they were married at the same time they were born. It was not so in my case. ("Amen!"—Laughter.) This is certainly just as true in the spiritual domain as in the natural. There must be a spiritual being,—a spiritual existence, before this text could apply.

Then he proceeds, beginning with the ninth verse, to give his experience in connection with the law. Here, we have a testimony that has become so common. People rise and say: "Brethren and sisters, I am like good old Paul." I never hear that but what I am startled. (Laughter.) I turn to hear what it is he has done. I listen with all the ears I have, only to hear him say: "I am like good old Paul, 'for the good that I would do, I do not: but the evil which I would not, that I do. O wretched man that I am! who shall deliver me from the body of this death?'" I say, "Is that the best good old Paul had?" I confess I had a more exalted opinion of good old Paul, Paul used that language.

"For that which I do I allow not: for what I would, that do I not; but what I hate, that do I. If then I do that which I would not, I consent unto the law that it is good."

Well, Paul! What is the difficulty? The difficulty apparently is not in the law. Then what is the difficulty?

"For the good that I would, I do not: but the evil which I would not, that I do."

Is that the best thing we can promise to men to-day?

In the next verse he tells us: "It is no more I that do it, but sin that dwelleth in me." What sin dwelleth in him? You see he recognizes the presence of indwelling sin. The sin committed may be repented of and forgiven, but He cannot ask us to repent for being born into this world with sinful tendencies, or what is termed in the Scriptures as the "old man," "the law of sin," "the flesh," spoken of as original sin, as inbred sin, the Adamic nature, etc. I submit that God cannot forgive inbred sin. I cannot repent for something that I have not done. ("Amen!") Here is something, not a result of your volition,—something born within you. We do declare, however, and love to publish to the world that there is efficacy and power in the blood of Jesus to wash and cleanse that out of your heart. Glory be to God! ("Amen!") Said a man, in a meeting I was holding some time ago, "When God forgave my sins, He forgave all of them. God didn't do any half-way work." That is true: He will forgive every sin you ever committed.

Regeneration and justification consist of four complete works within themselves, and is no half-way work.

1. The pardon of every sin you ever committed.
2. It comprehends the washing of regeneration, cleansing from the acquired pollution resultant from your sin.
3. The quickening,—the impartation of new life.
4. The adoption into the family of God, and receiving the Spirit of adoption, "whereby we cry, Abba, Father."

These four things take place when a soul is converted to God. When God converted you He did a complete work. One reason He did not sanctify us at conversion is that we had not realized our need of it. But we had not gone long before we became painfully conscious of this thing, the sin that dwelt in us. It matters not what your theory is, what your persuasion or what your denomination, after you were soundly converted, you never went any great length of time, until you came across something within you that gave you trouble. The manifestations of inbred sin are so varied, it is hard to locate them. With some, it is ill-temper; with some fear, or pride; with others jealousy; with others "prone to wander, Lord I feel it." All of these are manifestations of indwelling sin, and you have had some of these manifestations after you were converted. I needed no holiness teacher to tell me that I needed another experience after I was converted. I had such a "sky-blue" conversion that Satan could not make me doubt that I was converted through and through. ("Amen!") Glory! I was a new creature! But I don't need to tell you that after I was converted, that uprising, man-fearing spirit still belonged to me; and that there was something in my heart I knew ought not to be there. I was distressed. I wept bitterly. I asked God to help me. I didn't know what it was, but I knew it was something contrary to my new life. This is the thing Paul speaks of. He says: "Now if I do that I would not, it is no more I that do it, but sin that dwelleth in me." There is then such a thing as sin dwelling in you. He says: The law is all right. I delight in the law, but there is something in me that is not subject to the law. He says: "I see another law in my members warring against the law of my mind, and bringing me into captivity to the law of sin which is in my members." But is there no deliverance? Hear him: "I thank God, through Jesus Christ our Lord." Here is the answer: It is deliverance in Christ.

Then look at the eighth chapter and second verse: "For the law of the Spirit of life in Christ Jesus hath made me free"—free from what? From condemnation? ("No, sir!") Free from the law of sin and death. Where? "In my members." What did this "law of sin" do? It led him captive; hence he was coming under condemnation. But "what the law could not do, God sent His Son to do." Beginning with the ninth verse He gives his experience in connection with the law, and noting the weakness of the law then tells us what the law failed to accomplish God sent his Son to do.

What is the difficulty with all law? The law may prohibit and prevent a crime in the overt act. But the law cannot eradicate the tendency to commit the crime. There was the trouble with the old law. In Hebrews 7: 11, we read: "If therefore perfection were by the Levitical priesthood (for under it the people received the law,) what further need was there that another priest should rise after the order of Melchisedec, and not be called after the order of Aaron?" And, again, in the nineteenth verse: "For the law made nothing perfect: but the bringing in of a better hope did: by the which we draw nigh unto God." "Wherefore He is able to save them to the uttermost that come unto God by Him, seeing He ever liveth to make intercession for them."

The law, in itself, had no power to eradicate or eliminate the sin that dwelt within. Certainly men were forgiven and had pardon, the remission of sins under the former covenant. If this remission of sin is the best that comes under the new dispensation, what advantage have we over the former dispensation? The Old Testament stands for justification. The text says, in the third verse: "For what the law could not do, in that it was weak through the flesh, God, sending His own Son in the likeness of sinful flesh and for sin condemned sin in the flesh."

The law, itself, does not carry with it the power to eradicate inbred sin.

Some, looking through the types and shadows by faith, saw the Lamb that was slain from the foundation of the world. They were saved on credit, looking forward to this realization which we have in reality to-day,—the cleansing from all sin.

Brethren, what the law could not do, in that it was weak, God sent His Son to do. God sent His Son to eradicate inbred sin. "For the law of the Spirit of life in Christ Jesus hath made me free from the law of sin and death."

Since he declares he has been made "free," I will ask Paul to take the witness stand again and tell us how it is now. (Romans 8: 37:) "Nay, in all these things, we are more than conquerors, through Him that loved us." There is no more of his doing the things he ought not to, making crooked paths, and wanting prayers that he might continue. If I were living in the seventh chapter of Romans, I would move over into the eighth. ("Amen!")

I was casting about for an illustration of being "more than conqueror" and this occurred to me in the life of

David. He had been tending his father's sheep, and went over where the battle was going on, and there was a certain giant holding the Israelites at bay, and defying them, and they all seemed frightened to death about the Honorable Mr. Goliath! So David made a challenge to Goliath, and Goliath said: "Come to me, and I will give thy flesh unto the fowls of the air and the beasts of the field." Goliath came swinging his spear and making his boast. I fancy that I can almost see him, for I have met some of his kins-folk. David didn't stop to argue the science or the philosophy of the matter. You will remember as he passed the brook with his grip (knapsack or haversack, the thing he carried) he stooped and gathered five smooth stones, and slips down to where Goliath is, swings back his sling, gets in a center shot, and Mr. Goliath turns up his toes. David had enough ammunition left to kill four more like him! He was "more than conqueror." ("Amen!") He didn't bring him down simply with his last shot. That is the thought in this experience. It places you where you don't get through "by the skin of your teeth," but you have grace enough and some to spare.

When God sanctified you, your up and down experience came to an end.

I have confidence in the brethren here in this Assembly. I want to tell you what they are saying. They are saying that there is such a thing as the second blessing; that after our sins are forgiven, there is left in the heart, original sin. Then they come again and ask God to take that out of the heart, and the blood of Jesus does that. I want to ask if there are any witnesses here to that fact.

Bro. Fowler: "I can say that He did it for me."

Do you mean to say that there is such a thing as a second experience, after your sins are pardoned?

Bro. Fowler: "Yes."

And that this inbred sin can be suppressed and held down?

Bro. Fowler: "No, sir!" Several voices: "No!"

Do you mean to say that this inbred sin can be cleansed out of the heart?

Bro. Fowler: "Yes, sir."

I would like to know if there are any witnesses to this fact.

Bro. Fowler: "Here is one. God did that for me."

Do you mean to tell this congregation that, after you were converted, you grew into this?

Bro. Fowler: "No, sir."

Do you mean to say that after your sins were forgiven and God had accepted you, you were still conscious of inbred sin in your heart?

Bro. Fowler: "Yes, sir."

And you asked him to cleanse that out of your heart, and He actually did that?

Bro. Fowler: "Yes, sir."

Then you got this second experience, as a second definite work in your heart?

Bro. Fowler: "Yes, sir."

We have plenty of witnesses here. I want all who have that experience to raise their hands. (Scores if not hundreds of hands went up in response).

After the sermon, the invitation was given, and fifteen seekers came forward, and a large number gathered with them about the altar in prayer and supplication.

Friday, May 10.

MORNING SESSION.

8:00 A. M., People's Meeting led by Bro. E. F. Walker.

9:30 A. M., The President, C. J. Fowler in the chair.

Prayer led by Bro. A. Sergeant: "O, Lord, we are here as Thy children. We are here in the interest of Thy cause. We are here as co-workers with Thee in the building of the Kingdom of Thy Son here in this present world, and we pray that Thou wilt give us a double portion of Thy Spirit. Give us wisdom that comes from heaven. Take control of every heart. May everything that is said and done, be with an eye single to Thy glory.

We pray Thee that Thy blessing may rest upon every member of this Assembly. May our hearts be united and knit together in the bonds of perfect love. May nothing come in by any way or means to distract, or take our minds and hearts away from Thee.

God bless this meeting. God bless the President of this Assembly. Give him wisdom as from above, that he may do everything to Thy glory; and Thy name shall have the praise forever. Amen."

Following the order of the day, the Report of the Committee on Deliverances, was taken up, and was adopted by a unanimous standing vote. This report will be found under the heading, "Holiness Assembly General Address."

The President, by order of the Assembly, appointed the following Committee on the Publication of the Proceedings of the Assembly:

Bro. S. B. Shaw, Chairman.
Sister Sarah A. Cooke, Chicago, Ill.
Sister Kent White, Denver, Colo.
Sister Charlotte Dudman, Chicago, Ill.
Sister M. J. Harris, Evanston, Ill.
Sister Hattie Livingston, Des Moines, Ia.
Sister Etta E. Shaw, Chicago, Ill.

On motion, the Chair was authorized to appoint a committee of three to have the report of the Committee on Deliverances published in pamphlet form in time for distribution on Saturday, if possible, the expense of publishing same to be paid out of the General Assembly Fund.

The Chair appointed the following persons as such committee: Bros. Geo. A. McLaughlin, S. B. Shaw and A. L. Whitcomb.

Bro. E. F. Walker moved, and the motion prevailed, that the Assembly, by a rising vote, show its appreciation for the great sacrifice and labors of Bro. George Hughes and Bro. and Sister S. B. Shaw by which the Assembly was made possible and successful.

The Committee on Permanent Methods made its second report, which was accepted by the Assembly, and final action deferred, while a portion of the report went back to the committee for further revision. At this juncture, Bro. Fowler left for the East, and Bro. E. F. Walker took the chair. The Committee to nominate the members of a "Committee on Preparation," as provided for in the Report on Permanent Methods, made the following nominations: Bros. C. J. Fowler, Massachusetts, J. McD. Kerr, Canada, A. M. Hills, Texas, P. F. Bresee, California, H. C. Morrison, Kentucky, Geo. M. Morse of Connecticut, and A. L. Whitcomb, Illinois.

A set of resolutions was presented to the Assembly by Bro. B. S. Taylor, on the subject of Prohibition, and referred to the Committee on Permanent Methods.

An expression of fraternal sympathy from Bro. B. R. Jones, a General Superintendent of the Free Methodist Church was received and read by Bro. W. T. Hogue.

A letter of greeting from Bro. J. B. Atkins of Ireland was read and Bro. Geo. Hughes led the Assembly in prayer in behalf of this brother and of Ireland. On motion, Bro. Hughes was authorized to reply to said letter on behalf of the Assembly.

The Assembly thereupon listened to reports from different sections, as follows:

Sister M. J. Harris of Evanston, Ill.: "I truly praise the Lord for the privilege of being in this Assembly and for the blessings which the Lord has been pouring on my heart. We have had a hard winter's work, and I was tired when I came here, but the Lord is resting me as I go along. This has been the most wonderful winter, with us, in all our lives. At a series of meetings at Wabash, Ind., the Lord permitted us to see more than 700 souls either reclaimed or gloriously sanctified. ("Praise the Lord!") I find the people just as hungry as ever, and when the truth is presented rightly, they are ready to receive it. I am glad that the doors are not closed against us, as we walk in the light and present the doctrine as it ought to be. ("Amen!") We do not find it so. We have three calls where we can fill one. At the last conference we attended, we received enough calls to occupy our time for three years.

My soul is on the wing for Christ, and I am expecting this to be our greatest summer, as last winter was our greatest winter. I praise God for the advancement we are making in the holiness cause." ("Amen!")

Bro. J. M. Dustman of Urbana, Ind.:—"I heartily appreciate your kindness in permitting me to have a place in your proceedings. The Lord is wonderfully blessing the work in my part of the country. We have five or six camp meetings in the Northern District of Indiana, which bring five or six hundred souls a year to Christ for pardon and entire sanctification. We ask your prayers.

Benediction, pronounced by Bro. A. McLean.

AFTERNOON SESSION.

2:00 P. M., Bro. E. F. Walker, presiding.

After a word of prayer by Bro. Hiram Ackers, the Assembly proceeded with a continuation of presentations of holiness literature and schools as follows:

Bro. B. S. Taylor came forward as proxy for Bro. H. C. Morrison, representing "The Pentecostal Herald" (16 pp., Louisville, Ky.,)—Assistant Editor, Bro. H. B. Cockrill. Bro. Taylor stated, that the paper was always filled with original holiness articles, and had a staff of editorial writers. He also called attention to "The Pestecost Century," having reached No. 4 of Vol. 1, and spoke of the efforts through its columns in behalf of Cuba. Bro. Taylor mentioned also the fact that this firm had issued a number of books and tracts along holiness lines.

Bro. J. S. McGeary of Greenville, Ill., spoke briefly of the College of the Free Methodist Church located at Greenville, Ill., describing its pleasant location. Bro. McGeary confined himself to the Theological Department, devoted to the training of students for the work of God, "its faculty being devoted, sanctified, Christian men, and holiness being represented in the college 365 days in the year."

Bro. Thomas H. Nelson presented the "Pentecost Herald," (8 pp., Indianapolis, Ind.,) of which he is Associate Editor, and Mrs. Flora B. Nelson, Editor. Bro. Nelson stated that it contained "red-hot articles along Scriptural holiness lines," and called brief attention to his books "Marvels in Metaphor," "The Midnight Cry," and book of songs "Garden of Spices."

Col. F. E. Peck of Dutton, Mich., represented "The Herald of Salvation," (8 pp., Mount Pleasant, Mich.,) the organ of the Crusaders, which has its department for reports from the field and a page given largely to holiness.

Bro. G. W. Ridout represented the "Christian Standard," (20 pp., Philadelphia, Pa.,) Bro. E. I. D. Pepper, Editor, and Bro. Joseph H. Smith, Associate Editor. Bro. Ridout stated that the Standard had the reputation of "being a strong, sweet, holiness paper," calling attention to publications of the firm: Cornell's "Hints to Fishermen," "Songs of the Living Way," etc.

Bro. W. E. Shepard represented "The Nazarene Messenger," (8 pp., Los Angeles, Cal.), Editor, P. F. Bresee; Associates, J. P. Coleman and W. E. Shepard, "a small paper but representing big things." Bro. Shepard called attention to his books, "Holiness Typology," and "Wrested Scriptures Made Plain."

Bro. W. P. Olmstead told of some of the merits and advantages of Spring Arbor Seminary of Michigan, and stated it had a blessed holiness faculty, teaching the doctrine of entire sanctification.

Bro. S. B. Shaw spoke of his publications, calling attention first to "God's Financial Plan," which he regarded as his best production, "Dying Testimonies of the Saved and Unsaved," and "Touching Incidents, and Remarkable Answers to Prayer." One half million of these books, or something like two hundred and fifty tons or a freight train load are already in circulation and all in answer to prayer.

Bro. B. S. Taylor presented his publications, mentioning his "Full Salvation" Series and different tracts, also calling attention by request, to his book trunk.

Bro. Ridout called attention to a work by Bro. E. F. Walker, entitled "Sanctify Them."

Bro. E. F. Walker represented "The Way of Faith," (Columbia, S. C.,) edited by Bro. T. C. Ligon, to which Bro. Walker is a contributor.

The Chairman of the Assembly called for "single-sentence" testimonies, with responses as follows:

"Saved to-day."

"Praise the Lord for conscious salvation."

Bro. S. B. Shaw: I have not testified in this Assembly before, but it is not because I didn't know how. ("Amen!") I have been preaching holiness for about twenty-six years, because I enjoy the experience. When I can't preach it that way, I will quit. ("Amen!")

"Praise the Lord for sanctification."

J. A. WOOD.
Pasadena, Cal.

C. M. KEITH,
Greenville, Texas.

WILLIAM JONES,
(Deceased.)

JOSEPH DEMPSTER,
Washington, D. C.

A. M. HILLS,
Greenville, Texas.

B. S. TAYLOR,
Stewart, Iowa.

ALBERT JACOBS,
Chicago, Ill.

MRS. ALBERT JACOBS,
Chicago, Ill.

"Saved and kept by the power of the blood of the Lamb."

"Happy on the way."

"Sweetly and blessedly sanctified."

"Glad I can say I am saved and sanctified."

"Filled with the Holy Ghost."

"I live for Him who died for me."

"How can these things be? If you do not understand earthly things, how can you understand heavenly things? I am glad that I understand these things which I hear."

"Saved to the uttermost through the blood of Jesus Christ."

"Glad I can say: Jesus saves even me."

"The blood of Jesus cleanses me."

"I enjoy full salvation."

"Hallelujah, He cleanses me."

"Jesus satisfies the longings."

"He fully saves me now."

"The great transaction's done."

"I am standing on the Rock."

"Jesus is my all-sufficient Saviour."

"I have the assurance that I am saved and entirely sanctified."

"Sanctified and resting on Him."

Bro. Haney: I can testify that I am profoundly and increasingly charmed with holiness.

"Well, I am on the sanctified route."

"Thank God for full and free salvation."

"I praise the Lord that He received a poor sinner like me."

"I thank God for two births: one, natural; and a second, spiritual."

"He saves me now."

"I was a sinner saved by grace."

Prayer, led by L. B. Kent: "O, Lord, Thou art our

God. Thou art our Father, and we are Thy children. We have been born of God and we have come into Thy family. We have come into spiritual life and into communion with Thee. We have come into that experience of life that has made us Thine eternal worshipers. Glory be to God. We bless Thee that we are brethren and sisters of all Thy children of all ages and all lands.

We praise Thee that we have learned through Thy blessed Word, under the light of Thy Spirit, that it is our high calling to be fully saved from sin; to be sanctified; to be Thy spiritual children; to be brought finally to dwell with Thee in heaven.

We thank Thee for this delightful gathering and for Thy presence with us. We pray that Thou wilt help the speaker this afternoon. May many souls be saved and sanctified this hour, and we would ask Thy special blessing on all the meetings to follow, and may there be cause for soul rejoicing.

Bless us all, and receive us finally into Thy home in heaven. We ask it for Christ's sake. Amen."

Singing, by Bro. and Sister Harris, "Let Him have His way with Thee."

SERMON BY BRO. W. E. SHEPARD.

Now, I hope God will limber us all up, and save us from being stiff and starchy which prevents us from saying "Amen," or shouting "Hallelujah," or doing anything else the Lord has for us to do. ("Amen!")

There are a great many people continually asking the question: How can one tell when he is all the Lord's? How can he tell when he has reached the end of consecration, so he may step out on the promises and get under the blood? Now I don't believe I have ever been guilty of trying to preach a big sermon or of trying to do anything else impossible, but I do want to preach a plain, simple sermon to help some one. I want you to pray the best you can. I am going to preach the best I can; God will do the best He can, and, if every unsanctified soul here will do the best they can, we shall have a number of seekers. ("Amen!") If you feel that you can't stand it to wait for the call to come to the altar, if you will do just what I tell you to do, you will get sanctified just where you are, this afternoon. I am sure I can make it clear enough for any one to get sanctified.

I want to take up first, the thought of the Old Testament line of priesthood and its offering, and run a parallel with the New Testament priesthood and its offering, and then by a practical object lesson, show you what entire consecration, or dedication to God is.

We are going to build a structure and will move in with the furniture a little later. Possibly it may seem a little dry for a few minutes, but we will try and get it watered soon.

"For the law having a shadow of good things to come, and not the very image of the things, can never with those sacrifices which they offered year by year continually make the comers thereto perfect." (Heb. 10:1.)

I have read this to get one thought, and that is that the law represented the shadow of the good things to come. We haven't the shadow any more, but we have the substance of the good things. ("Amen!") The substance of a good thing is a great deal better than the shadow of it. If I were real hungry and you offered me a slice off of a loaf of bread or the shadow of it, I would say: "Please give me a slice off the loaf, it will stick to my ribs better!" ("Amen!") We have now the good things to come, the substance, the real salvation of God.

I wish to push out two parallel lines:—one, representing the shadow, and the other the blessed substance.

In the first place, under the Old Testament dispensation, there was a priesthood. There is no need of reading Scriptural proof; we all understand it.

Is there a priesthood today? I refer you to Rev. 1: 5, 6: "Unto Him that loved us, and washed us from our sins in His own blood. And hath made us kings and priests unto God and His Father." Every child of God, everybody that has had the blood to wash away his sins is made a priest unto God. ("Amen!")

What was the duty of the priesthood under the Old Testament dispensation? A part of it was to offer sacrifices. The first text I read speaks of those sacrifices which they offered "year by year, continually." Under the present dispensation, what does the priesthood do? We do the same thing, but in a different way. In 1 Peter 2: 5, it says: "Ye also, as lively stones, are built up a spiritual house, an holy priesthood, to offer up spiritual sacrifices, acceptable to God by Jesus Christ." So, the priesthood of today has a spiritual sacrifice to offer unto God.

What kind of a sacrifice did the priesthood offer under the old dispensation? If you turn to the first chapter of Leviticus, you find what that was. The sacrifice may have been one from the herd, or from the flock, or from the fowls. Could they have a choice? No, everyone had to offer the best he could. If he was able to do so, it must be one from the herd. If not able to offer one from the herd, then one from the flock, or from the fowls. Nobody was exempt. Anybody could give turtle doves. The requirement was that he should offer what he could. God's commands never transcend one's ability to perform.

Under the new dispensation, what is the sacrifice? It is not some animal. Read Rom. 12: 1: "Present your bodies a living sacrifice." Our sacrifice to-day is ourselves. We make an offering of ourselves. We give Him our bodies and everything that pertains to us. ("Amen!")

Where did they place the sacrifice in the old dispensation? They had to have a place, so God provided it. An altar was provided. We read in the first chapter of Leviticus, that if the sacrifice was from the herd, it had to be placed upon the wood that was upon the fire that was upon the altar. In like manner, if the sacrifice was from the flock or from the fowls. What does this teach us? It teaches that no matter what the offering, it had to be given the same way and be placed upon the same altar. If one was able to offer a large sacrifice and another only a small one, it was brought to the same altar. All had to come to one common level here. There was no room for caste; no chance for "big I and little you" in the worship.

Under the old dispensation, they came to God through their altar. We come to Him by Jesus Christ. Christ is our altar to-day. They were made acceptable through their altar; we are acceptable through Jesus Christ according to 1 Pet. 2: 5. In Heb. 13: 10, we read: "We have an altar, whereof they, have no right to eat which serve the tabernacle." The Jews who kept up the old service of the tabernacle and who rejected Jesus Christ, had no right to partake of Him. The Bible says that they who wait upon the altar have the right to partake of the altar. The Jews who rejected Christ could not wait upon our Altar, hence, had no right to partake of Him. Jesus said: "Except ye eat of the flesh of the Son of man and drink His blood, ye have no life in you."

Then, Christ is the Altar upon which Christians place their sacrifice.

If there was a priesthood under the old dispensation, and that priesthood offered animal sacrifices on that altar, what did that altar do? God pronounced the altar holy. He said it would do something in a ceremonial way. We read in Matt. 23: 19: "The altar sanctifieth the gift." Exodus 29: 37 says: "Whatsoever toucheth the altar shall be holy." Their altar sanctified the gift. God said so. But it was in a ceremonial sense. If we to-day, having a sacrifice, and that sacrifice being our selves, give ourselves wholly to God and place all on the Altar, Jesus Christ, will our Altar do less than theirs of 2,000 or 3,000 or 4,000 years ago? No. Our Altar does according to Hebrews 13: 12: "Wherefore Jesus, also, that He might sanctify the people with His own blood, suffered without the gate." Our Altar sanctifies. There never was a complete sacrifice offered; there never was a complete dedication of ourselves made to God, but what there was received the blessed fullness in the heart. It is absolutely certain if we get all on the Altar, we shall become sanctified. If you are going around saying, "I haven't got it," you would better ask the Lord to give you the light, and show you where you are lacking in complete abandonment to Him. "Present your bodies a living sacrifice, holy, acceptable unto God."

I want to illustrate this with an object lesson. Some one has said that we may speak into the ear of a person, and it may go out at the other, but if we speak into the eye, there is no way for it to pass through the head. I am going to illustrate the work of entire consecration. I will use the thought of the altar that sanctifieth the gift. ("Lord help us!") The word of God says: "Present your bodies a living sacrifice." I am going to let this box with its contents illustrate the body. We will use this desk for the altar. This is not sacrilege. We are employing it merely for the sake of illustration. By placing all upon this, let it be a representation of placing our all in the hands of God, letting Him do as He pleases with it. (Romans 12: 1) "Present your bodies a living sacrifice, holy, acceptable unto God." We will place this (object representing the body) on as the first thought. It says in Romans 6: 13: "Yield yourselves unto God, as those that are alive from the dead, and your members as instruments of righteousness unto God." And in another place it says that the feet, hands, eyes, etc., are our members. By giving our body, it takes in all its members and everything pertaining to it. Let the contents of this box represent the members. If you will follow out this consecration, you will get the blessing this afternoon. If God flashes the light on your soul, walk in the light. ("Amen!")

When I gave myself to the Lord, it took in my two hands. (Placing on altar objects representing the two hands.) If the Lord has blessed you with two hands, say, "Lord I consecrate my hands." ("Amen!") It is a good thing to have sanctified hands that will work for God; hands that will let the Lord use them in any way that he wants to; hands that will bless others; hands that will give out tracts, distribute papers, and in many ways find avenues of service. Do you know that you can bless a soul by a hand-shake, if you give the right kind? I have shaken hands before now when it seemed as if I had taken hold of a dead fish. Lord, put some life in these hands. ("Amen!")

Sanctified feet. (Putting objects representing feet on

altar.) We have two feet. Consecrate your feet to God. Say, Lord, let me have feet that will run on missions of mercy, carrying glad tidings of great joy. Consecrated feet will carry you wherever God wants you to go. They will not take you where God does not want you to go. They will not take you where you will have to leave Jesus Christ outside. ("Amen!") It means much to have sanctified feet that never walk in "by and forbidden paths," but are everlastingly going for God, and will stand on every promise of His.

Most people have two ears. Give them to God (placing objects representing ears on altar). Do you know that we can sin through our members? These are the avenues through which carnality can work. Consecrate your ears to Jesus. I want sanctified ears, that will be closed to the tattling, tale-bearing sin of the world Sanctified ears will not be running around after flattery. When some one has an outlandish tale to tell, such ears will not be open to it. ("Amen!") The world is full of slanderous stories about somebody or other. Pray for the party, instead of listening to more of the report.

Put your eyes on the altar. (Illustrating with object lesson.) Dedicate them to God. Consecrate them to be used to the glory of God. If you have sanctified eyes, you will read the Word when God wants you to. You will be all alert to see something that you can do for Jesus. ("Amen!") Sanctified eyes will be closed to impure sights. Sanctified eyes will have daily reading that is clean, and no time for lies and bosh in the newspapers. Sanctified eyes will have no time to read flashy stories, pamphlets and cheap-John trash. Sanctified eyes will not want to be running around for questionable amusement. ("Amen!") Sanctified eyes, pure eyes, will not look upon a woman to commit adultery with her in the heart. They will not lead you into sinful lusts. Do you know that you can scarcely walk a block in the business portion of the city without seeing enough nude and lewd pictures to backslide you if you would stop to look at them? It means much to have pure eyes. If you have a questionable piece of statuary on the mantel-piece, it ought to be ground to powder. If you have pictures, or anything that suggests impurity, anything in the home that does not savor of purity, burn it up. ("Amen!")

Then we have a tongue. (Laying object on altar). Do you know God reaches people through the tongue? A sanctified voice will speak when God wants it to speak. A sanctified voice touches souls. A sanctified tongue will deliver any message the Lord wants it to deliver, if the person knew he would die the next minute. You would pray anywhere, on the street, in the home, anyhow, any time. A sanctified voice is the channel of the Holy Ghost, given up to God, ready to do His bidding. ("Amen!") It will praise God, when the Lord wants it to. ("Praise the Lord.") It will be shut against a good many things. A sanctified tongue will be closed against tattling, talebearing, murmuring and complaining. I would no more think of complaining and finding fault than of swearing. How many people fret, and stew, and complain and find fault! By the grace of God, I will never do that nor speak evil of anybody. Nearly twenty years ago, I stood up in a Southern California camp meeting, with others, and vowed never to speak evil of any one. It has been a padlock on my lips for nearly twenty years. If you feel that you need to warn somebody concerning another, and that God leads, then do it.

Mind, intellect, thinking power; give these to God. Have sanctified brains, sanctified mind. It means much to have a pure mind, that thinketh no evil. A pure mind will put the best construction it can on people and things. The pure mind will not be the channel of impure thoughts. When God sanctified my soul, He didn't kill the devil. The devil does his best some times to put in evil suggestions. With God's help, you don't need to receive them. He will give you the victory. In passing along, somebody might thrust a cigar into my mouth. I could spit it out. I don't need to receive it. We do not need to receive the temptations of the devil into our heart, nor be subject to his wily suggestions.

If the Lord has given you one talent, or ten talents, put them on the altar. Let the Lord get the best use of your latent talents. There are people singing the Gospel to-day, who, before they were sanctified, did not know there was such music in them, and so in many lines of work.

Put your reputation on the altar.

You say: "What will my friends say?" You are giving up your will concerning your reputation and friends, saying: "I am going through with Jesus, no matter what my friends say or do." That man that cuts loose from his opposing friends and becomes one with God and the holiness people, gets the blessing of God. ("Amen!") You cannot be tied down to anybody or anything, and God at the same time. ("Amen!") You should be as free as the birds in the air. ("Amen!") Paul said that he had suffered the loss of all things that He might win Christ. When you have lost all, there is a kind of comfortable feeling, because you feel that you have nothing more to lose! ("Amen!")

If you want to win your friends, say, "Here goes, friends and all," and after you get through, you are better prepared to bring your friends around. What about the family? Will you consecrate them to God? Let Him have His way with your life companion, your child, give all to Jesus.

Then say, "Lord, I will go where you want me to go. I will do anything you want me to do. I will say anything you want me to say. I will suffer anything you want me to suffer. I will be anything you want me to be. I will drink, eat, dress, all to the glory of God." ("Amen!") Bless God! I wouldn't do anything I wouldn't be willing to do, if I knew Jesus was coming the next minute. ("Amen!")

Ask God to search your heart and show you if there is any thing more to give. He may say: "Will you give me your time?" Tell Him, "I will give you my time." Put that on the altar. (Placing time-piece on altar.)

"Is there anything else?" you ask. Yes. Your money, your possessions. You need to take God into your business. Put your pocket book on the altar. (Puts purse on the altar.) That reminds me of the preacher who was about to baptize a candidate by immersion. The candidate was about to hand his pocket book to a friend when the preacher said: "Let him be baptized pocket book and all." ("Amen!"—Laughter.)

Be systematic in your money matters. Give it all over to God, but see that He gets at least one-tenth and then as much more as He calls for. I believe that any one who will not give or rather pay one-tenth of his income to God is too stingy to be called a Christian. ("Amen!")

Then put your testimony on the altar. The Lord asks, "Are you going to tell out the glad news when I sanctify you, and will you give it a clear ring so that every body can understand?" Tell Him, "Yes, Lord," and let it ring out. (Puts a bell on the altar, and rings it loud and clear.) ("Glory to God.")

Do you know that many are afraid to do this? They hesitate to say they are sanctified. They want to testify some other way. They would say: "When in Chicago, the Lord gave me a big blessing: He gave me more religion. (Ringing bell with muffled sound.) Another says: "I consecrated all to the Lord, and received a deeper work of grace." (Rings bell with partly muffled sound.) That is only a little better. The devil is trying to close people's mouths on this question. I have learned a secret: If one gets his mouth open wide enough to let out the word "sanctification," the devil hasn't a plug big enough to close it up. ("Amen!") (Testifies clear and rings bell loud and clear.)

You will get where you can think of nothing more to consecrate. Then give Him all you can not think of. When He asks you if you are willing to sign a contract that everything you will have in the future shall be His, then answer, "Yes." Give Him all that will come up later on, that you fail to think of now. Put the "unknown bundle" on the Altar. (Putting larger bundle on.) That is a bigger bundle than the other. I don't know what is in it. That is the unrevealed will of God, until I get to heaven. ("Amen!") It may have in it, sorrow, suffering, ignominy, or death, and it may have blessing. Say, "Thy will be done."

I know nothing more to give up. I have put on the Altar, all I know, and all I don't know.

Having given up all, having reached the utmost limit of entire dedication, take hands off and say "I am thine, forever on the Altar." Step out on the promise, open your heart for the Holy Ghost, believe God, and you have the blessing. ("Amen!") If you don't put all on the

Altar, you will never get sanctified. If you don't keep everything on, you will lose it ("Amen!")

Now, concerning the unknown bundle: You will go along enjoying salvation, testifying, and somebody will point the finger of scorn and persecutes you for righteousness sake. The Lord says: "I knew that was coming. That was in the unknown bundle." That is something you hadn't thought of. That is known now, so you pass it over to the known bundle. (Transferring from the unknown bundle to the known.) You don't put this on the altar. It was there before. You never have to put anything else on. All you have to do is to transfer from the unknown bundle to the known. ("Glory!")

After awhile you may get a great blessing. You begin to fill up. The Lord says: "My child! I think you would better shout a little." ("Amen!") You say: "I hadn't thought of that before," and so let out the shout and quench not the Spirit. ("Amen!")

I think I see a young lady, perhaps. She has been gloriously sanctified. The Lord says to her: "You told me you would do everything to my glory." "Yes, Lord." You told me you would dress to my glory." "Yes, Lord." "I see that you have on some foolish toggery and jewelry and feathers. I think you would better begin to moult." "Must I lay aside these things, Lord?" "Yes, I want my children to be free from gaudy attire." She says, "Yes, Lord, I will lay aside anything that Thou requirest, and dress to Thy glory." (Transferring some feathers from the unknown bundle. Laughter and shouts from the congregation.)

I think I see a young person lately sanctified. The Lord says, "You are walking in the light. I want to tell you something for your good. I do not want you to get into trouble. You are keeping company with somebody who is not a Christian. You are anticipating marriage with a sinner. 'Be ye not unequally yoked together with unbelievers.'" (Another transfer from the unknown bundle.) So that loyal child swings around to the will of God, and forever pulls away from the thought of being yoked up with any sinner. ("Amen").

Do you think it wrong for a Christian to marry a sinner? ("Yes.") Well, what about the preacher that performs the marriage ceremony of such? I refuse to perform the marriage ceremony between a Christian and a sinner, finding out about the parties before I undertake the case.

Here is a brother who has lately been sanctified. Light comes to him about a certain thing. We think he ought to have known it before, but we will say it had not come to him. The Lord shows him that he is unequally yoked up with secret societies, and that he cannot spend any of his time nor money nor influence in that way. Having promised the Lord to walk in the light at any cost, he transfers that which he had not previously known to the known bundle, cuts loose from secret fraternities, gets more blessed than ever before and does more for the kingdom of God. ("Amen! Amen!")

Here is a young lady. The Lord says, "My child, you have been a good witness. I am going to send you across the sea to the heathen lands as a missionary and you can have more stars in your crown." She says "By the grace of God, where He leads I will follow." So, this is transferred from the unknown bundle to the known, and to the foreign fields she goes and wins many souls for Jesus.

You have a dear child in your home. Your heart's affections center around it. Sickness comes. Somehow you fail to get any evidence that God is going to heal. You wonder why, but He shows you that He is going to take the child to Himself. He transfers the precious jewel to heaven and makes it a loadstone to draw you stronger that way. You must be loyal to God's will and say, "Thy will be done."

The unknown bundle will constantly be getting smaller and the known bundle larger until finally the last thing will be transferred to the known, and you will be transferred to the glory world, having kept all on the Altar. From the heights of glory you will look down and bless God that you were ever permitted to consecrate all to Him and be sanctified and then kept in the blessed way.

It pays to be sanctified. ("Amen"). Every body in the house this afternoon that wants this experience, if you dare to get up from your seat and walk down these aisles, do so without any singing or persuading.

Eighteen seekers came forward, and a goodly portion of the congregation pushed forward to join in prayer.

EVENING SESSION.

7:00 P. M., Bro. E. F. Walker in the chair.

Scripture Reading, by Bro. J. M. Dustman.

Opportunity was given for requests for prayer, and the following subjects were presented:

"An unsaved daughter."

"An unsaved husband."

"A sister and a son unsaved."

"A son who once knew the Lord."

"An unsaved brother."

"My only child unsaved; the husband of a sister and five children in California unsaved."

"An unsaved brother and a great many unsaved friends."

"My child."

"An unsaved boy far away."

"A brother afflicted with a broken limb."

Bro. J. R. Allen led the Assembly in prayer in behalf

of these requests and the prayer roll, followed by Bro. O. Wendel and M. L. Haney.

Congregational singing: "Walking with Jesus," "It is for us All To-day," and "Beulah Land."

Prayer, led by Bro. Hiram Ackers: "Our Father who art in Heaven; hallowed be Thy name; Thy Kingdom come; Thy will be done in earth as it is in Heaven. We are exceedingly glad that we can, by grace through faith in our God and Saviour Jesus Christ, approach Thee as our Father, with the divine assurance that Thy parental ear is open to our petitions, and Thy loving parental hand toward the children in Thy care, to administer to their necessities. We realize that this is a time of great need. There are hungry souls here. There are souls here, no doubt, that know not God.

We pray that there may be such a manifestation of Thy spiritual presence and power to-night that every soul that enters this sanctuary shall be touched by that Spirit. Take possession of our minds and hearts. May God be glorified in this meeting, and precious souls saved and sanctified, and the cause of Thy kingdom exalted. Touch the lips of him through whom Thou shalt speak to-night, with the unction, wisdom and power of Thy Spirit. May Thy power rest on all in Thy presence. We ask it all through Jesus Christ, Amen."

Singing by congregation: 'He Brought me out."

SERMON BY BRO. J. McD. KERR.

Text: "And the very God of peace sanctify you wholly; and I pray God your whole spirit and soul and body be preserved blameless unto the coming of our Lord Jesus Christ." (1 Thess. 5:23.)

A lady, this afternoon in this congregation, a perfect stranger, looking at those strings of paper behind me, asked what that meant. I said to her that it was a prayer roll,—requests for prayer, and an announcement that individuals were praying for this General Ho-

J. M. HARRIS,
Evanston, Ill.

MRS. M. J. HARRIS,
Evanston, Ill.

C. B. JERNIGAN,
Greenville, Texas.

N. O. WESTERGREEN,
Chicago, Ill.

ALEXANDER McLEAN,
Brooklyn, N. Y.

WILLIAM BENKERT,
Davenport, Iowa.

U. WARRINGTON.
Harvey, Ill.

JOHN P. BROOKS.
Ft. Scott, Kan.

liness Assembly. There has been a great cry going up to God for His blessing on these gatherings, and since I came, I have had the consciousness that God is answering these petitions. We believe that He can and will answer prayer, and grant His blessing on souls far away. We want you to pray for all who have not yet found Christ, for those who have back-slidden, and also those that are in the congregation who want to know more of Christ, that they may be gloriously blessed in their souls.

The first part from the Revised Version reads: "And the very God of peace, Himself," putting emphasis on the word "Himself."

I believe there are more people enjoying the experience of the higher life than even before. I believe more people in all the churches are seeking this experience than at any former period of time. I believe that there is less preaching against this blessed doctrine of the Word of God to-day than there has ever been in the past, and I give the glory to God, for these have been my convictions as I have gone up and down the land. Yet, there is a little prejudice existing in some quarters, and, as a consequence, some persons go around the circle of unmeaning and unscriptural phraseology to avoid the terms which God has used, which are so expressive of the doctrine, and by which He often accomplishes His purposes. If you have a particle of prejudice in your mind, or anything akin to it, I would recommend that you take out your pen knife and eliminate from the doctrines of your church everything pertaining to this subject; such a course I know would make a very large elimination in connection with the standards of doctrine in my own church. Then take up your hymn-book and go through it. I do not know how many hymns on this subject are in other hymnals, but I know we have a great many that we hold in common in the evangelical churches. I have had occasion to stand in the pulpits of different denominations, and I have yet to find any difficulty in locating in their hymnals, songs to meet the particular thought of heart purity and holiness that I wished to present. These hymns and truths are all here to stay, and will stand when heaven and earth are passed away. Then take the Bible, and wherever you find the word "Holy," or anything pertaining to holiness, erase it; take out every word on sanctification and purity in the blessed Word of God, and you will be so sick before you get through with the process, that you will never want to see that penknife again, or that mutilated Bible. Take my recipe and you will get over your prejudice before we are through with this sermon, and I know it is possible for you to get the blessing before we are through with this service. ("Amen!") I don't know that I ever had any prejudice concerning the blessed Word of the living God. ("Amen!") I am glad to say that I can take all the theological terms, from "Higher Spiritual Life," down to "The Second Blessing,"—whatever you propose to call it; also all the scriptural terms from that presented by the Apostle Paul in my text: "Sanctified wholly," down to the Lord's statement of heart purity, in that inimitable Sermon on the Mount: "Blessed are the pure in heart: for they shall see God." I do not say that we are not to use other terms, but we may pare and cut and trim the truth, until it becomes a powerless weapon. Let us not only hold to scriptural doctrines but to scriptural phraseology as far as possible. I believe these are to be blessed by the Holy Ghost in the presentation of this theme.

While I may make reference to my church, it is merely for the purpose of illustration, and because of the fact that I am a little more familiar with my own than with other branches of the Christian Church.

Wesley wrote to Dr. Adam Clark that those who spoke against the holiness doctrine should not be allowed in the church, for he didn't see how they could be honest men and women, after the vows to God that they had taken. Every Methodist minister is asked at the bar of the Conference: 1. "Do you believe in Christian perfection?" 2. "Do you expect to be made perfect in love in this life?" and he answers in the affirmative. The man who does not stand by the principles he has espoused by his solemn and holy ordination vows is not honest before God or man. I am impressed with this thought by force of circumstances that every member of the conference with which I am connected, believes in the truth of a full and complete salvation. I want to say that I have presented holiness as strongly in every church to which I have gone, as I shall to you, by the help of God to-night. ("Amen!") I glorify His name for the privilege of declaring the truth as it is in Christ Jesus, our Lord.

One time, in the City of London, six hundred and fifty persons gave testimony to the experience as taught in my text. These were nearly all interviewed by Rev. John Wesley. It was found that some obtained it in a few months after conversion; some in two weeks; one in two days. None of these were found to have gotten it in a shorter period than that. I believe it is possible to bring it closer than this. I like to see a soul get saved by grace and then move over into the Canaan

Land at the same altar service. I believe that we may more easily enter then than at any other time.

I want to say that the experience of holiness and its adoption is not peculiar to any one church alone. It is found in all evangelical churches, and in some that we have not rated as evangelical. I wonder at any person leaving the church, when Madam Guyon could enter into this close experience, and live it in the Roman Catholic Church. Let us stand in our places where God puts us! ("Amen!") If our church people are not with us on this, I believe, by patiently practicing and living up to the full experience, we will, in time, bring them along with us. I was holding services in the city of Ottawa and a brother minister of my own church came to the services full of prejudice: but after he heard the word preached and saw the methods adopted, he said,—"I want to make an apology to you, and I want to unite heartily in the work." And so he did to the end of a four weeks' campaign. While we were engaged in these services in the West End three prominent ministers visited the city and opened up holiness meetings in the Congregational Church, and the interest grew until the church would not accommodate all the people. That went on to the close of the meetings, and many hungry souls found the blessed Saviour and entered into full salvation. God is spreading this work all over the world and throughout this land. Let us have faith in God. ("Amen!") Prejudice is going. Blessed be His name! I am glad that the truth is popular; I am glad that holiness is popular. I mean that in a pure and good sense. I believe it is more popular with the churches, to-day, than ever. I can remember, during the period of my own life, a time when men doubted the possibility of knowing that their sins were forgiven; but that time has passed away. I believe the truth of full salvation will be received as freely and fully as the doctrine of the new birth. Thank God! Prejudice is going. ("Amen!") I want you to pray earnestly that God may help us in the work to-night, that precious souls may be sanctified unto God.

My God! If Thou didst ever help me, help me now. If Thou didst ever speak through me, speak through me now. I believe I stand in that place, where I am willing to have my mouth closed, where I am willing to be silent as well as to speak just as it be Thy will.

I notice, in the next place, that it is just about as difficult to get Christians into this experience of full salvation, as it is to get sinners converted.

Why? Has not God made provision and given commandment concerning the same? "This is the will of God even your sanctification." "Be ye holy for I the Lord your God am holy." "Follow peace with all men and holiness without which no man shall see the Lord." We cannot set these and similar truths aside and be guiltless.

I heard of a Presbyterian minister's wife who was brought down near the gates of death. She had found the Lord Jesus, and followed Him in justifying faith, as taught by her husband, but when she came so near eternity, looking into that other world, there was a fear of death, a drawing back from the call she felt must soon come. She summoned her companion to her side and asked him if it were not possible to be saved from sin in the present life; if it were not possible to be cleansed from all sin before death. Perhaps the pastor had not heard such a question before. It came from his beloved companion in the hour of sorest and direst soul need. He began to recall the promises of God, until he reached this passage: "But, if we walk in the light, as He is in the light, we have fellowship one with another, and the blood of Jesus Christ His Son cleanseth us from all sin." "If we confess our sins, He is faithful and just to forgive us our sins, and to cleanse us from all unrighteousness." The pastor told his wife that he believed Jesus could fulfill His promises. She said: "Husband, if that is the case, will you not now kneel by my bedside and ask our Heavenly Father, for Jesus' sake, to do this in my heart?" He prayed with her and God answered the prayer. God fulfills His promises to-day. Mrs. Phoebe Palmer was very well satisfied with her experience of the new birth, and would have been content to live in a justified experience until eternity broke in on her soul, but the commandment of God came to be pure in heart, to be sanctified wholly, to be perfect in love. She knew that she did not have this experience, and, with her great, logical mind, she also knew that she could not break or disobey any of God's commandments and not be condemned. She saw that she could not be condemned and justified at the same time. It meant either to go forward in these truths, or to go back into spiritual bondage. Thank God! She entered into this experience. Thousands will bless her memory and life, and glorify God through all eternity as a result. Why do we not enter in? Is it because of unbelief? Moses got all Israel out of Egypt in 24 hours. It took 40 years to get them to a point where they were really ready to enter into the promised land. With two exceptions, none would enter in, but later when Joshua commanded the priests to go forward, although the Jordan had overflowed its banks, they stepped into the water, and the Israelites went over dry-shod into the promised land. It may be that a minister here and there will not go over. It may be that a few now will not enter in, but the rising generation will. ("Amen!") God wants you to possess this heritage.

If you have been five, ten, fifteen or twenty years, professing to be a Christian and have not been seeking after a full salvation, I have as much reason to believe that you are back-slidden in heart as I have to believe that you are justified before God. Is it not a fact that you had more zeal, more earnestness, more devotion to Christ and the study of God's word the first week, or month, or year of your Christian life, than you have had since? God help us that we may follow on, to know the Lord, and be led to receive His blessed redemption and sanctification. ("Amen!")

Many, instead of looking at the precious promises of the gospel, look at themselves, and do not understand why they do not realize freedom from sin. I do not mean freedom from actual sin in life, but freedom from the sin in the heart that remained after conversion. Some, because of subdued sin in the heart, conclude that no one can be delivered in the present life. A lady, who admitted that she was a member of the church, said that she could not live without committing sin every day. If that is the case, what is the difference between her condition before she was converted and her condition at the present time? I am not referring to actual sins, but to the sin in your heart—pride, self-will, love of the world and self-esteem. You should have these taken out, and know that the old man can be destroyed. "But now being made free from sin, and become servants to God, ye have your fruit unto holiness, and the end everlasting life."

It can and must be done here and now, in the present life. I trust it may be so in your case. ("Amen!") "And the very God of peace sanctify you wholly: and I pray God your whole spirit and soul and body be preserved blameless unto the coming of our Lord Jesus Christ." That means that Christ is able to sanctify us fully now and that you and I are to be preserved blameless until the Lord comes. I know that He has done it in my case, and what He has done for me, He can do for every heart here.

Dr. Godbey, who has been exploring down in the Holy Land, tells us that stones taken out from the lower strata, beneath the temple, where the sound of chisel or hammer was not heard, came out squared and hewn and polished for their places in the temple. So the Lord is chiseling and squaring and polishing us for a place in the glorious temple hereafter.

As I passed down the street, I saw a man preparing stones for one of the great public buildings. He had a huge hammer, which he was bringing down on a large block of stone. It looked as if he was trying to break it all to pieces, but I found that he was chiseling it. He was bringing his hammer down to break off the protruding points. So God brings down His great hammer of Truth to break off our protruding points, to take off the rough corners of sin. At Ottawa, I went into the great Parliament Buildings, and my friend said: "I want to show you one thing more,—the corner-stone of the building." He took me through a passage-way to a stone laid many years ago by the Prince of Wales. When I came to that stone,

I could see my image in it. I said: "I want to be a polished stone for Jesus, that I may always reflect my Lord and Saviour." I thought of that blessed woman, the queen, who, not a great while before her decease, was at the bedside of a poor woman, who was about to die, and she quoted this passage from the Word of God: "The blood of Jesus Christ, His Son, cleanseth us from all sin." If the Queen of England, with the blessing in her heart, could quote that passage to a poor dying woman, every minister and worker ought to be able to go out and proclaim: "The blood of Jesus Christ His Son cleanseth us from all sin." Hallelujah to His name! ("Amen!")

We want the face of Jesus Christ reflected from the bottom of our hearts, through our minds, through our very being and nature. We want everything from the depths of our inmost soul made so clean and pure and transparent by the blessed blood of the Son of God, that nothing shall be seen in the reflection but the lovely image of Jesus Christ. If I have any ambition, it is to be like Jesus; to think like Jesus; to talk like Jesus; to preach like Jesus, and to glorify Jesus in this body and soul, which are the Lord's. ("Amen!") I have heard of twenty or thirty leading members of a church, who took the obligation upon them to follow the teachings of that little book: "In His Steps;" to endeavor to lead a life, such as the Lord Jesus Christ would have them lead. This is not only our privilege, but our duty. He not only enables us to live it, but he comes and enthrones Himself in us, to help us live it. We are ready to give to every one that asketh a reason of the hope that is within us, with meekness and reverence.

Jesus came to destroy the work of the devil, which is sin. This, He cannot do, unless He has the power to free my soul from sin. I am here to say, by personal experience, that Jesus can do it. You surely see the necessity, the privilege, and the obligation of being cleansed through the blood of Jesus. ("Amen!") Come and give yourself a living sacrifice to God, this very moment, and He will sanctify you wholly. The very God of peace, Himself, will do it. The blood of Jesus cleanses us, and the God of Peace sanctifies us. ("Amen!")

During the altar service fourteen seekers came forward, and workers assembled about the altar, looking to God in earnest prevailing prayer.

Saturday, May 11.

MORNING SESSION.

8:00 A. M. Prayer and Praise Service.

9:30 A. M., Bro. E. F. Walker presiding.

Bro. W. F. Spreuill led the Assembly in a short prayer.

Minutes of Friday's session read and approved.

The Assembly voted that all names handed in during the balance of the session be added to the Roll, at the discretion of the Secretary.

By a vote of the Assembly, it was decided to add four members to the Comittee on Preparation. Bro. L. B. Kent moved, and the motion prevailed, that the Committee on Nominations report four names as additional members of said committee, by the election of the Assembly.

The Report of the Committee on Permanent Methods was read, accepted, slightly revised by the Assembly, and adopted as follows:

REPORT ON PERMANENT METHODS.

Resolved 1st. That as many of the holiness people throughout the land have been excluded from their churches, on account of the profession and propagation of holiness, we extend to them our sympathy and prayers and advise them, in order to avoid come-outism with all its evils, as far as practicable to unite with some other evangelical church; and, where that is impracticable, to make such other adjustment as may seem, under the guidance of the Holy Spirit, to be wise.

Resolved 2nd. To more effectively promote the spread of holiness, and unify our work, we recommend the organization of bands, and county, and state associations, with a uniformity of constitution and by-laws. That this Assembly, composed of members from at least twenty different evangelical churches, declare that these bands and associations are in no sense churches, were never intended to be churches, and are not to take the place of churches, but are simply a union of people for the promotion and conservation of holiness, sustaining the same relation to the churches as the Y. M. C. A., W. C. T. U., Missionary Unions and associations similarly organized.

Resolved 3rd. That this Assembly appoint a committee to prepare a constitution and by-laws for the use of such bands and associations, and report at the next Assembly.

Resolved 4th. That all such bands seek to systematically raise a fund among themselves for evangelism, holiness literature, defraying necessary expenses of delegates to General Assemblies, and other expenses.

Resolved 5th. That this Assembly ask the Committee on Preparation to submit to the Assembly of next year, a full constitution for adoption.

On motion, it was decided that the Committee on Constitution, provided for in Article No. 3 of the Report of the Committee on Permanent Methods, shall not include any of the members of the Committee on Preparaation.

On motion, it was decided that the Committee to draft a constitution for Holiness Bands, as provided for in the second resolution of the report of the Committee on Permanent Methods shall consist of three persons appointed by the Chair. The following persons were appointed: Bro. Alexander McLean of New York, Bro. L. B. Kent of Illinois, Bro. M. L. Haney of Illinois.

The Committee on Nominations reported the following names to the Assembly, and, on motion, they were added to the Committee on Preparation:

Bros. Isaiah Reid of Iowa, M. L. Haney of Illinois, E. F. Walker of Indiana, and J. M. Pike of Georgia.

The following resolution was offered by Bro. L. B. Kent, and on motion adopted:

Resolved that, in case there are efforts made to exclude from churches brethren or sisters, because of their testimony to sanctification, or their connection with the holiness work, it is their privilege and duty to claim the right of defense, personally and by counsel, as accorded always in cases of charges preferred for other causes.

The Assembly voted to invite the Salvation Army Corps of the city to unite with us in our all-night service, Sunday evening, and that they be requested to take charge of the services for one hour.

On motion, the Volunteers of America were invited to unite in the all-night meeting of Sunday.

On motion, it was ordered that, when the Assembly adjourns, it be to meet next year at such time and place as the Committee on Preparation shall decide.

It was moved, and the motion prevailed, that when we adjourn, it be at the close of the all-night service of Sunday.

The following resolution on Prohibition was offered

by Bro. B. S. Taylor, and, on motion, was adopted by the Assembly:

Whereas, The liquor traffic is the giant foe of God, and the chief ally of Satan to-day, therefore:

Resolved: That we kindly urge all holy people to unite with, and vote for the candidates of those parties, on county, state and national tickets, who declare themselves for the Principle of Prohibition.

On motion, a rising vote of thanks was taken to show our appreciation of the kindness of the Pastor of the First Methodist Church, and other friends for their kindness shown us during the Assembly.

Adjourned to meet at 2:00 P. M.

AFTERNOON SESSION.

1:45 P. M., Bro. E. F. Walker presiding.

Special prayer was made in behalf of the Prayer Roll.

Scripture Reading by Bro. Walker, 1 Cor. 13.

TESTIMONIES.

Bro. S. B. Shaw:—"There are a great many things I don't know anything about; a great many things I never heard about, but I do know something of love, and this love of which I speak is not the love of man, but it is the love of God that is shed abroad in my heart by the Holy Ghost, which is given unto me. I am in love with everybody. I love God's people of every name." ("Amen!")

Bro. J. McD. Kerr: "I am so thankful that I have this love in my heart. I have heard nothing here contrary to love. It seems that this spirit has been filling all hearts. I am glad it is filling my heart and soul and being. ("Glory!") I came here with that thought and feeling in my mind and heart. I have love for everybody. I bless God for His presence and power with us in these services."

Sister Boyce:—"I want to say, to the glory of God, that He abides in my heart. No trials, losses nor disappointments disturb my inner being. My soul is at rest, perfectly satisfied in Jesus Christ, and I am running up the shining way."

Sister Amanda Smith: "Everybody, I think, has found out that Amanda Smith is on the holiness line and in sympathy with the Book of God. I haven't a doubt in my soul. No one can save anybody, but they can say a little word to help somebody. ("Amen!") I heard a sermon by John Inskip, in New York, that impressd me, and led me into the light. Making the teaching of the indwelling of the Spirit as simple as possible, he said: "You don't find it any trouble to breathe, when you go to bed at night. You wake up in the morning, and you have breathed all night, without thinking about it, and you needn't think it is any trouble for God to live in you." Then I saw that it was God in me, the Holy Ghost abiding in my heart. It was God doing something in me, and I didn't have to do it. I let go of self and went and got it. I got through as clean as a whistle!" ("Glory!")

Sister Sarah A. Cooke: "I came all the way from the middle of England to Chicago to be at the first camp meeting I ever attended. I had read books on holiness and been much helped, but I shall never forget my feelings as I looked upon the shining faces of those that had got it. I said: "O, Lord, give me that experience." And the Lord said: "Will you pay the price?" Every time the cry of my heart went up, the answer came back: "Will you pay the price?" My eyes looked on those radiant faces, and I would say: "Lord, give me the blessing. I want to be as they are," and the same answer would come back. The first thing the Lord told me was that he didn't want worldly adornment and costly array. I decided that I would have my dress plain, but would have things good. The Lord did not stop at that, but when my consecration was made I had to put everything on the altar.

I will never forget that day and night. I don't believe that the physical death will be anything compared to what came in the midst of that awful struggle. The pain and anguish was almost intolerable. The Lord said: "I passed through Gethsemane and so must you." The next morning I awoke. There had been the resurrection, and the glory came into my soul. I remember when I looked out on the camp ground, I said: "My heart is so pure. This is the same earth Moses and Paul and John walked on, and I am as near heaven as they were." ("Glory!") I praise the Lord that He has kept me. Shortly after we had the Chicago fire; and, as everything went up in the flames, I said: "The Lord has given, and the Lord has taken away. Blessed be the name of the Lord!"

Singing, by congregation, "The Half Has Never Yet Been Told."

Prayer, led by Bro. J. McD. Kerr: "Our Father, we come to Thee now in the name of our Saviour and Redeemer. We thank Thee for all Thy mercies unto us. We praise Thee for Thy wondrous love revealed to us. We have been wondrously redeemed, purchased with a price,—not with corruptible things, such as silver and gold, but by the precious blood of Jesus, the Lamb without blemish or spot. We thank Thee that Thou hast given unto us Thine own blessed Word, as a lamp unto our feet and a light to our path. We praise Thee that Thou hast not only given us this wonderful revelation of Thy divine will, but Thou hast given us the blessed Holy Ghost to lead us and guide us in all truth. We have realized Thy presence here.

"We pray for a gracious manifestation of Thy power and glory this afternoon, and, as our beloved brother stands before Thee and us and delivers to us what may be his last message to many here, may the Holy Ghost overshadow this place. Come in Thine own mighty power and glory, and may the hearts of all here be wonderfully melted down. Our Father, we want all of our talents used for the saving of lost souls and the building up of Thy Kingdom. Be with us at this hour, and to the Father, Son and Holy Ghost, we will ascribe all the praise forever. Amen."

Song, by Sister Aura Smith: "When We Get to the End of the Way."

SERMON BY BRO. GEORGE HUGHES.

Bro. Hughes said: "Before I give you my text, I want every eye in the congregation to be turned toward these folds of paper in the rear of the pulpit. On those links of paper stretching from gallery to gallery, are the cries of hundreds of people,—I might say thousands, on the mountains, in the valleys, on the prairies, along the sea shores of our country, and in Canada,—saying, in God's name, help us; pray for our fathers, mothers, husbands, wives, and for our children that they may not go down to darkness and eternal ruin. That is the cry of this multitude of hearts. What are we going to do about it? Will we intervene between these that cry and their friends— these fathers and mothers, and husbands and wives, and, through united prayer to God, prevent them from going

MRS. E. E. WILLIAMS,
Roodhouse, Ill.

SARAH A. COOKE,
Chicago, Ill.

MRS. M. J. McKINNON,
Dallas, Texas.

MRS. BEATRICE BEAZLEY,
Chicago, Ill.

GEORGE HUGHES,
Orange, N. J.

M. L. HANEY,
Normal, Ill.

MRS. CHARLOTTE DUDMAN,
Chicago, Ill.

FANNIE J. HOWARD,
Chicago, Ill.

down to the pit? May God help us! The cry of the country must be heeded. A woman of God sent the first letter from Colorado with sixteen names, imploring us to help her with our prayers, and so the mails have come to us heavily laden. As we stand in silent prayer, if any are moved of the Holy Ghost to offer audible prayer, do so."

(After a brief season of silent prayer, Rev. M. L. Haney led in earnest supplication to God in behalf of the subjects of prayer represented in the prayer roll.)

Brother Huges then remarked, When I was coming from New York to Chicago, on the train, a passage of Scripture came to my mind with great suddenness and impressiveness. It seemed like a message from heaven to be given to the people on some occasion.

I had not thought particularly of its being used in the Assembly, but when the appointment to preach was made, rather pressed upon me, it was made manifest that the passage referred to was the message from God for the hour. It is this:

"And when they had prayed, the place was shaken where they were assembled together; and they were all filled with the Holy Ghost, and they spake the word of God with boldness." Acts 4: 31.

Peter and John, the newly anointed apostles of the Gospel Dispensation, had been cast into prison for the sake of Christ and for His truth's sake. What was the offence charged against them? It is specifically stated in the second verse. "As they spake unto the people, the priests, and the captain of the temple, and the Sadducees, came upon them, being grieved that they taught the people, and preached through Jesus the resurrection from the dead."

A terrible charge, indeed—"They preached through Jesus the resurrection from the dead." Well, these rulers found they had a heavy piece of work on hand by imprisoning these men. They feared the people. Rulers can only go so far—there are limitations to their authority. They feared the popular voice, lest an uprising might despoil them of their authority. So they brought the apostles out of prison the next day. After having questioned and threatened them, they set them at liberty, straightly charging them, however, not to preach in the name of Jesus. But the apostles made no promises or stipulations in the matter. Being set free, the record says, "They went to their own company." This is a notable expression. There are saintly affiliations which naturally draw them together, in the enjoyment of the blessed fellowship divine.

When they found their own company there were mutual congratulations and praises to God for the marvelous deliverance of the apostles. Then, as further dangers threatened they went to God in prayer. The exercises of this occasion furnish us with a theme for the present hour, viz:

A Primitive Church Prayer Meeting—How they prayed, and with what effect. It was a very peculiar kind of prayer meeting—a model for all the centuries. It was peculiar in its personality and exercises.

As to its personality, the two apostles mightily anointed of God on the Day of Pentecost, were the leaders of the prayer service of the hour. A company of the disciples surrounded them and participated in the exercises—how many is not stated. Let us see now

I. How they prayed.

1. They prayed in holy unison. The exact record is: "They lifted up their voice to God with one accord."

There were no discordant notes—no impediments in the way of a successful approach to the Throne. This unity gave promise of victory in advance. We can only briefly state the characteristics of the prayer offered, as we desire speedily to reach an application of the subject to the object of our present assemblage. We note

2. They distinctly and appropriately recognized Jehovah's sovereignty.

They knew to whom to pray, and with what mode of address to come to His footstool. "They lifted up their voices"—saying, "Lord thou art God, which hast made heaven, and earth, and the sea and all that in them is." Here we see a becoming acknowledgment of Jehovah's glorious being—"Lord, thou art God" —of His creative splendors, and universal dominion— "which hast made heaven, and earth, and the sea, and all that in them is." In these acknowledgments of the power and glory of the Lord Jehovah their eyes and hearts were turned reverently and adoringly toward the heavens, where He was seated upon His throne.

3. They appealed to David and his significant utterances concerning God's people Israel, and her predestined glory.

The mention of no name at the throne could have had greater potency, than that of David except that of David's Son, the beloved of the Father.

They quoted from the second Psalm where the Psalmist inquires, "Why do the heathen rage, and the people imagine a vain thing?" He declares the impotency of their combinations against the Lord, and His Christ, and the certainty of their overthrow. In presenting these things, they assumed an attitude of sublime confidence.

4. They offered specific and comprehensive petitions.

(a) They ask for divine observation—that He

would take a survey of the imperiled situation of the apostles. "Now Lord, behold their threatenings." The enemies of the truth could largely use that sort of weapon.

(b) They pleaded for Gospel boldness.

This is a priceless gift—indispensable to success—resistless in its potency. Not for rhetorical beauty or exactness, or logical precision or force—but for divine boldness—to strike home, to sucessfully assault the enemy's works, to win victories in the name of Christ.

(c) They also asked for miraculous accompaniments.

They said, "By stretching forth thine hand to heal; and that signs and wonders may be done by the name of thy holy child Jesus." The healing of bodies as well as souls marked the Apostolic ministry—and the day of such signs and wonders is not closed. They are necessary to rebuke the prevalent skepticism of the age.

II. The Stupendous Effects of Their Prayer.

1. A Physical Effect.

"The place was shaken where they were assembled together." How, or in what way the place was shaken is not stated. It may have been by earthquake shocks, making the whole building tremble. But we know not what were the particular physical manifestations. One thing we know—for it is on record—the place was shaken, palpably and awfully shaken, demonstrating the presence and power of God.

In all ages of the world, when God has made extraordinary manifestations of Himself there has been some stirring of physical forces. It was so at Sinai, at the giving of the Law. "There were thunderings and lightnings, and the whole mount quaked greatly, and all the people in the camp trembled."

It was so on Mount Carmel when Elijah called down fire from heaven upon the sacrifice, and all the people in the camp fell upon their faces, and cried, "The Lord, he is God! The Lord he is God!"

At Pentecost there was another demonstration of a similar character. "The sound as of a rushing mighty wind, and cloven tongues, like as of fire sitting upon each of them."

So here, the place was shaken in some marvelous way, demonstrating God's eternal power and Godhead.

2. A Glorious Spiritual Effect.

"They were all filled with the Holy Ghost." This was the crowning feature of the occasion.

But what is it to be filled with the Holy Ghost? I will answer this in as few words as possible. The Holy Ghost is a divine person, the third person of the adorable Trinity. He was given to each of them to be their abiding Guest, to dwell in them, of which fact they were blessedly conscious. In this internal revelation of the Holy Ghost—infinite Purity, Love and Power pervade the whole soul-temple. So all who are filled with the Holy Ghost are constituted Kingdom Millionaires. A great Trust Company is established within, of limitless capital, which will never break, it will stand "the wreck of matter and the crush of worlds." But had they not been filled on the Day of Pentecost? Yes, but this was an additional installment, a refilling after an enlargment of soul under Pentecostal auspices.

3. An answer to their prayer was given in precise form—in the impartation of Gospel boldness.

I shall have to leave you to examine the historic records in the Acts to see how this "boldness" was manifested in their wonderful ministrations. There is a sublime summing up in the 33rd verse. "And with great power gave the apostles witness of the resurrection of the Lord Jesus; and great grace was upon them all."

They went forth to storm the very citadel of hell, and God gave them power and victory. ("Amen!")

I told you when I commenced that the burden of the Lord was upon me. Before I came to the Assembly I had a vision of tidal waves. I thought and wrote of a mighty upheaval from the great depths of Infinite Love, for the salvation of multitudes sweeping with mighty and resistless energy this great city of Chicago. Well, we have had blessed times, in preaching, song and testimony—but, brethren, there has been no shaking of the house where we have been assembled. ("We must have it.")

Look at those empty galleries! They ought to be full of people. They have been full. Those who filled them came to Christ and were gloriously saved. Is it not time for this house to be shaken? (Amen.) Is it not time that the awful sepulchral stillness of those galleries should be broken by the tramping up stairs of an eager, thronging multitude? (Amen.) I have been almost impelled, at times, to go up there myself, and lie down on one of the seats and cry mightily to God to shake the house by His almighty power. I would rather see them filled with publicans and sinners, than with appalling emptiness. Why do not the publicans and sinners come in and fill them? Why?

What are we going to do about it? ("Pray.") God has given us large praying privileges. Jesus has said, "If two of you shall agree on earth as touching anything that they ask, it shall be done for them of my father which is in heaven." What a promise! Why, it puts the resources of eternity at the back of two people who know how to pray. Lord, teach us to pray and touch the eternal magazines of the unseen world! (Amen!)

My brethren, my sisters: This is no time to jump, or cut capers in the aisles. Jump and cut capers **when the house is shaken!**

I am awfully impressed that the place, here and now, should be shaken, and that the people of the city and of the outside world, should be made to know that God almighty has come down here in the glory of His power! ("Amen!")

I do not want to go back to New York and tell them this Assembly was a mere fire-fly spark, or, an ordinary revival meeting. I want to be able to tell them there was a moral earthquake — a veritable Pentecost within these walls.

The whisky power of Chicago is stupendous. Its havoc is seen everywhere. The devastation is enormous. This is the time to weep, and wail, and cry unto God. I wonder how many people in this house are ready to join me and let us get down upon our faces and cry mightily to God, the almighty, eternal God, for a revelation of His mercy and power that will shake the house, and sweep things? In every part of the house let us get down—down before the almighty God, and cry unto Him.

In response to this fervent appeal, the congregation was prostrated before God and around the altar there arose a deep and awful cry. Some were prostrate on their faces in the aisles—prayer was ardent, opening heaven and the results will not be known until the day of eternity. Brother Hughes was exhausted and retired to the choir loft, and requested Brother S. B. Shaw to push the battle. To God be all the glory.

EVENING SESSION.

We have no report of this service, except the sermon which we give. We remember that the service was a very blessed one from beginning to end and characterized by very much of the presence of the Spirit of God.

SERMON BY BRO. ALEXANDER McLEAN.

I have been so immersed in the business side of this Assembly that I would prefer, greatly, to have anyone of half a dozen or more different brethren speak tonight than that I should, but the Lord's will be done.

It is Saturday night, and, if you please and the Lord will help, we will try to gather up the fragments of the week that might otherwise be lost. God help us to gather the fragments!

To speak of Union in Holiness two passages of Scripture will be used. In the last chapter of the book of Daniel, and the last clause of the seventh verse, are these words: "And when He shall have accomplished to scatter the power of the holy people, all these things shall be finished."

Daniel, among the prophets, gives us noticeable indications (and at the best, they are very uncertain,) when the end of the world shall be, and, in this last wonderful prophetic declaration, he says that when he shall have accomplished to scatter the power of the holy people, all these things shall be finished," as though it was the consummate will of the great enemy of all good, to try to scatter the power of the holy people and as though he would be satisfied when he saw such a scattering accomplished. And, when he shall have done that, look out! the end is near. That seems to be the trend of Daniel's utterance.

Then I invite your attention to what our Lord says in John 17: 21:

"That they all may be one; as Thou, Father, art in me, and I in Thee, that they also may be one in Us: that the world might believe that Thou hast sent Me."

Injury to Christianity results from scattering the power of the holy people. Advantage and blessing to Christianity will be brought by concentrating the power of the holy people. The Lord Jesus, in His great high-priestly prayer, cried to God from the depths of His soul, that all

His people, those who believed on Him in His day, and all who, through the ages, should come to believe in His Word, might be one in Him, as He was one with the Father, "That the world may believe that Thou hast sent Me." In His infinite stretch of thought and knowledge, He saw that nothing would so thoroughly cause this world to accept Him as the Messiah, as the unifying concentrating power wrought among believers by the Holy Ghost. When scattering is accomplished, destruction is nigh. Jesus seeks to unify, concentrate and bring believers together in Him, inaugurating thus the millennium. How emphatic His words "He that gathereth not with Me scattereth abroad." Jesus must be the center of attraction and union among all men and this union is the test of all methods and measures.

Oh, how my soul has gone out in prayer for this Assembly, and still goes out in earnest supplication that God would concentrate the power of the holy people, and so help the world to see what the Lord Jesus prayed for but a little before He was to render up His Spirit to God— "That they all may be one." ("Amen!") Not to effect a loose sense of union which men of the world may hold, but in that complete sense of union which He held, and which He received from His Father "that they may all be one in me as I am one with the Father;" as though He said then, and not till then, will this world "believe that thou hast sent me," as the Messiah.

Efforts that scatter, and dissuade from Holiness need not be sought alone in ancient history. We can see so much of it now,—this disposition to scatter and divide; to decry; and not to have faith in others, who are professing and striving to be all the Lord's. We need not go very far into history to see that. We are here, members of at least twenty different evangelical churches, ("Bless the Lord!") believing in holiness, striving with all our hearts for that union which the Lord Jesus Christ prayed for, that we may be one with Him as He is one with the Father. When that comes, in a broad sense the world will have to believe (it hasn't believed up to date, because that hasn't come) that Jesus is the Messiah. There are hearts here beating hard against the heart of the Lord Jesus. They are often before God on their faces saying, "O, Lord, grant that my brothers and sisters may be one in Jesus." "O, Lord, vouch-safe that we may be one in Thee. We are not worthy. We are infinitely undeserving. We can do nothing to make ourselves worthy of that high and wondrous privilege. For Jesus' sake, make us one with Thee, even as Thou art one with the Father." I confess that I am staggered at the thought. We must get very low before God when we utter that prayer. We may be one absolutely, now and henceforth and forever, one with Him, as He is one with the Father. It staggers me! Does it stagger you? Have you ever gone into the depths of that with the Holy Ghost, to find how much is meant? It cannot be realized by sending up a casual prayer or desire. It is only by deep contrition and the most earnest yearning as though you were about to go into His presence, or as though it were the last prayer you would utter to the Lord, "Make me one with Thee as Thou art one with the Father."

Let me retrace my steps a little, that we may, by the help of God, better understand the meaning of the Word. This is a great subject. Jesus prayed it. As certainly as Jesus offered this, He wants it answered. ("Amen!" "Blessed be God!") Help us Lord to get in a higher altitude and a purer plane to-night. One way of overcoming a great conflagration is by scattering; by putting dynamite and powder into adjoining structures. If they cannot overcome the flames in any other way, they do it by scattering the combustible portions, that they may subdue it piece by piece. The devil can get at you and me, and more effectually quench the Holy Spirit when we are separated in feeling the one from the other. He cannot accomplish this sad work, if we are united to the Lord and our brethren. "United we stand; divided we fall." Remember the cause of Ireland, as they speak of it over there. Their representatives in Parliament were unable to accomplish anything for their Emerald Isle, and "Johnnie Bull" paid very little attention to them, because they voted discursively. England was united. She said: "Let them remain scattered. We can thus handle them very readily." But there came an Irish statesman on the scene. He turned their disconcerted action into voting solidly, as one man. England trembled and Ireland won many victories.

God bless the people whose hearts the Lord has filled with His Spirit. ("Amen!") How we have allowed the enemy to scatter the power of the holy people. O, how my heart has bled through the years past, over the serious lack of solidarity in the Holiness cause. How thankful I am that God is opening our eyes to the tremendous meaning of concentration and union along the line of loving God with all the heart. ("Amen.") Pray about it in your closet. Next year come yourself and bring someone else with you, to the Assembly for the promotion of Holiness, and see if concentration will not mightily help us on these lines.

You will remember that a number of small and feeble independent states were congregated and united by Bismark into what constitutes, now, the powerful German Empire. O, Lord, send us a great leader to concentrate these holiness people that we may be one with Jesus and with each other. ("Amen!")

I am profoundly glad, this Saturday night, to see young men and young women coming forward to push Holiness. God bless them, in the accomplishment of more than they who soon shall be crowned! ("We'll stand by the cross.") Holiness must live. I can't see in the Bible that God has a mightier factor for the salvation of the world than holiness. ("Amen!") I repeat that I can't find anywhere in the Word of God a more potential factor for the salvation of the race than is found in holiness. Reverently let us realize that God knows of nothing to employ for the salvation of this world like holiness. ("Amen!") Let us appeal to Jesus. He says: "Thou shalt love the Lord thy God with all thy heart, and with all thy soul, and with all thy mind. This is the first and great commandment." That is Christ's version. The second is like unto it, "Thou shalt love thy neighbor as thyself. On these two commandments hang all the law and the prophets." By these remarks every theologian understands that this includes all scriptural requirements. He doubtless had in mind the method of the Romans. On a hook upon the outside of public buildings they hung the statutes of the realm so no man could have excuse for not knowing the law. On this hook of love were found all the law and the prophets. I repeat it, without any fear of contradiction, that our Lord knows of no power so potential in the salvation of the world as holiness. ("Amen!") That is the version of the Lord Jesus Christ on that subject, and we cannot justify ourselves in the neglect or perversion of this truth after our Lord has so emphasized it.

There can be no escape from the conclusion that Jesus wants unification. Whoever drops a firebrand of dissension, whoever seeks to scatter the power of the holy people by any process, is as directly hostile to Jesus Christ as possibly he can be; he is against the success of Christianity: and against the grace which God claims is the mightiest factor for the winning of this world.

You have heard of an elderly clergyman when approached by some young minister inclined toward holiness, saying "You had better let it alone." That young man takes the advice of the elder and says: "I guess he is giving me sound advice. I will let it alone." I believe rather than give such advice, a man had better have a millstone around his neck and be cast into the sea. For holiness is the greatest factor God employs for the salvation of race. ("Yes, sir!") We ofttimes hear it said and the thought frequently shapes the course of churches, "Get people converted; that is enough. If they are converted, all the rest will come out all right." That seems to be on the theory that you can get people converted by unsanctified persons more readily than by the sanctified; that those who are but imperfectly informed as to the things of the kingdom make the best religious instructors; in other words, you need hickory trees that have borne the hickory-nut, from which fruit in turn to raise young trees of the same kind. The Master may say of a fruitless Christian as of a fruitless tree, "Cut it down, why cumbereth it the ground?" There is no one so competent to help people into Christ as the sanctified. ("Amen!") They have walked along and carefully studied the whole length of both justification and sanctification and are thereby the better prepared to assist others. I was in Illinois at a camp and was sent for to a holiness camp meeting some miles away. It was dusty and the weather warm, and when I reached the point, one of the brethren hastened me. I inquired "What is the matter?" He said: "An able minister is going to preach this afternoon, and he is sure to give a strong sermon against holiness. We want you to be there to hear him, and, if you can, to answer him." Well he preached his sermon, quoting quite definitely from John Wesley on Justification, and he sets justification very high. No one that follows Wesley can minify justification. Following the preacher, I said: "That is right. In the grace of justification we are glad to follow John Wesley closely." But my sanctification helps me to keep my justification. What we want is sanctification to help us keep our justification. God help us to keep up to John Wesley's high mark." ("Amen.") I am glad to say my justification is ten times clearer and stronger because of the added grace of sanctification, than it could possibly be apart from entire sanctification. ("That is so!") I expect to go through on my justified line because God keeps me on my sanctified line." ("Amen!")

Let me stop to tell you a little about my own case. I was created with a good, strong Scotch will. Although I never was but a very brief visitor in Scotland, I have inherited a strain of Scotch blood. Those who know me well say: "What a tremendous will that fellow has." I bless God that I have a strong will and that it is all over on the side of God. ("Amen!") I strove, before God sanctified my soul, with all the intensity of my will power, to hold on. I found the more I wound up my will power, the more my spiritual thermometer dropped. I said: "This will not do." I would read the Scriptures and try to overcome my lost ground. I said: "How shall I avoid it?" I was trying to go through on my will power. The first thing I knew I was sprawling in the dust. I would get up and brush off the dirt and say: "I will go at it again." My spiritual thermometer kept dropping, and I would say to myself, "Perhaps you didn't wind up your will power tight enough." And I would say: "Now, will power, you have got to be well wound up! But it was only to go through the same sad experience as before. It is thirty-five years or more since God sanctified my soul, and I am a witness that a futile reliance on my will has ceased. ("Amen!") It is not my will power any more. If it were, I would down again. It is because I have a little more of the oneness in Christ. I said to the Lord, I can't keep myself. Behold some difficulty coming up like a cloud, O, how the Spirit can reveal difficulties, as if he would say, "Look out! There is danger ahead." That was the condition precisely that I was in after sanctification. I would see the cloud, and would get down before God. When the supposed difficulty and I came to meet, God had taken all the lightning out of it. I went through beautifully, as though in a clear sky.

Don't you remember there is something in the Scripture about standing up straight? After a Christian is sanctified, how he can stand up straight, walking like a king! ("Amen!") How triumphantly you can go forth! Some might put the question: "Would you say you have not sinned during all those thirty-five years?" I wouldn't like, myself, to say I have not sinned during all that time. When God has flashed a warning upon me, that I might be doing something wrong, I have plunged in the fountain and come up clean and rejoicing. Try it brother! I cannot say what is to come up before me, but I can say: There is the fountain. When I was a boy, I learned to dive, and when I have the slightest hint of impending harm, I go into the fountain head first, and, glory to God! I come up clean. There is a fountain open in the House of David for all sin and uncleanness. On the other hand, do not tell me that you can say "The Lord's Prayer" every day, in the expectation to go out and repeat sin. ("No!") You cannot pray "Thy will be done in earth as it is done in heaven," and go out and sin and come back saying, "I pray Thee forgive." Nothing of the kind. If, while you are watching and praying, you find you have thought or done something you cannot believe Jesus would have you do, get into the fountain. Don't stop to argue. Plunge into the fountain, get clean, and go on your way rejoicing in the name of the Lord of hosts.

I do not know as there is any one who can say they have not sinned for thirty-five years. I know I cannot, before God. I try to be as honest before you, as I am honest before God. But these thirty-five years—how blessed they have been!

I remember a July morning in New York. I had to go out and look up a parsonage myself. I had been sent in the middle of the year, without knowledge or consent on my part, to a charge in that city. That Sabbath was a hot day, and pretty nearly everybody had gone down to the seashore or out to the country. I said in the morning: "If the Lord lives, and will help me, this up and down religion in my soul has got to end," and a voice seemed to say, "When?" I said, "Now." "Where?" I said, "Right here. There is only one way left. I will make a complete surrender to God." I had not stolen; I had not sworn; I had not committed any outrageous sin, but, somehow, there was a dropping in my spiritual thermometer. I said: "That has got to stop." "How?" "By a new and unreserved gift of myself to God." "When?" "Right here and now." "Suppose it means starvation to you?" I said, "I am going to have it. I will die, but I will have it." The Scotch will got up that time. ("Amen!") (Will you pardon this little personal experience?) I said, "I may have a clear deed to properties now, but I will not own a thing when the breath has gone out of my body two minutes. Henceforth all I have must come from God, and must be acknowledged as a loan from Him to me." The Lord said to me: "What are you going to do with that nice sermon you have prepared?" I said: "I am going to put it in the waste basket. I am going to tell those tony people in my church what I have experienced." ("Amen!") I said to them: "Brethren, you don't see any increase in my height or my avoirdupois, but I know there is a difference in here. (The heart.) There is a sweet peace in my soul that tells me God has sanctified me." They did see a difference before long, so much so, that they wanted to get rid of me, and did at the end of that conference year. I said: "Lord, if you don't give me any special joy or peace or any great illumination for forty years, I am going along saying: It is settled. It is done. The great transaction is done. I am not going to worry about that." I went three or four days, on the streets and in the cars, up and down the great city of New York, saying, "It's done! It's done! It's done!" What a task I had! I attended a holiness meeting. As I began there to say "it's done," "heaven came down my soul to greet." Was I sanctified then? I was sanctified several days before when I took God at His word; when I laid all on the altar; when I ungrudgingly said, I don't want it back: but if the Lord wants more he shall have it; I will hunt up-stairs, down cellar, and every where to find something additional to put on the altar. It is so good to have all on the altar. I am glad to be a cipher in the hands of the Lord. I believe God has made ten times more of me, than would have been made, had I continued along the justified line exclusively. I don't know how much time God has given me on earth, but, if He were to let me have a million years, I would say: "Lord grant them so that I may preach holiness."

My brethren, you cannot do your best for Jesus, without sanctification. You may not be giants when you are sanctified, but you will be infinitely more successful in His cause with perfect love than without it.

O, brother! O, sister! Come to Jesus that He may give you this peace. Perhaps there is some soul here that don't know about His pardoning grace. I pity you. God help you to come and learn of Him.

This sermon was followed by a blessed and victorious altar service, numbers of seekers pressing to the front.

Sunday, May 12.

This closing day of the Assembly was glorious from beginning to end; and we would gladly furnish our readers every testimony and song—every exhortation and prayer with a full report of its sermons and a full description of its large and blessed altar services. Yet either through the failure of our stenographer or loss by our printer we have no connected report of the day's sevices with the exception of the all night of prayer, a report of which is given in the following chapter.

The morning love-feast was such an occasion as might have been anticipated after such a blessed week of victory. The morning sermon was preached by Bro. H. C. McBride and was spoken of by those who heard it as one of the crowning blessings of the whole Assembly. Special mention of this service will be found in Bro. Burlison's report in the chapter entitled "The Best Thing in the Assembly." Bro. McBride's sermon was written up by our stenographer and sent him for correction but if returned it never reached us.

Bro. Walker preached in the afternoon and Bro. Aura Smith in the evening, to large congregations. Both of these were excellent sermons followed by altars crowded with seekers; but it was thought best to only report one sermon from each speaker, and we have already given our readers a sermon by each of these two brethren. During this same day over thirty appointments were filled in different parts of the city by delegates of the Assembly and with glorious results; and then many calls for speakers were left unsupplied because of the hesitacy of many to take street cars on the Sabbath as would have been necessary in this city of great distances. At the services of the Assembly and those held in the city that day by members of the Assembly, there were many scores if not hundreds of seekers, and a large number converted, reclaimed, or made perfect in love.

Altogether, this last day of the Assembly, ending in the all-night session of waiting upon God which was so blessedly and so gloriously owned by the Spirit, was indeed a day never to be forgotten by those who shared its precious privileges and one of the richest seasons of grace in which it has ever been our privilege to participate. And we believe that beyond question our feelings were shared by a very large proportion of those who gathered together that blessed Sabbath day in that upper room down in the very heart of this great city of nearly two million human souls.

The Second All Night of Prayer.

The first all night of prayer was such a signal victory resulting in so much visible fruit, that it was thought best to have another at the close of the Assembly. We have attended many all nights of prayer, but this was the best and by far the largest we have ever known. Stirring songs, thrilling testimonies, glowing exhortations and powerful altar services occupied the time. No sermon was preached after the regular evening service, yet the hours passed so rapidly that many failed to get the opportunity of unburdening their hearts.

At twelve o'clock Sister S. B. Shaw gave the following exhortation:—

Beloved! This ought to be,—I believe it is, already, to all of our hearts—a solemn time. The eternal God, the unchangeable God, has a purpose in thus bringing us together, in laying it upon our hearts thus to wait upon Him.

We have been singing the words: "A charge to keep I have, a God to glorify." How wonderful, how past finding out, that He, through His wondrous love should commit unto us a part of His own blessed work— the work of salvation, the work of redemption, the crowning work of Christ! It was by "having respect unto the recompense of the reward" and looking forward to the joy that was set before Him—the joy of saving lost souls from an eternal hell and making them partners of His throne, that He was enabled to endure the cross, despising the shame, and is set down at the right hand of the throne of God. He wants to make us sharers of His eternal joy, but in order to do that, He must make us sharers in His toil and sharers in His suffering. If we want to know much of His joy, we must go with Him down into the Garden of Gethsemane and share His agony. We must get where our hearts will bleed for souls. It is glorious to shout praises. It is more blessed still, in the intercession of the Holy Ghost, to go down low into the garden all alone with Jesus, and allow Him to give us to drink of His cup and share His baptism and His sorrow for a lost world.

O, what a charge God has given to us! Who dares to say none will be found among the lost, because you and I have come short of the glory of God and have failed to keep, fully, the charge committed into our hands? We see everywhere, scores and hundreds and thousands of lost souls! Lost souls!! Lost souls!!! pressing their way down to eternal despair, and who cares? ("God help us!") Who takes it to heart? Who weeps over the desolation?

O, beloved, we come short of the charge that God gave us in the hour when He first spoke peace to our souls. So surely as you were ever converted; so surely as you ever knew your sins were forgiven, and your name written in the Lamb's Book of Life, God gave you a charge to save souls. ("Amen!")

Who of us in this house, dares to say that from that hour we have walked in all the light of God, and gone down to the depths of His Love as He would have us?

> "A charge to keep I have,
> A God to glorify;
> A never-dying soul to save,
> And fit it for the sky."

How sadly we come short! I am not bringing a harsh charge against you. It is only by the infinite mercies of God that He has spared my soul. O how sadly we come short of being what we might have been for God! How long ago our hearts ought to have been enlarged to know more of Him and His wonderful love! O, the souls that are being lost all about us! It is a time to go down before God; it is a time to weep over the places where we have come short of His will and His glory. ("Amen!") It is time for us to say, from the very depths of our souls, God helping us, we will work for His cause as never before; ("Amen!") That we will watch and pray as never before; that we will open our hearts to the love of Jesus, as we never opened them before. We haven't sounded the depths, nor measured the breadth of this wonderful Word of God. ("Amen!") Souls! Souls!! Souls!!! for whom Jesus shed His very life-blood, dropping, dropping, dropping, by our side, next door to us and all around us. Dropping, dropping, dropping, into an eternal perdition!

I tell you there is not one of us here tonight, but needs the blood. ("Amen!") Thank God there is atonement for everyone of us. But when you and I stand before the judgment bar of God, and He lets us see souls go out to an eternal night, that we might have brought to Christ had we permitted Him to use us as He would—how shall we feel about the souls, the lost souls, that it is then too late to win? ("God help us!") Now, we have the opportunity. They are all about us, and God has spared us for the work. If we fail to win souls to Christ, it is because our love is so small. O may the power of the Holy Ghost get us down tonight where we may receive a mighty baptism of holy love that will melt our hearts down at the foot of the Cross of Jesus, that He may send us out to do His bidding! ("Amen! Glory to God!")

The small hours of the morning witnessed a most

glorious altar service and among the seekers for holiness were several young men, some of whom were students from Moody's Bible Institute. With glowing faces and hearts aflame with their new found perfect love, they rang out their testimonies with no uncertain sound.

One of the touching and stirring experiences of the night was that of a young lady who lay for a long time under the power of the Spirit. Then she arose and it seemed by real inspiration began to exhort the Christian workers in a manner that was simply marvelous, thrilling the hearts of all present.

There was a freedom among the saints which was very marvelous. Sister Sarah A. Cooke, seventy-three years of age, one of the two women who was used of God in showing Mr. Moody his need of the baptism with the Holy Ghost was present. The Spirit fell upon this little woman and with the nimbleness of a little child she skipped back and forth in front of the altar in a way that brought the glory down and became a real blessing to the people. Bro. Frank Hall of the Moody Bible Institute danced up and down the aisle in an ecstacy of delight, while some were shouting and others were weeping and prevailing with God in prayer, and yet all things were done decently and in order.

The following is copied from an article written by Evangelist Hattie E. Livingston to the Pentecostal Herald:

"While each and every session was precious and full of spiritual help, the all night of prayer was to me the crowning service of the Assembly. While there had been many wonderful tokens of the divine approval and presence, the all night of prayer excelled in the mighty presence of the all-conquering Christ. Brother Aura

Smith preached in the evening with great unction. The sermon was followed by an altar service of wonderful power. The altar was packed. In fact, many could not get to the altar.

Brother S. B. Shaw took charge of the all night meeting which was turned over to the Holy Spirit and He had right of way during the entire service. The night was spent in prayer and songs and altar services. Many souls bounded into great liberty and victory. The tide rose higher until the morning hours. Tears, groans, songs, and shouts of victory made us realize the Holy Spirit was present not only in melting hearts together and lifting Christians into Heavenly places in Christ Jesus and revealing unto them some of the heights and depths of the love of Christ, but many souls leaped into glorious victory finding the pardon of their sins; others the cleansing fountain and the mighty power of the Holy Ghost.

The crowning service was about 4 o'clock in the morning. After a season of prayer that touched the throne, an invitation was given to those who wanted healing and the altar was again packed and some were healed. Thrilling testimonies of Christ's power to keep, cleanse, and fill, with marvelous answers to prayer for soul and body, were given. As we separated in the morning we felt it had been a night spent wtih God "in the more excellent glory' and the Assembly had been indeed a ten days of waiting on God."

Bro. G. W. Ridout in an article to the Christian Standard relative to the all night of prayer says, after giving a glowing report of the sermon and altar service of the evening: "This was next succeeded by an all night of prayer, under the leadership of Rev. S. B. Shaw.

It was entered into most unanimously. People came in from other churches to participate in it, and the people of God from everywhere met in one place, being of one accord, to pray for another Pentecost. They began to pray—preachers, evangelists, workers, all classes—for the outpouring of the Holy Ghost. Just past midnight there was a heavenly cloudburst. The power of God fell upon the company, and a holy tumult ensued, in which many of the saints cried aloud for joy. This service gave many the assurance of great victory in the coming days for the cause of holiness.

"The Assembly closed in the spirit of faith and praise. 'Glory be to the Father and to the Son and to the Holy Ghost.'"

The Open Air Work of the Assembly.

One of the most important branches of the work of the Assembly was the open air services. This very important work has been much neglected by Christian workers generally. The holiness people, above all others, ought to be an example in this line of religious work. Multitudes never go inside a church to hear the Gospel, neither do they go to any other place of worship. We should live so near God that if people do not come where we are we should go to them. If we are in the divine order, God will constrain us to seek after lost souls wherever they can be found. Humanity, without grace, are prone to evil and that continually. If we let them alone, their evil natures will lead them away from God, and they will surely stumble over each other as they throng the broad way to death and eternal night. There was once a picture in a Salvation Army War Cry illustrating this sad thought. It represented the teeming mass of humanity filling the broad way and rushing on towards the precipice of hell. There were the Salvationists, some on their knees and others with uplifted hands, trying to stop them from awful destruction, illustrating the fact that the world had stampeded for the pit and they were trying to head off as many as possible.

Some of the greatest opportunities of a life time are to preach the Gospel to the masses on the streets of our cities. Many of the mission workers are preaching to more people during a summer on the streets than the pastors of the largest churches.

The open air meetings were greatly blessed of God, and this effort was used of the Lord in increasing the attendance of the Assembly. In these street services a goodly number of people manifested a desire to be saved, and some knelt on the street to be prayed for and then followed the workers to the church.

Earnest prayers, powerful exhortations and inspiring songs were the order of these open air services. The labors of Sisters Sarah A. Cooke and Beatrice Beasley, who had charge of this department of the work, were greatly blessed of God. Colonels Peck and Mayhew with several other Christian Crusaders with a brass band furnished excellent music which was used of God in drawing the crowds and adding to the interest of the meetings.

This little band of open air workers was not ashamed of their colors, for they carried a large banner on which were words which could be easily read at a distance, advertising the Holiness Assembly and the work of God.

By request, Sister Sarah A. Cooke furnishes the following:

As our Holiness Assembly gathered from the north, south, east and west, consisting mostly of those who had not only tasted of the Bread of life but were well able to break it to others, our hearts began to be moved for the multitudes all around us, perishing for lack of knowledge. Soon, we mentioned to Bro. Shaw our conviction that we ought to hold street meetings. He at once responded and it was brought before the Assembly. Sister Beaseley and myself were placed in charge. Right in the very center of the city is this First Methodist church, which is but a good stone's throw from the Court House. Permission was granted by the Supt. of Police to hold meetings there every night before the evening service. When the weather permitted, we were there each evening as well as on each Sabbath, on which days we held two or three meetings.

Our right hand helper was Bro. A. Jacobs, a man full of faith and of the Holy Ghost. He was the son of a saloon keeper and formerly served behind the saloon bar, when the Spirit of God arrested and through the Word gloriously saved him. Since then he has been greatly blessed in saving others. From his daily labors he would join us, but it was hard work to get our preachers out on the street. Is not this one of the greatest lacks of our times? They tell us there are forty-eight millions of people in the United States who attend no place of worship whatever, and the command, mostly unheeded, is, "Go ye out into the highways and into the streets and lanes of the city and compel them to come in." Jesus, Himself and His own apostles led the way. "Go ye into all the world and preach the Gospel to every creature and lo, I am with you alway."

Here have been won the great victories of other days. It was said of Geo. Whitefield, the earth was his pulpit, the heavens his sounding board. Five hundred trophies of God's grace and power to save, snatched in one day from the power of the destroyer. It was a Fair day at Moorfield, in the suburbs of London. In vain his timid friends told him he would never come out of that place alive. It was the annual Fair where the scum and blacklegs of London gathered once a year. Three or four times in the course of the day his platform was overturned and built up again, and that God-filled voice would keep drawing the crowds around him. Nothing on earth is so attractive as the Gospel to the restless multitude when preached with the Holy Ghost sent down from heaven; nothing much drier than the mere letter without the Spirit. No out of door congregation can long be held or interested without it. Charles Finney and Charles Spurgeon, were twin brothers in their mighty exhortations to their students never to preach without it. This was as the secret of their own marvelous success.

The greatest sermon ever preached on this green earth was preached by our Lord on the mountain. The sermon of Peter on the day of Pentecost when three thousand were launched into the kingdom was preached on the streets of Jerusalem.

May the language of our hearts be that of the sainted Wesley:

> "The love of Christ doth me constrain
> To seek the wandering souls of men;
> With cries, entreaties, tears, to save,
> To snatch them from the gaping grave.
>
> "Give me Thy strength, O God of power;
> Then let winds blow, or thunders roar,
> Thy faithful witness will I be:
> 'Tis fixed; I can do all through Thee.
>
> "Yea, let men rage; since Thou wilt spread
> Thy shadowing wings around my head;
> Since in all pain Thy tender love
> Will still my sure refreshment prove."

The Best Thing in the Assembly for Me.

Sarah A. Cooke, Evangelist, Chicago, Ill: To me there was much of interest in the Assembly in the gathering together of so many of God's elect. Many were there of the princes in God's Israel who had long borne the heat and burden of the day. Amongst the first was Bro. Hughes, so long the editor of "The Guide to Holiness" whose pure streams have refreshed and gladdened many hearts. Bro. Doty, of Cleveland, Ohio, who told us that twenty years ago he might have landed in glory but knew it was more important for the church's sake to remain here. Yes, dear brother, heaven will be the richer for your stay on earth, weak and frail in body, but strong in faith, an able minister of our Lord Jesus Christ. Bro. Haney, we had not seen for many years, grand Captain on many a camp ground, a leader and commander of the people; no police force ever needed when he took charge of a camp meeting. We see danger in all the work of God, of our preachers choosing an easier part. How they need to brace up by reading the lives of our great leaders. Their unceasing toil and self sacrifice, the one path to insure victory and the very Spirit of our divine Lord. Bro. Allen, of Iowa, and many others were with us, who bore legibly on their foreheads, "holiness unto the Lord."

One marked feature much impressed me: The commencement inaugurated by a night of prayer and closing on the Sabbath by another all night meeting. Beginning at 7:30 p. m., without any intermission, it ran on till 4:30 Monday morning. O, what a night of victory!

> "While heaven came down our souls to greet,
> And glory crowned the mercy seat."

There was no program, which is often a great hindrance to the Spirit's work. Prayer, preaching, exhortation, songs and altar services; the joy of the new born soul, mingling with the sobs of the penitent, and then the glowing testimonies of those who had long walked with God; the touches of divine glory making them shout aloud with joy, dance or leap before the ark of the Lord. True as ever, the joy of the Lord is the strength of his people in body as well as in soul.

Reaching my home at 5:30 Monday morning I felt just as rested as if I had slept all night.

Mrs. C. A. West, Chicago: That part of the Assembly that was the most strikingly blessed to me was a portion of the illustrated sermon of Evangelist W. E. Shepard of California. He was preaching on the line of consecration and when he came to the unknown bundle, showing what might come up after one's sanctification, he touched on the dress question. Suddenly a flood of light beamed in on my soul, revealing the fact that I had not been careful to follow the Scripture injunction concerning modest apparel. I went home and began to arrange my wardrobe so as to correspond with the profession of holiness, and now by the grace of God I am enabled to dress plain as becometh one professing godliness.

Rev. H. S. Willing, Indianapolis, Ind.:—My strongest impression during the Assembly was following a preaching service when a sister delegate from the western frontier country delivered a stirring appeal for workers for that needy and neglected field who would not make money an object in going, but who possessed

> "A soul inured to pain,
> To hardship, grief and loss."

She declared (scripturally) that a true man of God would not be bought nor sold nor require a stipulated salary to work for God and souls.

Minnie R. Willing, Indianapolis, Ind:—The thing most noticeable to me during the Assembly was, that the preaching service was crowded out one morning because of the spirit of prayer that rested on many hearts. The leaders of the meeting gave way to the Holy Ghost. Near the close of the prayer service many came to the altar. Thank God for the possibility of prevailing prayer.

E. Goodman of Chicago:—We have many reasons for which to thank God because of the Holiness Assembly in our city. Among the foremost of its benefits to my soul was the intense and continued spirit of prayer that prevailed. The early morning prayer meetings were characterized by the "fervent, effectual prayer of the righteous" which availeth much. The altar services proved that the old time power in travail of soul had not yet died out. The long prayer roll which Brother Geo. Hughes brought with him, stretched twice across the church and the many requests for prayer daily showed that God's holy people still believe that prayer in the Holy Ghost is the greatest factor in promoting the life and experience of holiness. The good that has been effected by the Assembly in promoting the revival of Pentecostal praying and thus hastening the Millennium cannot be over estimated. To God be all the glory.

Evangelist Hiram Ackers, Big Prairie, Ohio:—The best thing to me was the continual presence and manifestation of the Holy Ghost in keeping us all one in Christ Jesus, holding us in the unity of the Spirit on the Bible doctrine of justification and entire sanctification.

Evangelist W. E. Shepard of Los Angeles, Cal:—"The best thing in the Assembly." The good part was to be there. The better part was the presence of the Holy Ghost in our midst. The best part was the salvation of sinners and the sanctification of believers which the presence of the Holy One brought to so many.

The direct pointed thing that most impressed me during the Assembly was at the close of Bro. Hughes' sermon. With the burden of souls upon his heart and the sense of their need pressing in upon him, that aged, white-haired saint of nearly four score years, with upraised hands and pleading voice, left the pulpit and rushed down the aisle calling upon the people to come to God. Quick as a flash, Bro. S. B. Shaw leaped upon the platform, and, with stentorian voice, called the people to the altar and to get down before God. It seemed as if volts from a mighty dynamo had struck the people and with one accord we went down before God. Oh, for more shocks from heaven's battery that set things in motion! Amen!

Evangelist C. J. Fowler of Haverhill, Mass: Among the not a few things that impressed me and were a genuine blessing to me in the Assembly, was the spirit of unity which prevailed. I had not gotten fairly away from Chicago, when I received a letter from a good and intelligent friend of holiness, asking me to do him the favor of taking the time to write him, giving the exact facts concerning the divisions he saw mentioned in the secular papers somewhere, which he regarded as a very serious reproach to holiness and the Assembly particularly.

I was glad to write him that the report was utterly unfounded; that the Assembly was of the greatest harmony. Of course this should be expected. If holiness is what it is preached to be, and certainly as taught to be in the word of our God, the coming together of holy people can but be the gathering which above all others, is an object lesson of the truth itself. The delegates were quite a number (219) and from all quarters and from all denominations and from no denominations, representing diversified views relative to many important yet minor questions, but in this Holiness Assembly were all one; and this, when the meeting was deliberative, as well as evangelistic. A purely spiritual, or evangelistic meeting, would not present the opportunity for the manifestation of differences, which might seem to present a very divisive spirit, that a meeting would, which was somewhat devoted to the discussion of doctrines and methods, as was this one; but even here, there was manifest the fact that the heart experience of genuine holiness, causes people who have it, to see alike on the great essentials of salvation, and agree to disagree, in a genuinely Christian spirit, relative to all else.

I am blest not a little in such a meeting as the Assembly, as I see this spirit of the Christ manifest. I see it nowhere as do I among the people whom God has sanctified. This is the purpose of sanctification, according to our Lord's own prayer. He declares that the salvation of the world depends upon the unity that Christian sanctity gives. The Assembly illustrated it. It was a blessing to be there.

Capt. Otto Wendel, Peiro, Iowa:—What impressed me most at the Assembly was, First: Meeting so many old co-workers and so many of whom I had read but had not seen,—a type of the grand reunion in heaven.

Second: The progress in the holiness work. In July, 1878, I went 180 miles to Clear Lake, Iowa, to hear my first sermon on holiness at a camp held by Inskip, Wood and McDonald. Here I received the experience definitely. Later I traveled with the first tabernacle campaign in Iowa to spread Scriptural holiness.

The unity, spirit, wide representation of the Assembly, and above all, the outpouring and manifestations of the Spirit in blessing to soul and body, will go with me through eternity.

Sister M. J. McKinnon, Dallas, Tex.:—I shall ever be thankful, that in the providence of God, I was privileged to attend the holiness assembly. The unity of the Spirit that prevailed was marvelous. The most impressive and helpful service to me was the last Saturday morning of the Assembly, when, Jacob like, the saints prevailed with God, and His Spirit was poured out upon us. Sister S. B. Shaw was for hours prostrated under the power of God; after which we witnessed the salvation of souls, the reclamation of backsliders and the sanctification of believers. Many were the demonstrations of God's power too numerous to mention.

Evangelst S. B Shaw, Chcago, Ill.:—The thing that made the deepest impression on my mind was the weeping and crying to God on the part of some of the saints for souls and the desolation of Zion. The unearthly burden for souls, and the prevailing prayers brought waves of glory to many hearts. I was greatly moved while listening to the sermon of Bro. Geo. Hughes: I was so moved during his talk that I could not keep still. Near the close of the sermon I had an unearthly burden to exhort, When he left the pulpit and rushed down the aisle, I was thrust forward and constrained to cry aloud to the people to fall on their faces and pour out their hearts to God. The people rushed to the altar and many began to weep and to cry to God. The glory of God was revealed in a wonderful manner. Many seekers found their way to the altar.

Evangelist H. L. Jones, Wild Cherry, Ark.:—Above everything that impressed me was the oneness of the leaders.

Bro. Fowler said he hoped the proceedings would not be too parliamentary.

Sister Amanda Smith said on one occasion, when they were making quite a fuss in the altar: "Still the people, Lord, so Thou mayest speak to them."

Sister Sarah Cooke said after a long prayer without much fire: "Don't pray too long. Just speak what is in your heart and believe God, and give some one else a chance to pray."

I would like to attend another Assembly like it.

Rev. James Harris, Guelph, Canada:—It was good to be there. It is hard to say what was best when all was good. The thrill of the soul as it felt the precious unity in the beautiful diversity of an assembly of saints from so many places and so far from each other, and yet all of whom had experienced the entire sanctifying power of the precious Spirit of God; the beautiful and timely singing led by our dear Brother and Sister Harris, where choruses, repeated again and again by the joy-filled Assembly, lifted our souls to heaven. The experiment of our dear Bro. Hills of Texas in starting a Holiness College for the training of the youth under the overshadowing of sanctifying power; the preaching of the Word, presenting the great truth of holiness as the duty and privilege of every Christian believer, especially the clearness with which the preachers showed that sin existed in the soul of the justified believer, and that entire sanctification was the cleansing of the soul from this "filthiness of the flesh and spirit" by the blood of Christ, and that the spirit would then fill the cleansed spirit, soul and body; the Pentecostal baptisms which we experienced as we bowed together around the consecrated altar, feeling as we did, that God was putting His seal upon our proceedings, by filling and empowering us afresh to go forth and spread holiness throughout the world; these were among the best things in the Assembly for me.

Rev. B. Winget, Chicago, Ill.:—The best thing in the Assembly for me was the object lesson it gave of the fulfillment of our Lord's prayer found in John 17: 21. Surely, if a company of people, like those who constituted this Assembly, gathered from many places, widely separated, and who had been educated so differently, and who came from such varied environments, having never met before, all taught the same doctrines, telling the same experiences, and worshiping, together in the Holy Ghost, what possibilities, in accordance with our Savior's prayer, may be realized on the part of the church!

Evangelist J. R. Allen, Waterloo, Iowa:—"The best thing in the Assembly for me," was the united, rapt, long continued prayers of the hundreds of God's truly sanctified people.

Here they were from every part of this great land and from other lands, men and women of deep piety, victors over self and sin, looking to God alone, and while they invited the Holy Spirit's rigid heart searching, they plead to be made more like God in character.

Is it to be wondered at, that at that time, no other business could be done, that no man of God could preach, that all song was hushed, that that wise and blessed man, Dr. Fowler, President of the Assembly, could only throw himself upon his knees and give up all direction to the only master of holy assemblies, the Holy Ghost?

Great leaders forgot all leadership and cried aloud to God. Men and women of various callings, ministers and laymen alike, forgot all surroundings, were oblivious to men and things, while they prostrated themselves before the divine One.

What men saw and felt and heard by supernatural sense could never be expressed. Wave after wave of divine power seemed to pass over the people. Now and again great shouting and hand clapping prevailed, and then almost perfect silence, to be followed again by loud demonstrations of holy joy.

It seemed to this writer that the people generally who were interested in the promulgation of gospel holiness, and were able to come to this gathering, came expecting the opening of a new and far more successful epoch in the "Holiness Movement." For this they had prayed at home; for this they came to Chicago to wrestle in prayer together. Hence, the answer of the Holy Spirit was to be expected in some supernatural way. The Assembly felt that God assured it that His presence and power should attend the special work of holiness as never before.

The holiness people were shown their individual weaknesses. They saw that the chief obstacle to mighty advance lay in themselves. The fearful opposition of a carnal church, the contempt of worldly people, the voice of detraction and persecution were nothing, when holiness people not only taught but always felt and exhibited perfect love.

They saw that the desire to be leaders and, hence, the separation into factions, and the mutual criticism of these leaders and factions, led people to lose the true spirit, and sink the true object in the desire to be great in leadership. They saw also, that the zeal of many was not united with deep humility, constant forbearance and perfect love.

Oh, how the people prayed for that Spirit which would unite and not divide! How clearly they saw that any individual or body of individuals who gives way to a harsh, criticising spirit, in the work of spreading Scriptural holiness, will defeat that object, and themselves sooner or later will imbibe and teach gross errors.

How easy for weak men to substitute their own ideas for the teachings of God!

How certain it is that they will do this, when they give way to desires for personal prominence, rather than that of living alone to the glory of God! Oh, that all of God's sanctified people may continually cry to be kept from a resurrection of self and sin! Amen and Amen!

Evangelist C. B. Jernigan, Greenville, Tex.:—"The thing that most forcibly impressed me at the Holiness Assembly was, that the people from the North, South, East and West, all told the same story of their joyous conversion, then of their awful struggle with the "old man," and of such complete deliverance from his clutches by the baptism with the Holy Ghost. The testimonies all had the same ring. I have always preached that entire sanctification was a complete cure for sectarian narrowness. At the Assembly I met with and heard preachers of many different denominations, and they all preached, shouted and sang a full salvation by faith in the all cleansing blood of Jesus as a second experience. Oh, how I do praise God for such unity as I saw in the Chicago Assembly! Surely, the prayer of Jesus was answered in this case, making all one.

Rev. C. M. Duryea, Holland, Mich.:—The best thing in the Assembly for me was that it reached beyond my expectation. All seemed to be of one mind and one spirit, yet so many different denominations represented.

Rev. J. McD. Kerr, Toronto, Canada:—I entered the old, historic First Methodist Church, Chicago, in connection with the Holiness General Assembly on Thursday morning. I had traveled all night to reach the city, and was somewhat weary in body. Many were present at the morning hour of prayer and I went forward and knelt among them. There was immediately a conscious sense of the presence of God; a restfulness, peace and sweetness which seemed to pervade the place. Jesus was in the midst, and His glorious presence in spiritual fulness and power continued to the close.

My soul was wonderfully filled as Brother and Sister Harris sang with much unction, "His way with thee." I had long ago given Jesus His way, and now resolved evermore to let Him have His way with me.

It was a great joy to look into the faces of brethren of whom I had heard and whose writings I had often read, and to hear the Word from their own lips. Dr. E. F. Walker's impromptu remarks at the close of that first service to me, were most inspiring.

"Cease from man, that God may be all in all.

"Let the Holy Ghost have His way, not let me have my way.

"Don't seek recognition. We used to pray, 'Make me little and unknown.'

"God teaches, that he that will be least shall be the greatest.

"May He give us the spirit of meekness and of fear and of love and of a sound mind."

Another thing which impressed me was the number of young ministers connected with this movement. Steady, sober, zealous, level-headed, young fellows, full of faith and the Holy Ghost. This augurs well for the future. The aged men must soon retire. Thank God, the young men are ready to carry forward the standard. If you were to ask me which service I enjoyed best, I think I should have to say, the all night meeting. I shall never forget those victories at the altar, nor those soul-on-fire testimonies from the young men on the platform.

My spirit is ready for another campaign. By all means let us make it an annual affair.

Bro. John Kirn, Owosso, Mich.: "That which interested me most was seeing so many from different parts of the land, manifesting so much interest in the great work of God and such a tender spirit among themselves. I rejoiced also in hearing the truth regarding the sanctification of the soul set forth with such clearness. Surely when such a fervent spirit is planted through the land, much good must result. I believe the Kingdom of our Christ and His work has taken advance steps because of our coming together. I feel wonderfully strengthened spiritually since I came home and I believe this is the result of the Assembly. May God help His people to live where the unity of the Spirit will prevail, and the world be compelled to acknowledge how Christians love one another. Just to the degree that we have the spirit of the Master, will we love our brethren—though they may differ from us in many things. God send a mighty baptism of love upon the holiness people everywhere! I trust we may see many more Assemblies of the saints and that our next coming together may be even more owned of the Holy Ghost than the one just closed."

Brig. S. L. Brengle, Salvation Army Headquarters, N. Y. City: "It was only my privilege to attend portions of two business sessions of the Assembly on the last Saturday, so that my opportunities for judging of the character and work of the Assembly would hardly justify an expression of opinion. I was however deeply and most favorably impressed by the sweet and earnest spirit that prevailed in the discussion, and I have no doubt the influence of the Assembly will be felt far and wide for good and only good. It has been my frequent privilege and great joy in my wide wanderings through the States to meet many of the workers who were then present and I do not see how it would be possible for such a body of men and women to spend a week together without a mighty quickening of the forces that shall surely win the world for God. Praise the Lord!"

Bro. Jonas Brooks, Des Moines, Iowa: "How I praise the dear Lord for the privilege of attending that great Holiness Assembly and seeing so many of the dear ones I love—Brother and Sister Shaw, and my dear Deacon Morse (that I never expected to see again) and my old friend Brother Foote and many others. Am so thankful for the kind entertainment provided and the new acquaintances I was permitted to form and for the blessed, straight holiness sermons and the rich testimonies and the mighty faith exercised and the real salvation of so many souls! Glory to God!"

Bro. A. E. Burlison, Chicago, Ill.: "The most blessed part of the Assembly to my soul was the last Sabbath morning service as dear Brother McBride from New York told us in his child-like, simple way of perfect love according to Matthew 5:48: 'Be ye therefore perfect, even as your Father which is in heaven is perfect.' When in closing he described the death-bed scene of the sainted Alfred Cookman and told how as he knelt by that bed-side Brother

Cookman shouted 'I am sweeping through the gates—washed in the blood of the Lamb,' there were few dry eyes in that large congregation and when Bro. McBride gave the call to the altar, many came weeping their way to Calvary and many, I trust, were there made perfect in love. Brother Shaw, that day's service paid for all your labor and sacrifice in behalf of the Assembly."

Evangelist C. W. Ruth, Indianapolis, Ind.: "What most impressed me at the General Assembly was: First, the spirit of unity, which was so manifest in all the business deliberations and service. Notwithstanding the fact there were present those who had widely divergent views, representing a score or more of the different denominations, and all sections of the country, they all seemed perfectly agreed to disagree, on non-essential points, and agreed to disagree in an agreeable manner; whereas, there was manifest the most delightful fellowship, and the perfect agreement of testimony regarding the experience of entire sanctification. It was in every particular an illustration of the "oneness" for which Jesus prayed. Second, the gladsome, hopeful, cheerful, expectant outlook for the work of holiness in the future. No pessimism nor thought of retreat, but a confident, concentrated, and eager looking forward to yet greater victories. The inspiration and enthusiasm for pushing the battle was exceedingly contagious, and made one feel like running through a troop and leaping over a wall. Praise God! The tenderness with which reference was made to antagonists, (only when it seemed necessary) the humility and simplicity of our leaders, the unctious sermons, the glad shouts of victory, the earnest prayers, ending with the all night of prayer, would all furnish chapters full of interest, and would fully justify a trip across the Continent in order to enjoy it all. Amen!

Personally, my soul received a great uplift, and boost heavenward. Glory!"

Wm. Oettinger, Chicago: "I was not able to be present at the Assembly with the exception of a part of one service, nevertheless it was made a great blessing to me through the brother who was sent to my home for entertainment. He was a minister of the gospel who had lost the experience of sanctification but who found it again during the Assembly. His teaching and the conversations we had at home were a means of great blessing and encouragement to me. The love and humility he manifested made me desire to be like him but O—even more—to be like Christ!"

Evangelist E. F. Walker, Greencastle, Ind.: "That which especially impressed me and filled me with gratitude and thrilled me with joy, next to the fact of the many souls blessed, in connection with the Holiness General Assembly; was the evident oneness and harmony in the Lord of the people who composed the gathering. It is not recognized as it should be that the meeting was deliberative, as well as evangelistic. As a rule, deliberative bodies of men and women, even when all are connected with exactly the same organization, do not, always see eye to eye. Frequently in such, there is much disputation and sometimes divisions in conclusions. This is so, even among good people engaged in the Lord's work. It was thus even with that 'son of consolation' and him who 'was not a whit behind the very chiefest apostles: Barnabas 'determined' and Paul 'thought not good.' 'And the contention was so sharp between them, that they depared asunder one from the other.' (Acts 15: 37-39.)

"But there was little, if any, of this manifested in the Assembly. Of course there were of necessity differences of opinion and preferences among so many minds; but there was little disputation, and no contention. Not an uncharitable word against any holding to different views did we hear. Not an unkind reference was made to any who could not see their way clear to unite in the meeting. No contention except against sin."

Bro. F. H. Brookmiller, Pastor Evangelical Church, Red Oak, Iowa: "It was my privilege to attend the General Holiness Assembly fifteen years ago. I have been in the holiness movement for twenty-seven years. When I saw the call for this last Assembly my heart was glad, and I felt a strong pull in my soul to go. So I went in good time to be there at the first service and in the opening service felt the divine presence and felt sure the meeting would be a glorious success. O the beautiful spirit of holiness in the manifestation of brotherly love when I saw brethren like Brother Morse and others embrace each other and give the holy kiss! It seemed to me as never before in my life I understood what Paul meant when he said 'Greet ye one another with an holy kiss.' Thank God, there is yet in the world a real primitive spirit of Bible holiness. O how much it needs to be conserved and spread throughout the whole world! In these days of coldness and formality in the churches, how refreshing to one's spirit to get in a real Holy Ghost atmosphere like there was in the Assembly! To me, personally, the meeting was a real blessing and benediction such as I have not enjoyed for years. I know I shall be a better man because of contact with these holy men and women, the real elect of God! I hope the good report of this Assembly will stir hundreds of others to be present at the next. O how these gatherings make us long for the coming of Jesus when in that great holiness assembly we shall meet to part no more."

Brother Alexander McLean, Brooklyn, N. Y.: "The

precious memories of the General Holiness Assembly fade not away as the days pass by, but its love and fire burn in my soul most blessedly. Praise the Lord! He would have us enjoy even a better one in the coming year. Let us all work and pray for a mightier baptism of the Holy Ghost then, than at either the first or second of these great seasons of outpouring. It surely is in the direction of convincing the world that Jesus is the Messiah!"

Bro. Isaiah Reid, Des Moines, Iowa: "Having attended the Jacksonville convocation in 1880, and the first Chicago Assembly fifteen years ago, I have some wideness of the conditions in mind that some others do not. At Jacksonville the dew of youth was on us. We had not then met many of the issues that have since confronted us. The ecclesiasticisms of the day had not then so used their combined power to oppose the movement. The general public were eager to attend our camps and various meetings. We always had the benefit of large congregations. We also had the conscious uplifting that the knowledge of general unity and harmony brings the heart. In a few instances had there been discovered tendencies and signs of wildfire on the one hand, and church oppression on the other. At that time our main stress was the formulation of our belief as to the doctrine of holiness and related teachings, and the status of our teachers. The statement was sound and satisfactory. It helped form the basis of the first Chicago Assembly and through that reached our late utterance.

"No one in that assembly had any thought of advocating the addition of any other issues to the holiness movement save those which had been presented from the camp-meeting platforms beginning with the days of the Palmers, and the national movement under the leadership of John S. Inskip. No one felt called to preach on second-coming or call an altar service for bodily healing. Doubtless there was not a soul there who did not believe in both, but not one considered these doctrines any more a part of the holiness work than the matter of water baptism or the creation of the world. I call attention to this to show that these issues have been thrust on the movement as innovations, and that it is not holiness that divides holiness, but the insistence of making that a part of the movement which for nearly half a century was never presented as a part of it.

"The report of the Committee on Teachers, that is preachers and evangelists, is very important and needed re-affiming in our late Assembly as we had nothing to take its place or cover the ground. It had nine special points. The 6th reads as follows: "That they should make such full proof of their ministry that souls be established in holiness, avoiding the introduction of such themes as would constitute a permanent diversion of the services, or essentially change the meeting from its proper object and work.'

This was evidently a Spirit led or suggested statement and heed to it would have saved us from much that we have to confront now. The ground covered by this report, the reading of a paper of marked pith and point on 'Current Errors,' by Rev. M. L. Haney, reveal plainly the fact that the heart of the holiness movement sensed the trend of coming events in a remarkable manner and did all that was possible for it to do in planning for the success and safety of the movement. I make special mention of the work of this convention because it certainly set the pace for both the assemblies that followed, and was an actual need of the time, and honestly and fairly met the issues confronting it. It was the result of the call of a committee appointed for that purpose by what was then called the 'Western Holiness Association.' It provided for the calling of a similar convention, which if I remember rightly resulted in the first Chicago Assembly. Sixteen different denominations were represented and in this it was the first of its kind.

"The Assembly of 1901 was like it in its fraternalism, and like it in sweetness of spirit and holiness unity. Both are evidence that holiness unites and the addition of something else divides. We had graver faces at Chicago than at Jacksonville because face to face with menacing difficulties. The fire of enthusiasm burned but the dew of youth was sobered by the broader views coming with the experience of years and the vision of manhood. In the face of serious complications in the ecclesiastical world; and at our threshold the factious spirit against which the Jacksonville Assembly had forewarned us; and conscious that the old-time holiness movement which we were standing for was denounced by some who evidently knew not Joseph, it was a time to be thoughtful and listen for the Spirit's voice in every move.

"Looking back, we praise God there was no jar, and no dividing spirit. The unity was blessed. The fellowship was owned of God. The results of our deliberations shine in the clear light of Spirit-led conference. The acknowledged need of the Assembly is manifest in the provision made for its successor. The manifest leading of the common heart of the assembled saints, gathered from all quarters, and from various branches of the vine, in practically abiding and continuing on the line of old-time holiness is a remarkable proof that God intends that these three assemblies shall continue to be one the successor of the other, maintaining the faith and unity of the saints, and the perpetuation of holiness as a special work. Amen. So let it be."

How Chicago Pastors and Churches were Helped by the Assembly.

As has already been mentioned, a very large number of services were held in various parts of the city by delegates in answer to calls from pastors, Salvation Army officers, Volunteer officers and Mission workers and the blessed results of these services greatly added to the fruitfulness of the Assembly itself in the salvation of souls. Numerous verbal reports of glorious results come to us from many sources and the following words from several of our city pastors will convey to our readers some knowledge of the blessed work accomplished. Bro. Brushingham's report we have condensed from an article in the Northwestern Christian Advocate published soon after the close of the Assembly.

Bro. J. P. Brushingham, Pastor of First M. E. Church, where the Assembly was held:

"We have been profoundly impressed with the conversation, piety and exalted motives of the men and women who made up the Assembly. A member of our regular First Church congregation said Sunday night: "This is old-fashioned religion. I have seen nothing like this for twenty years." Another said: "This is as it used to be fifty years ago." We are not surprised that some should stumble over the manifestations of enthusiasm at different sessions of the convention. We could see nothing to contradict the spirit of such Scriptures as: "Where the spirit of the Lord is there is liberty." Surely it is the same spirit but different manifestations. President Fowler said when he closed a very demonstrative meeting: 'You may not have felt the pressure that is on some hearts here; you may not have had upon your heart the burden that is with some hearts now—it does not necessarily follow that you are not right with God because you have not got it. You are not necessarily out of harmony with God; don't let the accuser take advantage of you there. But, if you have not been in sympathy with what you have witnessed here and look upon it as creature activity, as human manifestation; if you have been restless in the presence of this thing you want to look out. Brother, if you have been betrayed to merely look on, look out. God does not give us light to play with. He wants us to go forward with the swing of victory and the tread of a conqueror.'

The Assembly appointed a committee of seven to arrange for a meeting in 1902, when the body may be permanently organized. The declaration of principles opposed everything that looks like "comeoutism" forcibly and radically. The whole letter and spirit of the services breathed loyalty to the Church. A truly fraternal spirit was expected and realized. While sectarian and ecclesiastical uniformity was lacking, " the unity of the spirit and the bonds of peace prevailed." And why not? For emphasis was placed upon love, the very essence of religion. Not a hasty nor bitter word was spoken throughout the deliberations. The flush of anger did not mantle a single cheek during the sharpest discussions, but many faces shone with a light celestial and a radiance reflecting the power of an indwelling and abiding Christ. Christian courtesy and a sanctified common-sense prevailed throughout. There has been a real spirit of revival with an undercurrent of earnestness—a deepening of the spiritual life. There has been no wild fire, nor fanaticism. We do not say but that such assemblies are in danger of what Mr. Wesley called enthusiasm and we call fanaticism, because in old age John Wesley's heart cried out for the sweeping revivals of his earlier years. He pleaded that God might send them without the blemishes, but if not he would welcome them with the extravagances.

He prayed that they might come any way. It is hard to reach the heart of a great wicked city where the devil has meeting places (saloons) and a perpetual revival upon every street corner. Let us thank God when the city is stirred, whether by ordinary or extraordinary methods.

It may be truly said that the blessing of God has rested upon the General Assembly for the Promotion of Holiness. It has proven a Pentecost—a Jerusalem chamber to many souls. The First Methodist Episcopal Church, the mother Church of Chicago Methodism, could not but receive a spiritual uplift from the meeting. Several young people have been soundly converted and have united upon probation. The promise of the Father has been realized and, best of all, may be realized personally and in abiding presence.

Rev. J. O. Nelson, Pastor Second Swedish M. E. Church, "I was exceedingly gratified at the Assembly to find a spirit of brotherly kindness toward non-professors of entire sanctification and toward the different denominations of evangelical Christians—a grace not always found with professors of this wonderful experience. Brothers S. B. Shaw of this city and W. E. Shepard of California preached at our church and the impressions made by the word preached were blessed and reviving."

Rev. A. J. Lofgren, Pastor Oak St. Swedish M. E. Church, "I wish to say that our church was greatly benefitted by the Assembly. The evangelists who preached for us were Rev. M. L. Haney, Mr. and Mrs. S. B. Shaw, Thos. H. Nelson and wife and Miss Fannie Birdsall. We enjoyed the singing by the two last named ladies very much. We also had an evangelist the last Sunday of the Assembly but do not remember the name.

All the sermons were very strong and to the point and I, as pastor, and my congregation as a whole, feel very much obliged to them and to the Assembly for the interest taken in our Swedish Church both during the Assembly and before it convened, during the preparatory services."

Bro. J. H. Alling: "In a busy pastorate I found some time to attend the recent Assembly of workers interested in the higher Christian life and experience, held at the Clark St. M. E. church, and experienced a rich blessing. In forty-two consecutive years in the Christian ministry I have never been more pleased with the wise conduct, sweet spirit and evident endowment of the Holy Ghost which these gatherings constantly exhibited. A great work was accomplished for God's Kingdom—and as a pastor of one of the Chicago churches, I can testify the meeting had blessed and what promises to be lasting results among my membership. And this was largely contributed to by a sermon of great argumentative power preached in the demonstration of the Spirit by Bro. T. K. Doty of Cleveland, Ohio, in my pulpit. My sincere impression is that Chicago Christians, and Methodists in particular, owe a deep debt of gratitude to the chief promoters of this great convention, Brother and Sister S. B. Shaw."

Bro. D. B. Fay, Pastor Second Free Methodist Church, Chicago: "My soul was fed many times while attending the Assembly and very favorably impressed with the general agreement of the Convention to plain Bible holiness. I am free to say that my soul has not been stirred in years as it was upon that famous Wednesday morning when the awful power of God came down shaking nightily the whole place. The Lord give us more of the same kind."

Bro. J. D. Marsh, Pastor F. M. Church, Chicago: "The church of which I am pastor was greatly benefited during the Assembly by the ministry of the Word by three different members of that gathering who preached to us in power. We were also helped much by being in attendance at the Assembly."

Bro. G. D. Cleworth, Pastor Wabash Ave. M. E. Church, Chicago: The Wabash Av. M. E. Church (The Open Church) in two ways received much benefit from the Assembly: 1. Our people attended the Assembly services and several of them received there the blessing of perfect love. 2. We had a preacher from the Assembly every evening and kept our own doors open as usual. Brothers Jernigan and De Jernette of Texas, B. S. Taylor of Iowa, and G. W. Ridout of New Jersey, gave us red hot holiness sermons under which others of our people came into the light. Bro. Hughes preached Sunday morning May 5, and Bro. Haney May 12, splendid sermons that bore immediate fruit in earnest souls at the altar seeking the fire. The flame has burned right on. May 26th B. S. Taylor came for a two weeks' campaign and the fight is on at this writing June 7. Souls are being saved and sanctified every evening. Personally the Assembly was a feast of fat things to my soul. Many of the sermons were masterpieces — clear, definite, convincing, powerful. The result of the Assembly in Chicago will not be told to-morrow nor the day after, but will be seen in the life of the church for months and years to come. Amen, Hallelujah!"

The Assembly closed in a flame of revival and after its close quite a number of those who came to attend the Assembly remained for some time in the city and assisted in revival work. In addition to work in city missions at has been done and for what shall still be done to God the Father, and God the Son, and God the Holy Ghost be honor and praise both now and throughout eternity. **Amen and Amen.**

least five special revival services were conducted by Assembly workers with blessed and lasting results.

Sister Jennie Smith, of Washington, D. C., the railroad evangelist, conducted services daily for some time at Williard Hall assisted by others who remained after the close of the Assembly. The services were largely attended, numbers were saved and many helped.

Bro. T. H. Agnew of Virginia, Ill., tarried and held very succesful services at West Side Pentecostal Mission. Souls found victory at every service.

Rev. W. E. Shepard and wife and several other workers assisted S. B. Shaw and wife at a tent meeting in Irving Park at which souls were saved and sanctified.

Sister R. L. Wortheim of Denver, Colorado and Brother and Sister B. S. Morris of Derby, Iowa and others assisted Brother and Sister A. Jacobs in a tent meeting on the South Side and Bro. B. S. Taylor's successful work at Wabash Ave. M. E. church has already been mentioned by Bro. Cleworth.

Thus the General Holiness Assembly of 1901 and its immediate results passed into history. It was a glorious victory that more than repaid for all it cost in time and money and self-denying effort and left those who attended it eagerly looking forward to another such gathering of the holiness people in the coming Assembly of 1902, of which we trust definite announcements will soon be made by the Committee of Arrangement. In the meantime let constant prayer be made for the Committee and for the coming Assembly and for such an outpouring of the Holy Spirit upon workers and people as shall speedily result in the great wave of revival victory over our land for which so many are already laboring and praying. And for what

Weeping and Crying to God.
S. B. SHAW.

No language can describe the awful curse of sin. The human mind is unable to realize the terrible penalty that is visited upon this earth because of man's disobedience, to say nothing of the eternal punishment of the wicked.

Well may this world be called a "vale of tears." From the fall of Adam, humanity has been born weeping and crying; for we are shapen in iniquity and conceived in sin (Psa. 51: 5); and the inevitable consequences of sin are disease and suffering and agony and death. From the beginning, "the wrath of God has been revealed from heaven against all ungodliness and unrighteousness of men;" and in justice He has declared, "Whatsoever a man soweth, that shall he also reap." In all ages of the world in spite of God's offers of mercy, multitudes have sown to the wind and have reaped the whirlwind, and millions are doing it to-day. No ear but the ear of God can hear, no eye but the eye of God can see, no heart but the heart of God can comprehend, the pain and agony and wretchedness of desolate souls whose lives are to-day blasted by sin.

Nor is this all. While we write, millions of moral and physical wrecks are floating down the river of death to suffering greater than they have ever known, or ever can be known in this life. Ten thousand times ten thousand more of broken-hearted sinners, whose lives have been blasted by the drunkard, the harlot, the outcast who are filling the poorhouse, the jail, the prison, and the insane asylum, are getting ready for a rapid march to the lake of fire: and millions of unborn infants will take their place and follow in their steps in the near future. And their names are legion who are bewailing the wrath of God as revealed by the pestilence, by the famine, by the flood, by the earthquake, by the cyclone, and the tornado, and by the many wars, where humanity is butchered until rivers of blood are flowing from the field of battle, and the cries of the wounded and dying rend the very heavens.

And is all this suffering a merely arbitrary, penalty inflicted by an angry God for disobedience to arbitrary law? Nay, verily. All this woe, all this misery, all wretchedness of body and mind, is the inevitable consequence of the violation of the holy laws of a holy God, so inevitable that God himself could provide no way of deliverance from the power and curse of sin only through sacrifice—sacrifice so great that the angels of God look on with wonder and amazement, sacrifice that nothing short of infinite love would ever have made.

It was the knowledge of the awful and eternal consesequences of sin that moved the heart of God with such infinite pity that He was willing to sacrifice the brightest jewel of Heaven, even His only begotten son, the lamb of God slain from the foundation of the world, whose sufferings began when sin entered into the world and will endure until sin is swept from the face of the earth, in order that we might escape the awful suffering that sin brings both in time and eternity.

Two things moved the heart of Christ to offer Himself the just for the unjust, that He might bring us to God. First, our terrible need; second, the eternal joy that would come through His atonement to us and to Him, Who "for the joy that was set before Him endured the cross, despising the shame, and is set down at the right hand of the throne of God." He prevailed for us through suffering, for "in the days of His flesh when He had offered up prayer and supplications, with strong crying and tears, unto Him that was able to save Him from death," He "was heard in that He feared." "Though He were a son, yet learned He obedience by the things which He suffered. And being made perfect, He became the author of eternal salvation unto all them that obey Him." See Heb. 5: 7-9.

And God's plan of redemption involves not only the suffering of Christ but suffering on the part of all those who would partake of His work and His reward. Jesus said to His disciples who would share His honor, Can ye drink of the cup that I drink of and be baptized with the baptism that I am baptized with? (Mark 10: 38.)

Christ in infinite compassion bore upon His heart the weight of a world's sin and gave His life for its salvation; and it is only as we share in His spirit of compassion and sacrifice and intercession, that God can use us to help in accomplishing His work. The soul that has power to prevail with God, is the soul that has been quickened by the Spirit to see and to feel the world's need. We must see something of the suffering and desolation that God sees, and hear something of the wail of agony that God hears, and feel something of the compassion that God feels, and bear something of the awful burden of soul that Christ endured, if we would mightily prevail in behalf of a lost world. We too must drink of His cup and be baptized with His baptism, if we would be able to bring joy and peace and healing and blessing to hearts here, and share His eternal joy over souls redeemed. The multitudes that are weeping and crying because of sin and sorrow, are like the sands of the sea shore, innumerable; but oh, how few know how to pray! How few are crying to God with a pure heart! And if we regard iniquity in our hearts, the Lord will not hear us. (See Psalm 66: 18.)

We tell of the faith of God's servants who have mightily prevailed, but we perhaps have failed to notice the record of their crying to God in agony of spirit.

"Crying" is a stronger term and includes more than

shedding tears. It is weeping aloud and giving away to grief or pain with a loud voice. Sometimes the grief is so great that the mourning and lamentation may only be expressed by screaming, and sometimes the mental agony is unspeakable. The saints of God as mentioned in both the Old Testament and the New, have had such revelations of the wrath of a holy God against the workers of iniquity that no words or language could express their feelings, and their unearthly groans and cries, inexpressed in human language, have prevailed with God.

When the people of God were in Egyptian bondage, their burdens were greater than they could bear. We read, "The children of Israel sighed by reason of the bondage; and they cried, and their cry came up unto God, by reason of the bondage. And God heard their groaning, and God remembered his covenant with Abraham, with Isaac, and Jacob." It was their groans and their cries that came from their heart of hearts, with an unearthly desire for divine help, that reached the ear and heart of God, and how quickly He came to the rescue!

Many years ago, we heard Bishop Bowman illustrate the cry of a burdened soul as follows: "Let us imagine we see a child on the floor crying for its mother. The mother goes on with her work seeming to pay no attention. Her heart is touched, she hears the cry, but she is not sufficiently moved to leave her work and take the child. The child continues to cry, but the mother seems to pay no attention. While the child is thus crying, it beholds with awful fright and horror, a serpent with open mouth crawling nearer and nearer. Terrified at the sight, the child utters an unearthly scream. The mother is shocked, her heart is pierced, she hears the cry that comes from the child's inmost soul, and she grasps the child from the jaws of the serpent. So God hears and answers the cry that comes from the soul who realizes its desperate need."

The Israelites had been crying for many years, but they had not cried with all their hearts. It was their united, unearthly cry that brought the reformation through Moses. It was the unearthly cry of Moses' heart that brought him into favor with God and gave him such marvelous power with Him and influence with the people.

Moses so loved Israel that in the prime of his manhood, seeing them bound and oppressed and down-trodden, he had chosen rather to suffer affliction with them than to enjoy all the wealth and ease and honor of the Egyptian court. (See Heb. 11: 25-27). We have wondered at his faith and meekness and power; but have we realized that that same faith, meekness and power were born of the agony of soul in which he cried out to God when over and over again that people whom he loved dearer than his own life, turned against him and against God and seemed bent upon their own destruction? Notice how God tells us of the crying that brought deliverance.

When the Israelites came to the Red Sea, they saw no way of escape. The army of Pharaoh was in the rear, the mountains on either side, and the Red Sea before them. "And when Pharaoh drew nigh, the children of Israel lifted up their eyes, and, behold, the Egyptians marched after them; and they were sore afraid: and the children of Israel cried out unto the Lord. And they said unto Moses, Because there were no graves in Egypt, hast thou taken us away to die in the wilderness? wherefore hast thou dealt thus with us, to carry us forth out of Egypt? Is not this the word that we did tell thee in Egypt, saying Let us alone, that we may serve the Egyptians? For it had been better for us to serve the Egyptians, than that we should die in the wilderness. And Moses said unto the people, Fear ye not, stand still, and see the salvation of the Lord, which he will show you to-day: for the Egyptians whom ye have seen to-day ye shall see them again no more forever. The Lord shall fight for you, and ye shall hold your peace. And the Lord said unto Moses, Wherefore criest thou unto me? speak unto the children of Israel, that they go forward. But lift thou up thy rod, and stretch out thy hand over the sea, and divide it: and the children of Israel shall go on dry ground through the midst of the sea."

So, in his desperate need, Moses prevailed with God and brought deliverance to Israel in spite of the mountains on either side and the Red Sea in front; in spite of Pharaoh's army; in spite of the unbelief and murmurings of the people, with both friends and foes turned against him, and with no one but God to stand by him. What a rebuke to the unbelief of would-be soul-winners that are discouraged by unfavorable circumstances and look at difficulties instead of looking to God alone!

Again, after the Israelites had crossed the Red Sea and pitched their tents at Marah, they found they could not drink the water, for it was bitter; and again "the people murmured against Moses, saying: What shall we drink? And he cried unto the Lord and the Lord showed him a tree, which, when he had cast it into the water, the waters were made sweet."

After that they journeyed from the Wilderness of Sin and camped in Rephidim. There was no water in the place, and the people were dying with thirst. Again "Moses cried unto the Lord, saying, What shall I do unto this people? They be almost ready to stone me. And the Lord said unto Moses, Go on before the people, and take with thee of the elders of Israel: and thy rod, wherewith thou smotest the river, take in thine hand, and go. Behold, I will stand before thee there upon the rock in Horeb; and thou shalt smite the rock, and there shall come water out of it, that the people may drink."

Again, when the people, forgetting all that God had done, went into open idolatry and made them gods to take them back into Egypt, we are told how it was only after forty days of fasting and wrestling with God that Moses was granted the life of Israel. Why was this—because God was less gracious or less forgiving than man? Not that, but because, much as he loved them that forty days of prayer and burden and agony were necessary to fit Moses to bear with that rebellious people during forty years of wandering.

At another time, when Miriam and Aaron found fault with Moses because of his Ethiopian wife and were guilty of sedition, for which Miriam was smitten with leprosy, we read how "Moses cried unto the Lord, saying, Heal her now, O, Lord, I beseech thee." And God heard his cry. (See Num. 12: 14.)

Nearly half a century after the death of Moses, in the time of the Judges, "when the children of Israel cried unto the Lord, the Lord raised up a deliverer who delivered them, Othniel, the son of Kenaz, Caleb's younger brother." (Judges 3: 9.)

Again about a hundred years later, "the children of Israel cried unto the Lord" and He raised up the prophets, Deborah and Barak and delivered them from Jabin and Sisera. (See Judges 4: 3-17.)

Still fifty years later, "Israel was greatly impoverished because of the Midianites, and the children of Israel cried unto the Lord," and "When Israel cried unto the Lord because of the Midianites" God sent an angel with a message to Gideon who delivered the people of God from their enemies,

Another hundred years passed and Israel was oppressed by the Philistines; and God raised up Samuel. "And Samuel cried unto the Lord for Israel and the Lord heard him." "So the Philistines were subdued, and they came no more into the coasts of Israel; and the hand of the Lord was against the Philistines all the days of Samuel." (See 1 Sam. 7: 8-13.)

Two hundred and thirty years later. Elijah cried unto the Lord, and there was no rain on the earth for three years. He cried again, and the Lord sent rain. During the famine he was fed by ravens, and later by a poor widow woman whose cruse of oil and barrel of meal were kept from failing by a special miracle in answer to the cry of Elijah. Before he left, the widow woman's son died. Elijah cried to God and the son was raised to life again. We read in James 5: 16, 17, that Elijah was a man of like passions as we are, and so were Moses and all the Old Testament saints; but their prayers prevailed with God and so may ours.

A few years after the death of Elijah, "Asa cried unto the Lord his God and said, Lord, it is nothing with thee to help whether with many, or with them that have no power: help us O Lord our God; for we rest on thee, and in thy name we go against this multitude. O Lord, thou art our God; Let not man prevail against thee. So the Lord smote the Ethiopians before Asa, and before Judah; and the Ethiopians fled." (See 2 Chron. 14: 11, 12.)

King David spent much of his time crying to God. The records of his crying are marvelous. They convey to the people of all ages sublime lessons. He tells us: "The eyes of the Lord are upon the righteous and his ears are open unto their cry." (Psa. 34: 15.) His prayer was:

"Hear the voice of my supplication, when I cry unto thee," (Psa. 28: 2) and his testimony, "When I cry unto thee, then shall mine enemies turn back: this I know; for God is for me." (Psa. 56: 9.)

Three hundred and fifty years later, we find the weeping prophet, Jeremiah, crying: "Oh that my head were waters, and mine eyes a fountain of tears, that I might weep day and night for the slain of the daughter of my people!"

While Jeremiah, the weeping prophet, was crying, his contemporary, Joel, was calling: "Blow the trumpet in Zion, sanctify a fast, call a solemn assembly; gather the people, sanctify the congregation, assemble the elders, gather the children, and those that suck the breasts: let the bridegroom go forth out his chamber, and the bride out of her closet. Let the priests, the ministers of the Lord, weep between the porch and the altar, and let them say, Spare thy people, O Lord, and give not thine heritage to reproach, that the heathen should rule over them; wherefore should they say among the people, Where is their God? Then will the Lord be jealous for his land, and pity his people." May God help us to follow the example of Joel, and may every minister of the Lord, weep between the porch and the altar.

By the revelation of the Holy Ghost, Ezekiel pictures the sure and terrible judgments of God against all those who fail to sigh and to cry because of the abominations that are committed in Israel. In Ezekiel, ninth chapter, we read that God said to His servant, clothed with linen, which had the writers inkhorn by his side, "Go through the midst of Jerusalem, and set a mark upon the foreheads of the men that sigh and cry for all the abominations that be done in the midst thereof." Then the prophet adds: "And to the others he said in mine hearing, Go ye after him through the city and smite: let not your eyes spare, neither have ye pity: slay utterly old and young, both maid, and little children and women: but come not near any man upon whom is the mark; and begin at my sanctuary." God's judgments begin at His sanctuary. Then what of that minister that is at ease in Zion? What of those professors of holiness that are careless about souls? What of any that claim redemption through the sacrifice of Christ—yet fail to take to heart the terrible need of the unsaved all about them? How are any of us to escape if we have not the mark on our foreheads?

Ten days the disciples tarried in an upper room, pleading for the promise of the Father. That was no mere formal prayer. Their Lord had been taken from them; and with broken, pleading hearts they plead for the coming of the Comforter. When every other desire was lost in this, He came, and their sorrow was turned into joy, and that same day three thousand more had joined their song of redemption from the power of sin.

Paul, the chief of the apostles told, in few words, the secret of his power when he wrote to the elders at Ephesus: "Remember, that by the space of three years I ceased not to warn everyone night and day with tears."

In our own evangelistic work of over twenty years we have never seen any great revivals until our own soul was melted before the Lord and we plead with Him with strong crying and tears for the desolation of Zion and the salvation of the lost. Who has not read of John Knox's agony of prayer when he cried out, "Give me Scotland or I die," and of John Wesley's days and nights of weeping and fasting and prayer? And it was after some members of his congregation had spent a whole night in prayer that Jonathan Edwards preached that wonderful sermon,

"Sinners in the hands of an angry God," that has resulted in the salvation of thousands of souls.

Such is the experience of the saints of God in all ages. May God help us to follow their example and grant to us such a spirit of intercession that we may go on our faces and weep and pray until we prevail with God and with man. And, may God so possess and control our emotional natures that all our tears and groans may be the fruit of the Holy Spirit making intercession for us with groanings that cannot be uttered. (See Rom. 8:26.) The Lord grant it. Amen!

They that sow in tears shall reap in joy. He that goeth forth and weepeth, bearing precious seed, shall doubtless come again with rejoicing, bringing his sheaves with him.—Psalm 126:5, 6.

Chicago, Ill.

Failing to receive two of the sermons we had expected to publish, we have several pages of space unoccupied in the making up of forms. Believing that the great need of the holiness work is persistent and united and prevailing prayer we have decided to insert an article of our own which emphasizes this thought already touched upon in our introduction and in our exhortation already published —with a prayer that by its reading hearts may be stirred up to learn the secret of prevailing with God. S. B. S.

God's Financial Plan

OR

Temporal Prosperity

THE RESULT OF

Faithful Stewardship.

By Rev. S. B. SHAW,

AUTHOR OF

"TOUCHING INCIDENTS, AND
REMARKABLE ANWSERS TO PRAYER."

"Honor the Lord with thy substance, and with the firstfruits of all thine increase; so shall thy barns be filled with plenty." Prov. 3 : 9, 10.

"He which soweth sparingly shall reap also sparingly; and he which soweth bountifully shall reap also bountifully.' 2 Cor. 9 : 6.

TO AGENTS;

This book has over 300 pages, 5x8 inches, substantially bound in paper, price 35 cents. In cloth covers, sewed, price $1.00. Write for terms to agents and for special price for books to give away. Pastors and others who want books in quantities can have them at reduced prices.

S. B. SHAW, 275 Madison St., Chicago, Ill.

A Timely Book.

Review Notices from Leading Religious Periodicals concerning GOD'S FINANCIAL PLAN or Temporal Prosperity the Result of Faithful Stewardship.

The Independent: "This is a better book than 'Coin's Financial School'—better for bankers, traders, farmers, working people, and every one who cares to prosper in this world. It is based on solid principles; it has the whole history of the world back of it, the Bible under it, and is supported by examples and instances of which the author gives us a few in the volume named above. The doctrine of the book is nothing more nor less than the doctrine of the Bible, illustrated in the history of men in this world and enforced by it. Mr. Shaw's previous volume, 'Touching Incidents and Remarkable Answers to Prayer,' reached a sale of some 250,000 copies. This book deserves as great a success. It is a capital antidote to the gross and popular commercialism of the times."

The Herald and Presbyter: "The writer of this book, seeing the haphazard methods employed in the church for replenishing the treasury, or, rather, not keeping it replenished, was led to realize that God had a system in his Word for this part of the work, so he has made a simple exposition of God's plan for systematic and proportionate giving, and in this little volume urges Christians everywhere to adopt God's own methods, so that His treasury may be filled, and kept filled."

The Revivalist: "A running perusal of 'God's Financial Plan' by Rev. S. B. Shaw, convinces me that it is a radiant sun-burst on the subject. It will prove a spiritual and temporal blessing to all who will walk in its light. Pastors and official boards should read it, and it should be sown broadcast among believers. It is written in a taking style which the common people will gladly hear. I believe it is the best book I ever saw on the subject."

Michigan Christian Advocate: "It is a strong plea for the consecration by Christians of their substance to the Lord and the practice of systematic giving. Many incidents are given as incentives to a course of fidelity and trustfulness."

The Christian Messenger: "The name of the author is a sufficient guarantee to the worth of this book. The main object is to show that God does, as of old, bless with material prosperity those who meet the conditions of tithing and freewill offerings, as taught in the Sacred Scriptures. The book we are sure will prove a great help to all classes of Christian people who are passing through financial trial."

The Evangelical Messenger: "A useful and practical discussion of the important subject of Christian benevolence. There is need of teaching on this line. The conscience of many Christians is asleep, and their judgment woefully deficient. The era of universal Scriptural benevolence would hasten the millenium more than any other one thing we can think of. Mr. Shaw's book will do good wherever circulated."

The Religious Telescope: "The book is the outgrowth of over twenty years' experience as an evangelist. It is a forcible plea in favor of God's plan for raising money for the support of His church, as against modern devices, such as fairs, festivals, quilts, chain letters, socials, etc. It will well repay a careful reading, and will be of special value to pastors and church workers."

The Christian Herald: "This excellent little volume is worthy wide circulation and careful reading as an important and valuable contribution to the literature of a great subject, upon which there is a wide diversity of thought and belief, and in which a larger and deeper interest should be taken by Christians regardless of denominational lines."

The Christian Union Herald: "One thing in this author's presentation of the subject which I specially admire is that it urges systematic giving, not in a legal, but in an evangelical spirit."

The Morning Star: "A book written with an earnest purpose after much reading and research. The author shows God's plan from Paradise down to the present time, and he finds that God has always required a part of man's income for the support of His church. He proceeds to show what was required of the Jews, the temporal prosperity given to the faithful, obedient Israelite, the prophecies concerning the liberality of the New Testament church. He considers the question whether Christians should tithe their income and give systematically, and some of the advantages of systematic giving to the cause of God. He further considers the temporal prosperity promised to the obedient, and contrasts the temporal prosperity of the righteous and the wicked, and closes with the inconsistent excuses among professing Christians for not paying more to God's cause.

The Evangelical Review: "'God's Financial Plan' as unfolded in the Word, and in this book, will show how well He has provided for the financial interests of His church. The tone of the book is earnest, thorough, inspiring, candid, fervent, and its publication wise, timely, and eminently fitting to existing conditions. It is a helper, a teacher, a doubt-remover, a faith provoker, much too much good work that hitherto has not been undertaken in Jesus' name, that should and must be done for the glory of God in the salvation of men."

The Cumberland Presbyterian: "This is unquestionably one of the ablest and most convincing arguments for systematic and proportionate giving we have ever examined. It is othodox from preface to finale, and supported by so many authentic examples as to extort acquiescence, almost, from an unwilling mind. It covers practically every phase of the subject and brings together a wealth of illustrations and exemplifications. We commend it without reservation to all of our readers as worthy their perusal."

The Evangel: "No question of more pressing importance confronts Christian people at the present hour, than this of financial obligation to God. This book, by Evangelist Shaw, aims to point out the defect and suggest the remedy. The author lays the foundation of his work in Scripture, tracing the plan of God for the support of His cause through the Old and New Testaments."

The Pauline Advocate: "The author furnishes a fine illustration of the principles inculcated. While in comparative poverty he honored God by giving as liberally as his means would allow and God has wonderfully prospered him. It fills an important place in Christian literature, and solves a problem that has perplexed the minds of many good men."

Christian Neighbor: "The 'Plan' is amplified throughout the book (267 pages) in the light of the teachings of the Old Testament and the New. The author, in getting up this book, has 'quoted freely from many prominent works and leading writers of various denominations.' A partial examination of the book impresses us favorably."

Golden Censer: "The author makes an earnest plea for systematic and liberal contributions to the support of religious work. His own experience has assured him that not only spiritual blessing, but temporal prosperity will be the reward of those who honor the Lord with their substance according to the Bible standard."

The Pentecostal Herald: "There has been a lamentable lack of light and teaching among Christians on the management of finances, which this book will fill. It is the most thorough and sensible, and at the same time scriptural treatise on this important subject that it has ever been our privilege to examine."

The Christian World: "The author is well qualified for expressing his opinion, as he has for twenty years made this subject a study. He shows from history how closely God is connected with temporal prosperity, and gives convincing evidence that God does bless the righteous in his day."

Herald of Truth: "A new book, full of facts, instruction and advice, supported by evidences of God's dealings with His people at all times. Extremely fascinating reading, sound, logical and instructive."

The Christian Harvester: "A needful and a precious subject; a well-handled subject; a kindly illuminator of conscience and consecration; a book to read, and to lend."

Way of Faith: "We rejoice in the publication of this book, and believe that it will aid many in a correct settlement of the privilege and duty of liberal giving."

DYING TESTIMONIES
OF
SAVED AND UNSAVED.

A harvest for agents in selling this heart-thrilling and wonderful book. The book is uniform in size and appearance with *Touching Incidents and Remarkable Answers to Prayer*, which has had a sale of OVER A QUARTER MILLION in four years. This book will have a larger sale. It contains the most wonderful death-bed experiences of the saved and unsaved that can be found. **No religious book will sell faster or do more good.**

Rev. E. Davies, author of *The Contrast Between Infidelity and Christianity* and other works: "The Christian world is greatly indebted to Rev. S. B. Shaw for writing and publishing that most excellent book, DYING TESTIMONIES OF SAVED AND UNSAVED. It is the most complete work of this sort that I know of, and is of infinite value as a warning to the wicked and as an elixir of life to the saints. Ministers and Christian workers should have it on their tables for constant reference. A million copies of it would be a benediction to this generation. Many who think God is all mercy will find that God is infinitely and inexorably just by reading this book. Hell and heaven begin here, and this book is a constant testimony to one and all. Get the book and circulate it far and wide. It is a feast to the soul.

The Free Baptist: "A compilation of several hundred authentic accounts of the death-bed utterances of saints and sinners. On the one hand it is full of comfort and assurance to the righteous, and on the other of foreboding to the wicked. As people approach the confines of this life and the end of their probation, they place a truer valuation on the comparative worth of things temporal and eternal. They often have a foretaste of future blessedness or pain. To the frivolous this book will be sobering, to the sinful convicting and to the saint assuring."

The experiences are indescribable. It is hard to picture the awful contrast between the last words and actions of dying saints and sinners as given in this book. We think it the most complete work ever published on this subject. **Everybody will read it.**

Paper, price 35 cents, postpaid.
Cloth, price $1.00, postpaid.

Write at once for terms to agents.

Touching Incidents

AND

Remarkable Answers To Prayer.

Some books are for preachers, some for merchants, some for tradesmen. Some are for temperance people, some are for Christians and some are for the unsaved. Of those that are for Christians, some are for one denomination and some for another, but

This Book is for You!

and a religious book at that.

Words cannot tell the good that is being done by the circulation of these books. Even the unconverted eagerly read them through from beginning to end. To this end we have many testimonies. These books will bring sunshine and blessing into every home they enter. **Very few can read them without weeping.**

During the four years these books have been circulated over

A Quarter Million

have been sold or given away.

Paper Binding, price 35 cents.
Cloth Binding, price $1.00.

Furnished to agents in lots of six or more at a time, half price. Now is the time to begin the canvass. Send in your orders at once.

☞ We also have a children's edition, illustrated with 42 cuts. Price board covers, 35 cents; cloth, 60 cents.

A Fine Group For Framing.

We have just published a **Fine Group for Framing** of half-tones of 60 of the leaders of the **Modern Holiness Movement**, **20x24** inches, on heavy half-tone paper, which should be rapidly placed upon the walls of thousands of homes of holiness people.

Christian people should honor, and in every possible way, teach their children to honor, those whom God honors. The pictures upon our walls and the books upon our tables and in our homes should tell for God. The world will honor its own. Let the children of light be as wise in their generation as the children of darkness.

Price of group, without frame, postpaid, 25 cents.

Price put up in beautiful 3 inch solid oak frame with gold glass, $1.50.

Great inducements to Agents. Write at once for terms.

S. B. SHAW, Publisher,
275 Madison St.,   **Chicago, Ill.**

FOUR GOOD HOLINESS SCHOOLS

Are you looking for a good school to send your children where they will be under good Chris- influence? If so, we would like to recommend the four following schools named below:

GREENVILLE COLLEGE, Greenville, Ill.
W. T. HOGUE, Pres

Texas Holiness University, Greenville, Texas.
Rev. A. M. Hills, Pres.

TAYLOR UNIVERSITY, UPLAND, IND.
REV. T. C. REED, Pres.

ASBURY COLLEGE, Wilmore, Kentucky.
J. W. HUGES, Pres.

The majority of the unconverted students that attend these schools are converted before they leave. We have a son in each of the first three named and know them to be first class schools. Write for catalogues and pray for the prosperity of each school.

There are a number of Holiness Schools in different parts of the country, but none that are any better than the four we mention.

TITLES in THIS SERIES

1. THE HIGHER CHRISTIAN LIFE; A BIBLIOGRAPHICAL OVERVIEW. Donald W. Dayton, *THE AMERICAN HOLINESS MOVEMENT: A BIBLIOGRAPHICAL INTRODUCTION.* (Wilmore, Ky., 1971) *bound with* David W. Faupel, *THE AMERICAN PENTECOSTAL MOVEMENT: A BIBLIOGRAPHICAL ESSAY.* (Wilmore, Ky., 1972) *bound with* David D. Bundy, *Keswick: A BIBLIOGRAPHIC INTRODUCTION TO THE HIGHER LIFE MOVEMENTS.* (Wilmore, Ky., 1975)

2. *ACCOUNT OF THE UNION MEETING FOR THE PROMOTION OF SCRIPTURAL HOLINESS, HELD AT OXFORD, AUGUST 29 TO SEPTEMBER 7, 1874.* (Boston, n. d.)

3. Baker, Elizabeth V., and Co-workers, *CHRONICLES OF A FAITH LIFE.*

4. THE WORK OF T. B. BARRATT. T. B. Barratt, *IN THE DAYS OF THE LATTER RAIN.* (London, 1909) *WHEN THE FIRE FELL AND AN OUTLINE OF MY LIFE,* (Oslo, 1927)

5. WITNESS TO PENTECOST: THE LIFE OF FRANK BARTLEMAN. Frank Bartleman, *FROM PLOW TO PULPIT— FROM MAINE TO CALIFORNIA* (Los Angeles, n. d.), *HOW PENTECOST CAME TO LOS ANGELES* (Los An-

geles, 1925), *Around the World by Faith, With Six Weeks in the Holy Land* (Los Angeles, n. d.), *Two Years Mission Work in Europe Just before the World War, 1912-14* (Los Angeles, [1926])

6. Boardman, W. E., *The Higher Christian Life* (Boston, 1858)

7. Girvin, E. A., *Phineas F. Bresee: A Prince In Israel* (Kansas City, Mo., [1916])

8. Brooks, John P., *The Divine Church* (Columbia, Mo., 1891)

9. Russell Kelso Carter on "Faith Healing." R. Kelso Carter, *The Atonement for Sin and Sickness* (Boston, 1884) *"Faith Healing" Reviewed After Twenty Years* (Boston, 1897)

10. Daniels, W. H., *Dr. Cullis and His Work* (Boston, [1885])

11. Holiness Tracts Defending the Ministry of Women. Luther Lee, *"Woman's Right to Preach the Gospel; A Sermon, at the Ordination of Rev. Miss Antoinette L. Brown, at South Butler, Wayne County, N. Y., Sept. 15, 1853"* (Syracuse, 1853) *bound with* B. T. Roberts, *Ordaining Women* (Rochester, 1891) *bound with* Catherine (Mumford) Booth, *"Female Ministry; or, Woman's Right to Preach the Gospel . . ."* (London, n. d.) *bound with* Fannie (McDowell) Hunter, *Women Preachers* (Dallas, 1905)

12. Late Nineteenth Century Revivalist Teachings on the Holy Spirit. D. L. Moody, *Secret Power or the Secret of Success in Christian Life and*

WORK (New York, [1881]) *bound with* J. Wilbur Chapman, RECEIVED YE THE HOLY GHOST? (New York, [1894]) *bound with* R. A. Torrey, THE BAPTISM WITH THE HOLY SPIRIT (New York, 1895 & 1897)

13. SEVEN "JESUS ONLY" TRACTS. Andrew D. Urshan, THE DOCTRINE OF THE NEW BIRTH, OR, THE PERFECT WAY TO ETERNAL LIFE (Cochrane, Wis., 1921) *bound with* Andrew Urshan, THE ALMIGHTY GOD IN THE LORD JESUS CHRIST (Los Angeles, 1919) *bound with* Frank J. Ewart, THE REVELATION OF JESUS CHRIST (St. Louis, n. d.) *bound with* G. T. Haywood, THE BIRTH OF THE SPIRIT IN THE DAYS OF THE APOSTLES (Indianapolis, n. d.) DIVINE NAMES AND TITLES OF JEHOVAH (Indianapolis, n. d.) THE FINEST OF THE WHEAT (Indianapolis, n. d.) THE VICTIM OF THE FLAMING SWORD (Indianapolis, n. d.)

14. THREE EARLY PENTECOSTAL TRACTS. D. Wesley Myland, THE LATTER RAIN COVENANT AND PENTECOSTAL POWER (Chicago, 1910) *bound with* G. F. Taylor, THE SPIRIT AND THE BRIDE (n. p., [1907?]) *bound with* B. F. Laurence, THE APOSTOLIC FAITH RESTORED (St. Louis, 1916)

15. Fairchild, James H., OBERLIN: THE COLONY AND THE COLLEGE, *1833-1883* (Oberlin, 1883)

16. Figgis, John B., KESWICK FROM WITHIN (London, [1914])

17. Finney, Charles G., LECTURES TO PROFESSING CHRISTIANS (New York, 1837)

18. Fleisch, Paul, DIE MODERNE GEMEINSCHAFTSBEWEGUNG IN DEUTSCHLAND (Leipzig, 1912)

19. SIX TRACTS BY W. B. GODBEY. *SPIRITUAL GIFTS AND GRACES* (Cincinnati, [1895]) *THE RETURN OF JESUS* (Cincinnati, [1899?]) *WORK OF THE HOLY SPIRIT* (Louisville, [1902]) *CHURCH—BRIDE—KINGDOM* (Cincinnati, [1905]) *DIVINE HEALING* (Greensboro, [1909]) *TONGUE MOVEMENT, SATANIC* (Zarephath, N. J., 1918)

20. Gordon, Earnest B., *ADONIRAM JUDSON GORDON* (New York, [1896])

21. Hills, A. M., *HOLINESS AND POWER FOR THE CHURCH AND THE MINISTRY* (Cincinnati, [1897])

22. Horner, Ralph C., *FROM THE ALTAR TO THE UPPER ROOM* (Toronto, [1891])

23. McDonald, William and John E. Searles, *THE LIFE OF REV. JOHN S. INSKIP* (Boston, [1885])

24. LaBerge, Agnes N. O., *WHAT GOD HATH WROUGHT* (Chicago, n. d.)

25. Lee, Luther, *AUTOBIOGRAPHY OF THE REV. LUTHER LEE* (New York, 1882)

26. McLean, A. and J. W. Easton, *PENUEL; OR, FACE TO FACE WITH GOD* (New York, 1869)

27. McPherson, Aimee Semple, *THIS IS THAT: PERSONAL EXPERIENCES SERMONS AND WRITINGS* (Los Angeles, [1919])

28. Mahan, Asa, *OUT OF DARKNESS INTO LIGHT* (London, 1877)

29. THE LIFE AND TEACHING OF CARRIE JUDD MONTGOMERY Carrie Judd Montgomery, *"UNDER HIS WINGS": THE STORY OF MY LIFE* (Oakland,

[1936]) Carrie F. Judd, *The Prayer of Faith* (New York, 1880)

30. THE DEVOTIONAL WRITINGS OF PHOEBE PALMER
Phoebe Palmer, *The Way of Holiness* (52nd ed., New York, 1867) *Faith and Its Effects* (27th ed., New York, n. d., orig. pub. 1854)

31. Wheatley, Richard, *The Life and Letters of Mrs. Phoebe Palmer* (New York, 1881)

32. Palmer, Phoebe, ed., *Pioneer Experiences* (New York, 1868)

33. Palmer, Phoebe, *The Promise of the Father* (Boston, 1859)

34. Pardington, G. P., *Twenty-five Wonderful Years, 1889-1914: A Popular Sketch of the Christian and Missionary Alliance* (New York, [1914])

35. Parham, Sarah E., *The Life of Charles F. Parham, Founder of the Apostolic Faith Movement* (Joplin, [1930])

36. THE SERMONS OF CHARLES F. PARHAM. Charles F. Parham, *A Voice Crying in the Wilderness* (4th ed., Baxter Springs, Kan., 1944, orig. pub. 1902) *The Everlasting Gospel* (n.p., n.d., orig. pub. 1911)

37. Pierson, Arthur Tappan, *Forward Movements of the Last Half Century* (New York, 1905)

38. *Proceedings of Holiness Conferences, Held at Cincinnati, November 26th, 1877, and at New York, December 17th, 1877* (Philadelphia, 1878)

39. *Record of the Convention for the Promotion of*

Scriptural Holiness Held at Brighton, May 29th, to June 7th, 1875 (Brighton, [1896?])

40. Rees, Seth Cook, *Miracles in the Slums* (Chicago, [1905?])

41. Roberts, B. T., *Why Another Sect* (Rochester, 1879)

42. Shaw, S. B., ed., *Echoes of the General Holiness Assembly* (Chicago, [1901])

43. *The Devotional Writings of Robert Pearsall Smith and Hannah Whitall Smith.* [R]obert [P]earsall [S]mith, *Holiness Through Faith: Light on the Way of Holiness* (New York, [1870]) [H]annah [W]hitall [S]mith, *The Christian's Secret of a Happy Life,* (Boston and Chicago, [1885])

44. [S]mith, [H]annah [W]hitall, *The Unselfishness of God and How I Discovered It* (New York, [1903])

45. Steele, Daniel, *A Substitute for Holiness; or, Antinomianism Revived* (Chicago and Boston, [1899])

46. Tomlinson, A. J., *The Last Great Conflict* (Cleveland, 1913)

47. Upham, Thomas C., *The Life of Faith* (Boston, 1845)

48. Washburn, Josephine M., *History and Reminiscences of the Holiness Church Work in Southern California and Arizona* (South Pasadena, [1912?])